The Autobiography of
GERALDINE FARRAR

Da Capo Press Music Reprint Series

GENERAL EDITOR

FREDERICK FREEDMAN

VASSAR COLLEGE

The Autobiography of
GERALDINE FARRAR

SUCH SWEET COMPULSION

 DA CAPO PRESS · NEW YORK · 1970

A Da Capo Press Reprint Edition

This Da Capo Press edition of *The Autobiography of Geraldine Farrar* is an unabridged republication of the first edition published in New York in 1938 by The Greystone Press.

Library of Congress Catalog Card Number 70-100656

SBN 306-71863-4

Published by Da Capo Press
A Division of Plenum Publishing Corporation
227 West 17th Street
New York, N. Y. 10011

Manufactured in the United States of America

SUCH SWEET COMPULSION

The Autobiography of

GERALDINE FARRAR

SUCH SWEET COMPULSION

THE GREYSTONE PRESS

New York

PRINTED IN THE UNITED STATES OF AMERICA
THE WILLIAM BYRD PRESS, INC.
RICHMOND, VIRGINIA

To
A Perfect Friend
C. A. E.

CONTENTS

		PAGE
Chapter One		3
I.	THE MOTHER, 1882-1897	
II.	THE DAUGHTER, 1897-1901	
Chapter Two		31
I.	THE DAUGHTER, 1899-1901	
Chapter Three		37
I.	THE MOTHER, 1901-1906	
II.	THE DAUGHTER, 1901-1906	
Chapter Four		93
I.	THE MOTHER, 1906-1907	
II.	THE DAUGHTER, 1906-1914	
Chapter Five		133
I.	THE DAUGHTER, 1914-1916	
II.	THE MOTHER, 1915-1917-1921	
Chapter Six		165
I.	SCREEN ACTIVITIES	

PAGE

Chapter Seven   189

    I.   THE DAUGHTER, 1921-1932

   II.   REMINISCENCES

Chapter Eight   215

    I.   THE DAUGHTER, 1932-1933

Chapter Nine   230

    I.   THE DAUGHTER, 1934-1938

Chapter Ten   266

    I.   THE DAUGHTER—L'ENVOI

Appendix   281

A Complete List of Miss Farrar's Operatic Roles   289

Index   297

ILLUSTRATIONS

	FACING
GERALDINE FARRAR	*Frontispiece*
AT THE AGE OF THREE MONTHS	4
THREE YEARS OLD	4
MISS FARRAR'S MATERNAL GRANDPARENTS	*Following* 4
HENRIETTA BARNES FARRAR, MISS FARRAR'S MOTHER	*Following* 4
MISS FARRAR'S PATERNAL GRANDPARENTS	*Following* 4
SIDNEY FARRAR, MISS FARRAR'S FATHER	*Following* 4
THE FIRST MELROSE CONCERT GIVEN BY MISS FARRAR	5
AT THE TIME OF MR. BOND'S INTERVIEW	5
CONCERT IN WASHINGTON, 1897	14
MISS FARRAR'S FIRST PARIS HAT AND GOWN, 1900	16
IN BERLIN, 1901	16
MISS FARRAR AS SHE SANG IN THE VOM RATH'S HOME	17
DEBUT PROGRAM, BERLIN ROYAL OPERA	32
DEBUT, BERLIN, MARGUERITE IN *Faust*	32
TWO SCENES FROM *Romeo et Juliette*	32
THE BERLIN *Manon*	33
ELIZABETH IN *Tannhauser*	33
ZERLINA IN *Don Giovanni*	40
MIMI IN *Bohème*	40
FEODOR CHALIAPIN	41
DR. KARL MUCK	41

FACING

Violetta in *Traviata* 44

Leonora in *Trovatore* 44

Nedda in *Pagliacci* 45

Mignon 45

Crown Prince Wilhelm of Prussia 52

Crown Princess Cecile 52

The Crown Princess with her sons Prince Frederick
Wilhelm and Prince Louis Ferdinand 53

The Kaiser with his grandson, Prince Frederick
Wilhelm 53

Herr and Frau vom Rath 53

Lilli Lehmann 58

Jules Massenet 59

Two scenes from *Manon* 59

Leo Slezak as Otello 64

Dr. Holbrook Curtis 64

Lillian Nordica 65

Nellie Melba 65

Isadora Duncan 68

Mata Hari 68

Violetta in *Traviata*, Act IV 69

Queen Elizabeth in *Don Carlos* 69

Farewell Concert, Berlin, 1906 80

Miss Farrar and her mother, New York, 1906 81

Debut Program, Metropolitan Opera House 94

Miss Farrar's American Debut as Juliette 94

Marguerite in *Faust*, Prison Scene 95

Thaïs 95

The Goosegirl in *Koenigskinder*, when live geese
were used 98

Kate Douglas Wiggin 102

x

	FACING
MISS FARRAR'S MOTHER	102
MADAME BUTTERFLY	103
GIACOMO PUCCINI	108
ARTURO TOSCANINI	109
ANTONIO SCOTTI AS SCARPIA IN *Tosca*	109
IN FRANZ LEHAR'S *Romany Love*	112
MME. SANS-GÊNE	112
TOSCA	113
LOUISE	113
MISS FARRAR LISTENING TO HER FIRST RECORDING	118
ENRICO CARUSO	119
GIULIO GATTI-CASAZZA	119
MISS FARRAR IN 1912	126
SARAH BERNHARDT	126
ITEMIZED STATEMENT OF INDEBTEDNESS TO MRS. ANNIE B. WEBB, PAID IN FULL BY MISS FARRAR IN 1909	127
MINNIE HAUK	128
EMMA CALVÈ	128
MISS FARRAR IN HER METROPOLITAN OPERA *Carmen*	129
LUCREZIA BORI	150
GIOVANNI MARTINELLI	151
MISS FARRAR IN *Zaza*	151
DAVID BELASCO	154
MISS FARRAR IN A LIBERTY LOAN DRIVE PAGEANT	154
MR. AND MRS. SIDNEY FARRAR IN 1917	155
LOU TELLEGEN, GERALDINE FARRAR, MR. AND MRS. FARRAR IN HOLLYWOOD	160
SCENE FROM MOVING-PICTURE VERSION OF *Carmen*	161
SCENE FROM *The Woman God Forgot*, WITH THEODORE KOSLOFF AND WALLACE REID	161

Two scenes from *Turn of the Wheel*, with Percy
Marmont, Violet Heming and Hassard Short   168

Two scenes from *Maria Rosa*, with Pedro de Cordoba
and Wallace Reid   169

Miss Farrar in *Joan the Woman*   176

Scene from *Flame of the Desert*, with Lou Tellegen and
Alec B. Francis   177

Scene from *Shadows* with Milton Sills   177

Miss Farrar in the sable coat that proved too warm for
desert wear   184

Departure on concert tour, after Metropolitan Opera
farewell performance   192

Interior of Miss Farrar's private car   192

Farewell Concert, Carnegie Hall, 1931   232

Miss Farrar and Milton J. Cross during Metropolitan
Opera broadcast   233

Miss Farrar at Fairhaven, in her Garden   280

Note on the Illustrations

The picture of Leo Slezak facing page 64, courtesy of Underwood & Underwood. The picture of Mata Hari facing page 68, courtesy of Times Wide World. The picture of Isadora Duncan facing page 68; the pictures of Minnie Hauk and Emma Calvè facing page 128, courtesy of Culver Service. The picture of Miss Farrar facing page 280 taken by Louise Dahl-Wolfe, courtesy of Harper's Bazaar.

All other pictures are from Miss Farrar's private collection.

Such sweet compulsion doth in music lie
To lull the daughters of necessity
And keep unsteady Nature to her law
And the low world in measured motion draw
After the heavenly tune, which none can hear
Of human mould with gross unpurgèd ear.

MILTON: ARCADES

SUCH SWEET COMPULSION

When from the recess of the mind
Arise fair images of days gone by,
And all unheeded is the body's vanishing
Beyond the reach of mortal eye,
Yet stir the senses, with still power to charm,
While in a low and sweet refrain,
Fond memories our bosoms warm,
And we are young and fair again.

No change to true attachment comes,
How truly did the poet sing;
Thru varied seasons, changing tides,
Staunch friendship's theme will ever ring,
Space matters not, in sky or sea,
The realm of thought, the span of years,
Some essence of a beauty lived, tho' gone—
Quickens the soul, and animates the spheres.

G. F.

CHAPTER ONE

I

THE MOTHER

1882-1897

I DIED in the beginning of the year 1923. That is, my spirit freed itself from its physical wrappings.

I have always been a "sensitive;" and since my departure to another realm, I have had the constant yearning to communicate with my daughter, and thus once again voice the note of love and encouragement that united us so closely while I was on the earth.

For the present, that urge seems possible only through the intermediation of a close friend, sympathetic to us both, and a "sensitive," like myself.

My daughter is not yet placed in such a frame of serenity that she will permit me a direct approach to her; but sometimes, when she is in a mood of retrospection, or dreaming, or engrossed in self-study, she suffers me to impinge upon her subconscious mind, and then she is sympathetic to reception. How correctly she will interpret me remains to be seen, but her heart is kindly, she strives for justice, and I know she will render due tribute to the efforts made for her career, that career which has been our inseparable glory and interest.

Now grown to full maturity, and quite removed from those early scenes of ambitious activity, I feel she will try properly to value that achievement in life we both worked so hard and so honorably to obtain.

Her background I consider very important for its hereditary content of those values, in mosaic pattern, that distinguish the individual, and lend a colorful note beyond the ordinary scale of human equipment.

I was born in the latter years of my own mother's life—the last of several children, with no particular artistic talent. Mine was a very delicate nervous system coupled with a none too robust constitution.

My father was an unsung genius of the violin—gentle, moody, impractical; a nature-lover and an instinctive musician. These artistic attributes were not looked upon favourably by the reserved and rugged New England neighbors. I alone understood him, in his dream world.

As a small child I enjoyed our companionship, which was one of harmony and music. Owing to him, an inherent love of music became my early obsession and delight. The straitened circumstances of our daily life, the placid acceptance and unmoving contentment of those about me, fomented a fever and rebellion; a restlessness for another kind of existence and an outlet for the urge within me, as yet unable to find an escape from oppressive surroundings. In the midst of bewildering fancies, at seventeen I met and married the man who was to be the father of this daughter of mine.

4

Three years old

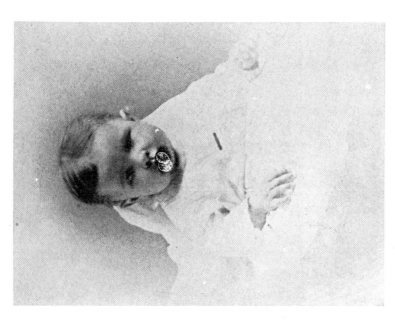

At the age of three months

ELVIRA WHEELER   DENNIS BARNES
MISS FARRAR'S MATERNAL GRANDPARENTS

HENRIETTA BARNES FARRAR
MISS FARRAR'S MOTHER

MARIA FARRAR   SIDNEY ALGERNON FARRAR

MISS FARRAR'S PATERNAL GRANDPARENTS

SIDNEY FARRAR

MISS FARRAR'S FATHER

AT THE TIME OF MR. BOND'S INTERVIEW

THE FIRST MELROSE CONCERT
GIVEN BY MISS FARRAR

Handsome, gifted with a lovely, natural voice—and best of all—endowed with extraordinary kindliness of heart, he was one to win every sympathy in all his contacts. This abundance of natural charm was to play an important part in my daughter's heritage, along with a remarkable endowment of vocal promise, that showed itself at an absurdly early age.

Thus, at eighteen, I was a mother, eagerly planning and full of hope for the ultimate musical development of my only child. How much beauty of thoughts and dreams I must have unconsciously carried in my heart along with that small embryo! Surely she was marked with a consecrated flame.

The activities of a small New England town in the early nineties were not without charm and interest. Our family trio was a happy, modest circle. My husband entered a small business, and in summertime, because of his magnificent physique and athletic ability, he became an outstanding baseball player. Meanwhile, I waited for our roly-poly baby to grow up. With what happy surprise I saw her toddle to the old-fashioned square piano—that great Titan with its yellowing keys. The tiny hands struck the notes in tune and harmony. She played by ear, catching melody and rhythm without fail.

The Sunday school class was her first audience; for them she sang loudly and joyously, never for a moment intimidated. I never allowed her to use a piece of music, but encouraged the habit of memorizing both songs and verses. In after years, we both had cause to be grateful for this early freedom from the printed page.

In her I soon began to formulate the dream I never could realize for myself. Gently but surely she was brought to a conscious knowledge of a career that would demand the ultimate in perception, discipline, and work. I had no difficulty with her. A youthful imagination lifted her into a dream world, beautiful and satisfying beyond the everyday routine that went on so monotonously about her. Her development was furthered by a healthy body and wholesome habits. A pleasant disposition, a nature easily swayed by affection, impulse overriding caution, and a stubborn loyalty were her marked characteristics. Books were her close companions; nor did I have any need to supervise a choice that was one of instinctive good taste and informative interest.

With all these excursions into a fairyland of her own making, she was not allowed to neglect her household duties! Like any other little New Englander's, they were many and not very romantic, but often I could hear her humming gaily as she went about the homely tasks, which were fairly well performed. She loved dolls to distraction, and all dogs were her friends.

Perhaps my own thwarted ambitions made me more than usually keen to watch the development of my child along musical lines. It was not entirely mother-pride that noted the maturity of Geraldine's voice at a very early age.

My young husband had a position in Boston. That meant an early morning awakening, particularly in our dark winters, and somewhat of an effort to prepare cheerfully his seven o'clock breakfast by the kerosene lamp—and sustain an equable mood throughout the busy day. It never occurred to me that my baby was unusual in her desire to join so early the small family circle; but we would find her wide-awake, so we placed her, well wrapped in flannels, in her high-chair, gurgling and crooning over her porridge, in invariably happy

6

spirits. Such a companionable little fat cherub, seldom out of my arms or sight. I rarely knew her to cry.

When she was three years of age, I allowed her to sing a little solo in the children's Sunday school class—and she not only carried the tune perfectly, with great poise, but asked me, upon conclusion, if "she had done well," to the amusement of the grown-ups present.

As time went on, I placed her with a local teacher for piano lessons. These were not very successful. Geraldine was impatient and had her own ideas about harmony, so that the drudgery of scale practice was a source of argument and little progress. The less alert-minded teacher had no defense to offer when confronted with the biographical statements, that often great musicians and composers were indifferent technicians, notably Richard Wagner. This glib alibi of my daughter worked wonderfully well. The cowed teacher said no more! Geraldine loved the thunder of great chords rather than the tinkling celerity of obedient fingers—too young to realize what makes a complete musical equipment, of course.

I subscribed to many musical biographies, and handsomely illustrated magazines, that fostered her interest in fine music and great names. Yards of cheese-cloth and calico went toward home-fashioned costumes. Fairy tales and Biblical stories were put into dramatic form for the children, at church and school festivals, and my girl fired her more phlegmatic little friends with her volatile spirits and energy.

The dancing class was like all such painful early efforts at a drawing-room manner, and highly unpopular with the children in general. Before little girls in stiffly starched skirts, with their locks straining at tight bows of brilliant ribbon, the boys stood first on one foot, then another, when the dances were called. Their white cotton gloves were a source of acute embarrassment, usually hanging shapeless, from imprisoned hands, while the outrage of scrubbed ears and plastered hair was in no way assuaged by a giggling partner, to be dismissed on the stroke of the last measure. Everybody felt the unaccustomed importance of patent-leather slippers, only donned for very special occasions, and in consequence of a normal vanity, generally uncomfortably tight. This somewhat mitigated against the swan-like glide prescribed for young ladies, and the measured step desirable for young gentlemen. The class waddled more or less like ducks on the waxed floor which, often as not, proved perilous.

As I fashioned all my dresses, as well as Geraldine's from her babyhood, we owned an indispensable wicker frame on which I draped my materials. Geraldine named this headless-armless travesty of the human form, "Sarah-Ann Wireback," and included her in the various dramas and poems she composed incessantly. These former were acted, in costume, by herself, me, "Nero" the cat, and "Jessie" the Spaniel, while "Sarah-Ann" was either an implacable witch or a benevolent fairy godmother. It was a delight to share my child's enthusiasm, as we cut cloth, pasted silver stars on night-gowns, or evolved blonde wigs from the shavings of a neighboring carpenter-shop.

These scenes naturally took place to a running accompaniment of music, both piano and song. In fact, the several men who used to depart by my husband's morning train, and return with him before suppertime, would ask him, sympathetically, how he withstood so much music in his home?

8

With wife and child constantly at this useless accomplishment, they were inclined to pity rather than compliment him! But he was proud of us both and gave little heed to such well-meant observations. Whatever I decided he agreed to and considered right in the education of our precious baby. I remember how infuriated I was as a young mother, wheeling Geraldine out on a first outing, when an elderly gentleman inquired if I were the baby's sister? Just turned eighteen and weighing scarcely one hundred pounds, I suppose I did not seem exactly the personification of maternal authority!

It was not long before the baby had outgrown the carriage and my arms, and become my sturdy companion, walking beside me, almost as tall as I was. However, she was a grown girl before we relinquished the sweet habit of the rocking-chair lullaby that put her in a drowsy mood, as she went stumbling to her own little bed every night.

She was ten when I allowed her to sing in a church social, and twelve when at a May festival she impersonated Jenny Lind before a large audience in our Town Hall. She did her part charmingly, and was quite free from affectation in her obvious happiness and ease in appearing upon a public stage. From one of my own silk dresses, I made a little evening frock, but gloves were taboo; nothing could confine those nervous hands. With the dark braids and flashing smile, she made a sweet and wholesome picture; and her voice was like a rich cello. I was proud and more than ever confident, and determined that my child should have all the advantages which her unusual talent dictated.

An important step had to be taken. Our small income was hardly sufficient to support those changes and expenses which

9

would have to be met in the consecrated and intense study for a professional career. Her voice was a voice of mature beauty in a child's throat—it was not too early to consider a careful routine for its development.

In the classroom, the urge for self-expression often brought her into disfavor with the school authorities. Music was the powerful magnet that drew her home, whenever the mood called, to the happy hour of absorption and outpouring of luscious tones at the piano. There was no curbing this instinct as sudden and as natural as a homing pigeon's flight. Meanwhile, I realized I had to cope with her strong sense of independence, and an individualism, almost obstinacy, along certain character lines. She was painfully frank—often brusque, but the impulsive expression of likes and dislikes has now noticeably softened with the years. She will not dissemble, but she will keep silent. Fortunately, the utmost trust and harmony prevailed, and bound us in common love and interest. To me, she voiced the one and only desire that actuated her every waking and sleeping hour: to be a great singer.

Through this channel, I was able to soften those manifestations of her exuberance and self-will that might otherwise have proved detrimental to our plans for her future. The usual careless play of her school friends was of minor interest when the choice lay between their pastimes and her beloved music. Every precaution was taken to keep the lovely mellow quality of her voice unharmed. Loud laughter, screams, dancing with attendant draughts, skating, horseback riding, tennis, swimming—all these usual gay doings were denied her. To be truthful, she didn't mind. She was an indifferent student, but loved history, literature and the languages. Impossible to mould her to the prescribed measure of mass tabulation.

10

In advance of our time, and with, perhaps, more freedom of thought than our friends of more conventional pattern, my husband and I, though of the Unitarian faith, never forced a religious formula upon our daughter's impressionable nature. She was not baptized, and I endeavored to have her realize from her early years that the deed, not the ritual, must be the standard by which to measure her life pattern. She was, by nature, a reverent spirit. She sought her own answers in self-examination; the effort to control a quick tongue and impatient spirit kept her aware of the benefits of discipline. She was never struck nor chastised by harsh measure; she was too high-strung and sensitive to risk such treatment. But isolation tormented her gregarious spirit—the closed piano— the absence of books—a day's silence—all such measures sank deeply into her active mind and reasoning-power. Thus I, as mother, did not represent the offended authority, but the *circumstance* in itself was the act that induced the penalty, and the afterthought.

As the years went on, this living expression of my hopes and dreams endeared itself to me in almost painful concentration. I was young and ambitious for her—and in her, perhaps, I hoped to find the complete expression of myself that had suffered a check in marriage and motherhood. My ambitious hopes began to take concrete form.

My husband's fine voice had placed him in our church choir, where I also had my place as leading soprano. He was as well, a valued member of the Amphion Club, an organization of male singers who were excellent amateur musicians. He was often the soloist at their concerts, and some great singer was always a guest artist during the season.

To these concerts I always took Geraldine, from babyhood. She was perfectly quiet, and never went to sleep as did some of the other youngsters brought by doting parents. She would ask questions about the selection given, and express pleasure or dislike in no uncertain terms. Often when her enthusiasm was not to be repressed she would hum with the singers. It was an unconscious impulse and disturbed nobody. That is—not much, I think. Though she may not recall it now in detail, she heard Lilli Lehmann, then in her prime; and our lovely Nordica who, delayed once by a snow storm, nevertheless arrived despite difficulties. In her pretty traveling gown, she apologized for lack of evening dress, remarking that as she was engaged to sing, she judged the wardrobe was of secondary importance, and rather than keep the audience waiting for baggage mislaid, she chose to perform at once. I often told Geraldine of the incident, and how much her gracious manner had endeared her to the listeners who had waited to hear her at considerable expense and discomfort.

Does anybody now recall those melodious cantatas and oratorios? For in them, my husband's beautiful barytone voice was in demand, while I had charge of the stage pictures and groups, also leading the chorus. Geraldine was always pressed into service, though I do not see how we could have kept her away, so insistent was she in her demands to sing and act—any and all things; if an infant fell ill, she knew all the parts, and could fill the vacancy in an eye-wink. I am not sure she didn't offer up a tiny prayer that a slight indisposition might affect each of the leading lights—just for the occasion—so that she might offer her ready services. She had absolutely no vanity, and it was quite remarkable to see how, once enveloped in some material to lend her line and grace, a pasteboard crown on her head, or a rose garland in her hands, she lost all semblance of a square little New Englander of no particular beauty, and became an arresting figure that drew all eyes. Behind the kerosene foot-lamps, embellished with the home-applied color from beet juice on lips and cheeks, and lamp-black to flatter grey eyes that sparkled gaily, I sometimes wondered if this transformation could really be my child. And so, it was not hard for my proud eyes to see what nature intended for my girl as she approached adolescence, and the surety of my purpose for her. For now it was time to begin thinking seriously of musical concentration to the exclusion of other things. Our good friend Janet Spencer, a soloist of note in one of Melrose's lovely churches, was responsible for the choice of the first vocal teacher, who had been her own.

The well-known Boston teacher received us one cold, rainy morning. Her opinion was not the usual superficial affirmation that the voice of the century stood before her! Slowly and carefully she listened to quality, volume, extension of scales, sustained tones. And above all, to that peculiar vibrant quality that was so unusual in its appealing tenderness, and so outstanding an asset to my daughter's vocal equipment. Tensely, we waited for that expert opinion of it. Its color and maturity, however, were less remarkable to her keen ear, than the unspoiled joyous spirit that animated the musical phrase, and gave it such poignant and spontaneous appeal. Appreciating my high hopes, and the potentialities possible to the highest standards—happily indifferent to the siren call of precocious exploitation—this honest teacher gave her opinion carefully and with true interest. I listened with beating heart.

We planned to have her continue in public school, let her

13

graduate with her class, and, save for the concentration on her musical activity, to follow a routine in no way different from that of the usual growing child in a small residential town. To manage on my husband's small means—and what the end would be if I seriously fostered her dedication to a professional career—was now the dream that colored my days and worried my nights. Both for ourselves and for her, I realized that only an adherence to the highest standards would bring us to the goal we sought. And I dared not fail. My organization must be the cradle in which she should flower. My hand must guide, my energy and courage sustain, all the efforts. Upon her obedience and trust in me alone would be formed the definite pattern, the character as woman and as artist, that I had to mould with her help. My husband, confident of my ability to manage a situation even so improbable as our family's successful dedication to our daughter's singing career, offered no resistance to a step that seemed radical indeed for our limited means. But I had before me the vision of a wide horizon, and my faith in the ultimate achievement of my heart's desire was so firm, I did not hesitate to put myself to any test.

On various occasions, at church services, funerals, and concerts, the precocious gift of my child had been noticed with more than usual interest and favor. A kindly Boston merchant, Charles H. Bond, had made many a beneficial gesture toward helping young aspirants. Geraldine had sung for him, on several occasions, and his own opinion of her ability and promise was heartily seconded by his charming wife, Belle Bond, herself a "reader" of note.

In those days, elocution as understood in public reading was

CONCERT IN WASHINGTON 1897

the popular step toward actual dramatic and stage experience. I confessed my ambitions to Mr. Bond, described our modest circumstances and the pressing need for Geraldine to have the complete educational benefits that should accompany such a career as I outlined. I related that Geraldine had recently obtained a favorable audition from Jean de Reszke, the idol of the opera-loving world. The Maurice Grau Opera Company was then in Boston and the tenor's artistry and distinction were acclaimed, with no note of dissension from a frenzied public all over America. This recommendation was helpful I am sure, and the Polish gentleman evidently felt an impulse to be kind to the little unknown school-girl, but I do in all honesty believe the shrewd merchant was more particularly impressed by my own belief and stubborn optimism in my daughter's future.

While I talked and talked, Geraldine was at home recovering from a tonsilectomy. It had taken weeks to persuade her to take this necessary step—and only when I pointed out that unless removed the offending tissues would spoil her singing did I obtain her consent. Trembling and tearful, the poor mite went through the very bloody and nauseous ordeal and was a very sick little creature for days. This temporary disturbance was almost forgotten in the result of my final discussion with Mr. Bond. His aid was assured—he was willing to gamble with me. So our first business transaction was effected with him. It was a generous loan of $500, which seemed fabulous to a mind that had reckoned always in cautious pennies! By careful planning I intended to stretch it to the utmost, keeping minute account of every expenditure, and the value received. With no further security than his trust in

15

my integrity, and judgment of my child's possibilities, my hopes were thus crystallized into definite procedure.

New York was our immediate aim.

II

THE DAUGHTER

1897-1901

I AM over half a century young, as I write these lines. Looking out over the tranquil hills, their quiet green an inspiration far removed from that operatic realm of youthful exuberance and endeavor where long ago I trod the pasteboard land of illusion, where the calcium challenges the sun and the canvas marvels of the designer and decorator call more insistently than nature's own colors and intentions. To recapture that fine aroma, and relegate the personal pronoun to impartial observation as much as possible, I shall try to vitalize the shadows that were once vivid and compelling sound, gesture, and fleshly apparition. As many others have done, I shall try to fashion the truthful story of a fortunate girl happily endowed with many of nature's choice gifts, that made her artistic life one of glamour and laurel.

A wise and imaginative Chinese poet once wrote:

"Life is the dream of a dream"—and so it seems in pleasant retrospection—may this soften the possible egoism of the writer. All the arts consort in sweet sisterhood and each tiny thread of individual achievement gilds the long chain of their enduring history.

16

MISS FARRAR'S FIRST PARIS HAT AND GOWN, 1900

IN BERLIN, 1901

MISS FARRAR AS SHE SANG IN THE VOM RATH'S HOME

Perhaps the gossamer pattern of song, so appealing, so personal, is all the more intense an expression by reason of its universal and transient utterance. And within these portals stand figures of Beauty, Hope, Inspiration and Poetry—fit companions of the the singing Muse.

The destiny of a spectacular achievement was reserved for this sturdy New Englander, in a small town of no more virtue or quality than is to be found in hundreds of such pleasant communities throughout our United States.

Modest circumstances, modest surroundings—but a fire and urge to soar on wings of song to a delicious, dangerous, unknown adventure.

Biographies of famous prima donnas often have a distressing and monotonous similarity, according to their written page. The Cinderella legend has a perennial appeal to adult as well as adolescent imagination. The early wonder-child invariably overcomes poverty, the ugly duckling period of awkwardness and juvenile plainness of feature, to find herself an alluring magnet of temperamental display, after the indispensable European sojourn has been heralded in the home gazettes, and one's home people are brought to a prostrate chorus of admiring approval and love.

Admirers swarm. Romance breathes. A bewildering train of amorous swains keeps her in the headlines, and her frocks and jewels invariably excite more comment than the precious vocal pearls that account for the extravagant worship.

If she marries—it need not be fatal error—it might well be conceded a passing fancy and by no chance allowed to interfere with the implacable routine of the singer's rigorous adherence to her scales and diet, and her public duties. Surprisingly enough, if there are children, the contralto provides the more generous figure of maternity and girth.

Perfumes, powders, candy and feminine apparel, often bear her euphonious name and yield her a pretty royalty in return for the small favor of her personal recommendation.

Her pets are either the smallest or largest; though one exuberant Latin artist never travelled without a cage of canaries, objects of her childish and devoted attention.

The world is ever-watching and critical; a reporter might linger in the person of a charming young girl across the way, or the broad-shouldered man who so gallantly retrieved a muff or handkerchief! He gets a smile—to be sure—often news, as well!

Glamour—glamour—and then glamour. She must play her stellar role from the moment she leaves her boudoir till she returns. No fatigue, no nervous tension, must mar the winning manner or cloud the smile, while on parade. *Noblesse oblige.* Her opinion is requested on every subject—always, she is "news"—during her reign, until a younger, fresher rival challenges her supremacy, to wrest from her the laurel diadem. Gala operas provoke the mad delight of her listeners, and charitable affairs clamour for her patronage. Crowds follow her home, hanging to the tail-end of whatever vehicle she chooses to honor. Life would seem a delirium of roses, shouts and perfervid affection. The gracious lady (well aware of the finale expected) bares her million dollar throat to the frosty winds, and after a homely ditty, is allowed reluctantly to retire to a well-earned repose.

Quiet she has not—for tomorrow is again the same day of vigilance—and so on throughout the years of a career. Her

18

success must be made along every line. She needs a level head and a stout heart, as well as most unusual vocal cords!

Now had one young hopeful envisioned all this, she would still not have faltered on that wondrous path chosen in her tender years. Life was rich in promise; it was fine to struggle, and a privilege to achieve! And there were odds aplenty to challenge one.

With high courage, devotion and faith, my young mother fostered her child's natural and independent approach to people and things, with a definite emphasis on that self-reliance which must be sustained with determination, and more, at the price of many a wound and experience.

Unhampered by *don'ts*, my childhood was replete with color and interest.

A world of musical sounds began to impress itself early upon a conscious and receptive ear:—the silvery splash of a rain-drop—the menace of a rusty door-hinge—the call of a flirtatious robin—the deep bars of a contented frog—the surge of the Sunday hymns—and the throb of the organ that spurred the most timid among us to congregational and hearty vocal endeavor. *Greenland's Icy Mountains* rose in a fantastic picture, likewise *Unfold Ye Portals Everlasting*—and a lusty young acolyte joined in the chorus with fervor and volume.

The long sermon—and how long they can seem to a restless youngster!—was but a murmuring undercurrent to the music of the swaying elms outside the tiny church. Their glorious branches caressed the stained-glass windows—and immutable Saints in soft colors and gracious attitudes glowed with life and radiance; Burne-Jones throats raised in impossible singing postures, glittering wings—a poetic and indefinite land of musical expression, as yet sensed and half-revealed, while the sermon droned on.

Tremulous and eager were these first conscious indications of a spirit's release from actuality. That early maturity of vocal urge gave this little girl a prominent place in musical activities.

The depth and volume of the middle voice—its most appealing register throughout a long career—easily placed her *one* lone second soprano against an entire class of high, piping, trebles. Never fear—out-sing them she could and did; lung power, exuberance, and instinct were there to time her ear to part-singing without additional aid from the blackboard and the school musical authority. Child of musical parents, both gifted with lovely natural voices and interested only in standard music, our young hopeful knew from her earliest approach to the Muse only the best; at the piano a rebel, and unwilling to follow dry and methodical outlines, she found an instinctive release of tone color from the keys, though she never mastered an acceptable piano selection, and ignored every advice as to proper fingering and pedaling.

She always maintained from even so tender an age—twelve—that she could sing best with her own accompaniment; this assertion was voiced frequently in her later years, when the question of that most subtle merging in Lieder of voice and accompaniment made it a task to find the required second artist of sensitive co-operation. Curiously enough, by no prescribed rules could this obstinate young energy be governed.

Punishment for trivial misdemeanors were sacrifices of independence; no book, no piano—silence and isolation. Reflec-

20

tion, rebellion—eventual contrition—and again restoration to the musical dream world that was growing in its intensity and urge.

The first piano—all one's own! A reward for conquering the hated arithmetic! An opera score as a commendation for household tasks! Dusting, washing of lamp chimneys—no easy task without breakage in those days of the kerosene beacon!—the making of one's bed with no wrinkles in the snowy sheets—or fold to mar a smooth counterpane. Books kept untorn and clean, stockings neatly mended, hair-ribbons properly folded, handkerchiefs clean in the morning pocket for 9 A. M. school, and many similar chores for a small-town New Englander of modest means. At fourteen, in 1896, a healthy desire to shine in some romantic world of musical expression. The pretty mother, young and graceful, a beautiful dancer at all the festivals of church and social gatherings. This young song-bird, an awkward fledgling.

There was the tedium of school routine—the boredom and restlessness—the flight toward freedom, if but for an hour! The raised hand—permission for a drink of water. The flight toward home and the piano—music—revery—the passing of hours in blissful solitude!

Many such infringements could not go without notice for long! We could not know then that in later year this sense of suffocation would come under the well-defined head of claustrophobia—the imperative need for space; space of mind, body and spirit! A reason we seek our hills today and receive their benediction of quiet.

Meanwhile, the sturdy body grows apace—a pair of wide shoulders that frame a big box for unrestricted lung play. In those days young females were put at an early age into the restraining steel of the old-fashioned corset—sheathed in this under cuirass, skirts to the heels, and one's mop of hair in a knob at the nape of the neck—this was the prescribed procedure for a "nice girl" approaching graduation and womanhood. But this young rebel was not forced to such a martyrdom; and later, at seventeen, a long braid still swung down her back when she embarked for the indispensable European teaching, and no iron confined the freedom of her splendid bellows.

At this time, several appearances in local towns were making it possible for a vivid, somewhat hoydenish personality to taste a few of the delights of early public acclaim, and the fascinating game of "being someone else." The question of serious study was a problem for the parents, cautious in their concern for their one ewe lamb; entailing as well sacrifices on their part to make possible the slim chance of a career.

If every girl might find a similar wholesome training at the beginning!

The ebullient, inexhaustible vitality was allowed such scope in singing procedure as kept the pupil's interest without injurious exertion of the voice; despite its maturity in appeal and color, it was still the voice of a girl in her 'teens.

Then came a real recital night; the first city concert in Boston! A frock, made by a mother's loving hands, from her own store of silk. Those days, material did "best" and "second best" for her, then similar service for her daughter! Had there been younger offspring, surely they too would have had their share of the lustrous material bought for such honorable service! All young persons hopefully eyed their elders' wardrobe . . . with "Diamond Dyes" to change and offset an ennui of color, if not of pattern.

I am reasonably certain that a mink that once found itself in my mother's Christmas package, never dreamed of an existence as long as he was to have in our family! For he swung season after season, first about her neck, then about mine! He was a prized ornament, and frequently journeyed to adorn a friend's costume, a loan that but engendered pleasant intimacy, extending to borrowed silver and linen when occasion and numbers taxed one's home stock for weddings, anniversaries and such! The pleasant exchange of small town intimacies.

Then came periods when one's school friends began to act in strange fashion; boys who had indifferently pushed one aside at class, or teased to tears an exasperated skater with their hockey sticks, suddenly wore slick hair, scrubbed red hands, and begged the privilege of carrying one's books . . . lingering on the doorstep with a foolish grin and inarticulate stuttering.

Girls became conscious of their oddities:—blushed and giggled, ostentatiously tucked away scraps of writing—chose partners at dancing school with the energy of an Amazon— and often appeared with beet juice and flour thick upon self-conscious faces.

These manifestations were no part of our own day-dreams. Singing, always singing—this fairy world occupied my every thought, day and night. I fear I gave myself airs then and there, as being "different" and destined for more exciting adventures.

The excited young heart was thrilled with the first introduction to opera!—a world of enchantment—heard and seen from the gallery. The opera was *Carmen*, that master expression to which musician and layman alike thrill with unconscious and joyful enthusiasm in all climes. Add the fascinating Calvè as the gypsy girl—the supreme and daring French woman never to be forgotten once heard!

This New Englander was conscious of the luscious excitation of thrill and color, the allure of the glowing score, and the provocative beauty of the fascinating singer. Upon this strong fare she steeped herself for weeks . . . from elementary high-school French, she evolved her own imitative pronunciation, as nearly as possible like the magic syllables that had issued in sensuous beauty from the lips of the gifted artist.

And now to serious work. Mind, body and voice were ready. This student was not an easy nor docile acolyte. There must be a reason for all that was told her, and, as well, an insistence upon her individual expression which she jealously defended, and on which point more than once she clashed with older and wiser heads! Rash, impertinent—disrespectful too, perhaps.

This questionable independence is only of value when followed through with self-confidence and faith; an urge that will not and cannot be denied!

There is no rule for this type. The self-invited criticisms and experiences are of the person's own volition; by such procedure, however, their own particular efforts stand or fall. No one mould ever succeeded in other than mass-production of wearisome replicas. Very good for an open-stock dinner set, perhaps, but far and away outside the domain of individual expression in any creative pattern. Even the most uninteresting of humans varies from the pattern in some fashion, even though the variation is not obvious to the casual eye.

24

One's first teacher is frequently one's most valuable aid; if the principles are proper, one's early steps are built upon an enduring foundation.

I found in Mrs. J. H. Long, of Boston, just such excellent counsel. The Italian *bel canto* was her ideal and to her I owe the constant routine of schooling that kept the voice sweet and flexible in those first years of study. It was but natural, after a time, that I was taken to be heard by the visiting great stars for expert opinion, both at home and in New York. I have often wondered at their kindness in listening to so many young hopefuls; just how much is accomplished by a sporadic audition is questionable, but in my case, at any rate, had I not enjoyed their encouragement I might not have had so early and favorable a beginning.

A winter in New York evolved itself. I heard opera constantly from behind the "standee" rail and upon paralyzed feet that seemed not to belong to my physical body, save when they refused locomotion after hours of standing in Elysium!

I recall the first acting lessons from a prominent woman who fondly imagined herself of paramount importance in what was then the heyday of "elocution" and Delsartian plastic grace. Herded into a class of a dozen, no more ungainly duckling than myself could have been imagined. In this company, on the stroke of a beat, hands, bodies and faces would try to respond to conventionalized attitudes and expressions as prescribed. Needless to say, I defaulted in every particular—first in silence, then in expostulation. Exasperated at the end of the term, the lady emphasized her opinion to my mother: "Never will this obstinate girl amount to anything"— which did not discourage me, but did remove the untalented one from the circle of obedient and dull nobodies. Hers was

25

not the only class I found so deplorably mechanical, and in which I could find no inspiration or learning for my individual needs.

The drawback with teaching, I find, is the fixed idea that all pupils must tread the same avenue of monotonous tradition. The intense individual will not be able to conform to set rules, but will have to evolve some training that fits her own particular wants and abide by it conscientiously. An inquiring consciousness will not be dampened.

Probably the two most exciting events were the occasions when I sang for Nordica and Melba.

It was my teacher of the moment, Emma Thursby, who made the meeting with these distinguished divas possible. The American prima donna was an example for all time of talent, perseverance and courage. She had achieved an enviable position in the German as well as the lyric repertoire, having, like Lilli Lehmann, developed from an easy coloratura to the dramatic values of these heroic roles. The Australian songstress had been miraculously endowed with the finest natural vocal equipment since Patti, which was not even rivaled by the dizzy cadenzas of the flute she shamed, to the delirious delight of astonished listeners.

Both women were kind. To Nordica I owe later connections that were to prove so valuable in Berlin, while to Melba, I am grateful for the introduction to a peerless gentleman and staunch friend, Mr. Charles A. Ellis, a wise manager, at that time hers, and later, mine.

Another friend who was to be kind and valuable throughout my professional career was Dr. Holbrook Curtis, the authority on singers' throats, as well as the larynxes of less

26

endowed mortals. That five hundred dollars which was Mr. Bond's loan, so preciously budgeted, could not last indefinitely, and certainly even my clever mother had not foreseen expensive treatments and operations on this very instrument with which we hoped to bring ourselves to stellar heights and achievements. But Dr. Curtis, whose brusque manner hid a tender heart, would hear of no delay—nor payment for urgent needs of the moment. When my mother, moreover, demurred, and said even for a career we could not accept such an obligation, he waved her away, even as the nurse prepared his delicate instruments, and muttered: "Well, if you insist, and this girl amounts to what you think she will, you can ask me then for a bill. But for Heaven's sake stop talking and let me operate!" Which he did—neatly and without further delay.

It is pleasant to relate that I was able to repay this particular debt soon after my Metropolitan appearance, some ten years later. But no fee could really have repaid him for the devotion and skill exercised at a critical moment when I needed help and his surgery. I was to be his grateful patient all his life.

As house physician to the Metropolitan stars, he owned a pair of orchestra seats most advantageously placed down front. When the less temperamental stars were scheduled to sing, he felt he could take an evening of rest away from his post, and in giving me and mother these seats he made it possible, now and again, actually to sit in blissful ease and enjoy the opera wonderland. Otherwise I paid my fifty cents and clung to the familiar old railing, always in a joyous daze.

If all the wives of impresarios were blessed with the kindliness and tact of Madame Maurice Grau, life for them and the singers would be comparatively peaceful in the operatic

27

aviary. I met Madame Grau through Dr. Curtis, and it was she who arranged the audition I had that winter at the Metropolitan. I imagine mother consented in the hope of interesting some prominent person in my further studies, for surely those five hundred dollars were fast diminishing, despite her excellent economy.

I made the audition and in doing so made several good friends who, indeed, seemed very desirous to advance material aid. For some reason, however, mother did not accept the offers. Nor the proposal to have me appear, as a *wunderkind* in a revival of *Mignon*, proposed for Melba in her desire for an additional role. I must add that she too wished me to succeed, and urged the debut. Fortunately, my mother's good sense prevailed. She was playing for bigger stakes than a brief flash of spectacular value only, and voiced her reasons for refusal with firmness and regret. So the Metropolitan debut was deferred until a more propitious moment made me worthy of serious consideration as a trained singer.

It would be ungallant to give in detail the events and minor contributions of the several professionals who were my instructors during this period. All had something of value to impart. They have since died, and perhaps are not even names to this reading generation. I am grateful for such kernels as I picked up from them for myself.

Always, some grist was to be added to my mill. Self-analysis was soon awakened. My mother's wise judgment and my own inherent love of the finest, kept us from too grievous mistakes along the trite or commonplace road of endeavor. Flattering were the many offers for early appearances in concert, and most welcome would have been the generous fees, but we were seeking more enduring laurels.

I was growing rapidly and too much attention was focused upon these trying 'teens; the prodigy halo became a menace! For a season I was placed in a charming home in Washington, to continue piano and singing lessons in a less exciting atmosphere, and in company with girls my own age, with no fiery urges. Opportunity to develop thus under wholesome conditions fitted in with my mother's plans for later Continental flight.

Madame Melba was partly responsible for the eventual decision to go to Paris, but again there was need of a permanent guarantee to sustain this expensive move.

On my return home, in the summertime, I had the good fortune to sing for Mrs. Annie Webb. Another Bostonian, she interested herself in young aspirants along all lines of creative endeavor. Her Paris home saw many of her protégés in the avenues of the sister Arts.

On no other security than a philanthropic gamble, and my dear mother's integrity, there was arranged a loan that was to cover expenses for two years abroad. My mother refused to separate our small family and the sum involved had to provide for the living expenses of three persons, as well as sustain my incursion into untried fields of musical and cultural development.

With my father's consent, my mother placed as collateral with Mrs. Webb, our modest home property, his business, and further assured her of our good intentions to repay by an insurance, in her favor, on my life. On the other hand, her conditions were more than generous. There was no date set for repayment, and a written agreement, very loosely worded, was made between Mrs. Webb and my parents (I was still a minor), that when and if my professional career warranted,

29

the loan would be repaid in sums and at times comfortably commensurate with my earning capacity. Surely this speaks eloquently for the kindly interest of Mrs. Webb, and the persuasive arguments of my mother.

So, armed with letters to various musical authorities, we set sail. I was just seventeen and happy as a lark. On a cold, misty morning we left Boston harbor on such a humble conveyance as a cattle boat. With many a protesting beast below, a few selected passengers enjoyed spotless quarters on the upper deck. No later princely suite on a super-liner gave me such a thrill! Our purses were thin, but our hopes boundless. That valiant little ocean traveller later served the Allies well in the Great War. She was called the *Armenian,* and safely landed her every cargo during the terror of the submarine warfare. Wherever her iron bones lie, she has our blessing and thanks!

CHAPTER TWO

THE DAUGHTER

1899-1901

PARIS—then, as now—was Fairyland! All was new, strange and exciting! Where we had at home leafy trees and shady gardens, the small-town cosiness of neighbors and friends, we now knew no one.

Atop the roof of a funny old Latin-Quarter house, we found a tiny apartment. A weary climb of four flights it was, too, though young feet never tire when hearts are light with hope and heads throb with ambitious plans. A solitary gas jet pointed the way with a pallid finger.

The grey wet days of a Paris winter were a far cry from the crisp snow and brilliant sky of our own frosty New England. The frugal briquette of evil-smelling peat barely warmed the rooms, each boasting a miniscule grate and mantle. Candles hung on the small upright piano; a festoon of flickering shadows by which one sang to the frequent tune of ill-repressed coughs and sneezes. Mr. Edison's unwinking Mazda brilliance was still in the future.

Once settled, an amusing round of auditions followed. Our first visit was to a dear old Italian of eighty, highly recommended. He sat at the piano, a veritable Patriarch—though too deaf to attempt even an opinion. His smile was seraphic, but—we left our gold-piece on the table, and departed.

The next authority was the favored Maestro of several stars, who had previously bestowed on us their cards of introduction. Rumor had it that as a valet he had acquired a glib proficiency from a certain beloved operatic tenor of the moment. At any rate, pupils were flocking, still embryonic but hopeful. His particular pet illustration was made by opening and closing an umbrella the while advocating vocalises, with a desperate push at one's stomach. A charlatan of easy address, he was of no use to us and one precious gold-piece was the first and last contribution.

A third on our list was a coach at the Paris opera, a charming and educated musician, but no real singing teacher and vague as to rudimentary requirements for vocal perfection.

I have always regretted I did not make use of a letter to that most noted vocal authority Marchesi, but despite Melba's recommendation to her favorite teacher, there was little to be gained, we felt, in submitting to a dazzling treatment whereby all voices were taught to shame the flute in impossible sky-rocket cadenzas or fall by the wayside when unable to do so. I had no true coloratura register and did not wish to change my own color in such mechanical attainment. I was even then aware of the monotony of beautiful even tones, when all dramatic expression was sacrificed to sound only. This seemed to prevail in the French school of that period. Diction was excellent and clean-cut, but the voices were far from appeal-

Königliche Schauspiele.

Opernhaus.

Dienstag, den 15. Oktober 1901.

212. Vorstellung.

Margarethe.

Oper in 5 Akten von Charles Gounod
nach Wolfgang von Goethes Faust von Jules Barbier
und Michel Carré.

Faust	Herr Grüning
Mephistopheles	Herr Mödlinger
Margarethe	* *
Valentin, deren Bruder	Herr Hoffmann
Martha, Nachbarin	Frau Pohl
Siebel	Frau Gradl
Wagner	Herr Krasa

Studenten. Landsknechte. Bürger. Frauen Mädchen.
Kinder. Heren. Engel.

* * Margarethe: Fräulein Geraldine Farrar aus
New-York als Gast.

Theater und Musik.

DEBUT PROGRAM,
BERLIN ROYAL OPERA

DEBUT, BERLIN, MARGUERITE
IN *Faust*

TWO SCENES FROM *Romeo et Juliette*

Elizabeth in *Tannhäuser*

The Berlin *Manon*

ing in quality and expression. I may have been presumptuous in criticism, but I was firm in my decision as to my own procedure. Finally, we decided upon a Spaniard—Trabadello— and certainly my season with him was very pleasant, but without the solid evidences of the progress that we felt I should be making.

Circumstances and needs were shaping other plans. Germany seemed more promising, with the great Lilli Lehmann, provided she would accept me, as the Ultima Thule of vocal mastery. It is an old story that I wrote her several letters, to which she sent no reply; when finally my mother supplemented them in her precise pretty little hand, an answer came instantly, with the crushing observation that previous communications had been undecipherable. However, I was still to wait before her own professional engagements would permit our uninterrupted study.

My manner of arrival in Berlin had been the outcome of a quick decision. It was because of Madame Nordica's continued interest that I had the friendly introduction to her German friends, the vom Raths, in a letter that was highly complimentary to my talents, and, acting upon this, we lost no time in giving up our Paris domicile, and proceeding to Berlin.

Written upon a slip of paper was the address where I was to stay—the American Women's Club—until we could settle ourselves permanently. These later quarters were found at a charming pension de famille (which sounds so much nicer than a family boarding house!) where a large group of American students held forth. Presided over by the traditional and economical German lady of uncertain age, we were all pleasantly housed and found ourselves busy as bees in a hive!

33

Potsdamerstrasse 13 is now no longer in existence, but it still holds youthful memories for me!

Three other young hopefuls from America were vocal pupils at Graziani's also, and our combined pleasures were many, if on a modest scale. My mother was chaperone, and father, who had returned from his camp in the Adirondacks, a handsome escort. The fare was not always as abundant as our wolfish appetites dictated, so we were always eager when friends came to Berlin on a visit. When they asked what we would like to do, we all invariably shouted, "Eat at the Bristol!" At that time, it was the finest hotel, only to be rivaled in later years by the Adlon, so popular in its catering to Americans that it is not unlike a national institution. Sundays, four of us pooled our resources and rode for an hour in the beautiful Tiergarten. What matter that the cab was decrepit, of third-class vintage, the horse a truck relic, and the coachman a garrulous bewhiskered grandfather? It was all fun, and we had ample opportunity to view the dashing cavalry officers exercising their steeds. The Kaiser would dash by, a handsome figure bowing to left and right from a prancing equine. The Kaiserin, too, might be seen in her victoria, her sweet face shaded under a lace parasol. And on New Year's Day, the parade of the Diplomatic Corps and Foreign Officials was a fairy-like scene of splendor, comparable on a smaller scale to the recent English coronation. There was plenty to bewitch my young and impressionable heart.

So, we were settled in Berlin, quite another atmosphere than Paris. I wanted without delay to meet Lilli Lehmann and get on with serious work. The Russian-Italian Graziani endorsed by Nordica proved of much help, understanding just

34

that breathing support and tone color that I found so lacking in other methods. His counsel was valuable to me, but not so to other voices of lighter calibre, which proves my contention that all teachers have human limitations. At any rate, I began seriously to think of roles and a debut; but that was to be effected in Italy, since I was trained in *bel canto* and anxious to sing only the melodious Italian repertoire. At that moment, it never dawned on me that my career was to be made upon that very soil, in a theatre only a few avenues beyond my temporary lodging!

Jmperial Germany of 1900 was a magnificent country, and Berlin quite measured up to one's earliest dreams of royalty and picturesque glitter. There was the military elegance of Court life, the dynamic Kaiser, a dashing young Crown Prince, and divine music for only a few pennies to enchant one's enthusiastic spirit. Great names abounded in opera, concert and recitals. Dr. Karl Muck, great Wagnerian authority; Dr. Richard Strauss, pre-eminent as conductor and composer; Leo Blech; Joachim's exquisite chamber quartet; Nikisch's glowing orchestral interpretations; Gustav Mahler; von Schuch and a host of others were guests in the Prussian Capitol. Americans were popular. Teddy Roosevelt was a friend of the Kaiser, and it was said each tried to outdo the other in friendly overtures; in evidences of mutual esteem in the press headlines, at any rate. Our ambassadors were wealthy and charming, commercial relations were successful and all was *couleur de rose*.

My first German friends were to be my staunch supporters all during my career and a helpful background in many an exciting, if perplexing, moment. Wealthy and dis-

35

tinguished, of an old Rhenish family, the vom Raths on the distaff side had a blood connection with that gentle Matilde Wesendonck of Wagner's immortal inspiration. It was in this house also that I met the dominant Cosima Wagner and that pallid, rather pathetic caricature of her great husband, her son Siegfried—no very lively table partner and save for the marked profile resemblance to his extraordinary progenitor, of little enough interest to warrant undue excitement on my part.

These early days of study and observation were full of charm and high enthusiasms. Not yet twenty, the days were not long enough to crowd into working hours all I hoped to accomplish. Musical discipline was no dreary round, but a pulsating current that bore one on toward the great highway of achievement and adventure, as yet only hinted at.

CHAPTER THREE

I

THE MOTHER

1901-1906

THE progress my child is making is highly gratifying. An impresario from Milan has heard her sing at Graziani's studio and is eager to present her in Italy this coming fall. There, it seems, one sings a role or two at various theatres as guest, with experience and travel to keep the artist busy enough, I should say, for each long season. At present she sings Violetta, Juliette, and Marguerite beautifully, with such feeling that, though I do not confess it to her, I sit in the neighboring room when she has her lessons and weep, for no explicit reason save that the tone quality is so appealing and lovely. She sings with the greatest ease and spontaneity in Italian and French; her youthfulness is so gay, fresh and unspoiled. Oh, if I could keep her so always.

But I do not favor the proposed excursion to Italy, nor a debut there. My child needs a firm hand and check upon her too exuberant nature that runs the risk of burning itself out before results are accomplished. I would like to see her disciplined by the great Lehmann. She is the artist par excellence, in the grand manner, in elegance and complete musicianship. This discipline will be precious. We shall see if she will accept Geraldine, once her arduous seasons allow freedom for teaching.

Meanwhile, our good friends Herr and Frau vom Rath, are urging us to let them arrange an audition at their house. They can effect a meeting with Graf von Hochberg, the opera intendant, and who knows if this might not be the better suggestion for Geraldine's interest, since she now should be seriously beginning a public career in opera, and so I shall agree.

How charming she will look in a pale blue evening gown, embroidered in silver, her glossy hair framing an eager face—the picture of happy girlhood. She will sing the waltz song, in French, from *Romeo and Juliette,* the concluding aria of the first act of *Traviata,* in Italian, and an English ballad, if an encore is allowed.

I regret she knows no German. This regret, I may mention, was voiced in the manner of a reprimand, when we met the distinguished Cosima Wagner previously, at the vom Raths'. Geraldine was asked to sing and complied in her most pleasing manner, being, as well, in excellent voice and mood. The *Traviata,* however, was not a fortunate choice. We learned later that the great lady did not favor Verdi, nor hold much regard for the several English selections requested by the hostess. It transpired that Cosima had been interested in her friend Frau vom Rath's praise of my daughter, and came with

38

the express purpose of offering her the role of Eva in Bayreuth's coming *Meistersinger* production, if Geraldine pleased her. By some singular fancy, Cosima desired, if possible, to present in the portrayal of this delightful and most naive of Wagnerian heroines, an actual virgin of flesh and blood. It seems this had been hitherto almost impossible to obtain in the singing world! Prima donnas, being normal, healthy females, were either married, widowed, or engaged in such emotional associations as apparently unfitted them and their vocal apparatus for the proper chastity of tone!

Meanwhile, I could not know that Geraldine was not at all impressed by the illustrious son, weighted, poor lad, by the background of a Titanic father, and a no less extraordinary mother. Such people can hardly be comfortable parents, I should think. At any rate, Bayreuth was not in our program, but Graf von Hochberg and the Royal Opera could be easily approached, it seemed, and so one day it all happened as if in a dream.

To be sure, the hour was changed, from the evening to the tea-time gathering of distinguished people. A Court ball that night was the reason. Alas! My child had but the one frock, and so our gracious and understanding hostess drew her curtains to provide a rich velvet background for the effect of night and brilliant setting. My Geraldine was at her best. Radiant and excited, she won all hearts, and in a corner my husband and I, whispering our hopes and plans, thought of the coming audition promised at the opera house, where a momentous decision was to be made.

Graf von Hochberg asked Geraldine if she could learn *Elsa's Dream* in German in ten days. The child confidently

39

promised, though she knew no German, and set herself to the task the following morning with a teacher, who was to become a firm friend and of inestimable assistance in the German language and its diction in singing.

The great day approached. The saturnine Karl Muck, at the peak of his splendid career, was at the conductor's stand. It was the first time Geraldine had ever sung with an orchestra! I thought the child would faint, she was so overwrought emotionally. However, onto the darkened stage she came, unaffected and charming in the waltz song of *Juliette*, the *Traviata* aria, and the Bird Song from *Pagliacci*. Then came the test in *Elsa's Dream*. Happily, her German was commended, likewise her musical phraseology. My husband and I were invited into the private cabinet of Graf von Hochberg, and actually before our eyes lay a contract! Our daughter was still a minor and our signatures were necessary to make a contract valid. We owed this to our good friends the vom Raths. The terms were generous in the interest of her musical freedom. Geraldine was to sing in Italian while she perfected a repertoire in German; she was to be carefully handled, and given the stellar roles that suited her youth and temperament.

This was the spring of 1901 and it was desirable to effect her debut the following autumn as Marguerite in *Faust*. The salary arrangement was a small guarantee monthly, and a fee for each of the eight monthly performances designated, for a term of three years, provided she pleased the Berliners! My heart held no fear for such a contingency! Geraldine's star was in the ascendant; our career was, at last, to begin!

That summer was spent in Switzerland, far from centers of

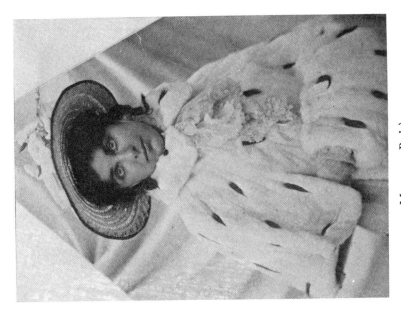

Mimi in *Bohème*

Zerlina in *Don Giovanni*

Dr. Karl Muck

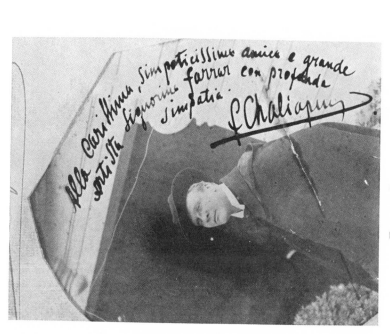

Alla Carissima, simpaticissima amica e grande
artista Signorina Farrar con profonda
simpatia.
F. Chaliapin

Feodor Chaliapin

excitement. A quiet routine and intensive study was our daily program. Geraldine evolved her own ideas of the acting values of Marguerite. Over these she had labored long and lovingly; her rich imagination and musical instinct prompted a self-confidence that used to irritate others less certain of their own powers, and perhaps less alert mentally. She went vigorously on with her particular understanding and approach to the important day that was to determine the course of our whole life as a family unit.

We met several notable musicians, all somewhat lukewarm in approval of so early a debut. I could not feel we were wrong, however. She was young, strong and ardent, mature in intelligence. She would never lose interest in work because of public claims; on the contrary, she would be inspired to further efforts toward their best fulfillment. Besides, youth is the time of singing.

I shall never forget our thrill when Geraldine was notified of the date of her debut, and called for rehearsals.

The opera house was, as is the usual case for these preliminaries, shrouded in protective linen covers; the golden eagles and glittering hangings blazon forth only when performances take place, and the theatre opens to the public. The company was assembled, the stage settings in place—with the piano at one side, serving for accompaniment till a later orchestral combination. Though the seasoned singers had been called expressly for Geraldine's benefit, proceedings were as meticulous as if the occasion were for their own first appearances. The routine and respect from soloist to dancer was an example of painstaking interest, accounting in the long run for the general excellence of ensemble work in the German

41

theatres. There were no haphazard methods, but strict adherence to the various supervisors.

Geraldine went through her rehearsals with fire and enthusiasm, unconscious of all but her own creative energy. She obtained many concessions on the stage, in her very personal conception of Marguerite which was her own, born of a lively fancy and youthful impulse. There was no mistaking her sincerity and the vim with which she attacked each act, developing a growing crescendo that brought spontaneous applause at the close of the trio from her colleagues who were carefully watching the newcomer, and reserving opinions. The tenor Grüning and barytone Hoffman were to become fast friends and partners, over a long period of happy association.

Dr. Karl Muck was at the conductor's desk, and his grim Mephisto countenance could not conceal his involuntary surprise at the newcomer's assurance, which needed no apology for her tender years or inexperience. Geraldine was sure of herself, her conception of the role, and the musical measures. The prompter gave up in astonishment. Not only did she not need his gesture to establish the time beat, nor attend his halting Italian cue; she ignored him completely. Later, this was to confound all those sibilant gentlemen who perspire generously in their service to art and dependent singers of treacherous memory, in their dreadful little prompter's box in the middle of the stage. Geraldine, however, contended she had "eyes in her ears" and could sense orchestra cues almost before they were actually played. This freedom naturally permitted her always to sing and act as impulse dictated, with happy relief from the agonized signals too frequently awaited by the uncertain performer.

The long-awaited night came at last. All day Geraldine was like a race horse, straining at the halter; carefully she practiced, and mentally reviewed her scenes, saving actual physical energy for the performance. A cup of tea and a poached egg on toast at five o'clock were her concessions to a nervous stomach. This was to be her usual supper for the coming years of professional routine. So down the Linden we rolled, in a very modest fiacre. Those were not the days of the convenient taxi, and it was to be some time before the family finances would permit a private equipage to arrive in real prima donna style. Geraldine was tense and nervous, but controlled herself well, humming softly to herself. Her father was to come later with friends, and occupy orchestra seats, while I stood near her, back of the stage, a special favor granted by the powers, through the kind offices of our friends the vom Raths.

There were pleasant wishes for *glück auf*, from the porter at the door to the various members of the company as they waited for the curtain's rise. It was like a dream and I kept pinching myself to convince an excited heart that my hopes were to be realized at last. The warning bell came—and Geraldine left her dressing room, a blonde vision of youth and beauty. I felt not unlike a Christian martyr who sees her daughter blindly descend to the Roman arena of chance, too late to realize she unwittingly has thrown her loved one to the lions of public opinion. I need not have worried, however.

On that breath-taking night of October 15, 1901, the curtain revealed this angelic figure as Marguerite, a role surely one of the most poignant in all operatic history. Lovely in her medieval costume, natural in bearing and gesture, the Berliners sat up with loud indications of approval and en-

43

thusiasm at this surprising apparition that won all hearts with its ecstasy of song! The language was mellifluous Italian, the singer an American, but the charm was undeniable and unusual. No meteor or dazzling comet, but a steady star was born that night. Back home to our modest hotel went a joyous trio—and our struggles were just begun!

The German *Times* says of Miss Geraldine Farrar's first appearance in Berlin:

We were all there, we Americans. We had recently heard and read much about anti-American feeling in the hallowed halls of the Berlin Royal Opera. We had been told of cabals and cliques, of plots and persecutions, of jealousies and jousts, and we were there to smooth the path for our young countrywoman, to howl down opposition if need be, and to see, before all things, that justice was done her, and she be given a fair, free, and full chance.

Miss Farrar needed neither our presence nor our applause. From the very first she established herself as a singer and actress so gifted, that she could hardly fail to conquer her audience, and as an artist so independent, that no degree of trickery on the stage could have shaken her confidence and repose.

Miss Farrar, about whose vocal future Melba is said to have been uncommonly optimistic, possesses a soprano voice of unusual richness and fullness in the middle and lower registers. The high notes sounded a trifle strained. This may have been due to the tension of a debut, but I am inclined to doubt it. Indeed, I should almost call Miss Farrar a mezzo-soprano. It was in the middle voice that she had her best moments, when her singing was of purest quality, and its timbre most convincing. Her voice reminds one greatly of Eames.

A faulty trill, and a tendency toward hurrying climaxes in the ensemble numbers, were the only blemishes on a performance really remarkable for a debutante.

Opinions as to her voice might differ, but on the subject of her acting there can be but one verdict. She has dramatic talent

44

LEONORA IN *Trovatore*

VIOLETTA IN *Traviata*

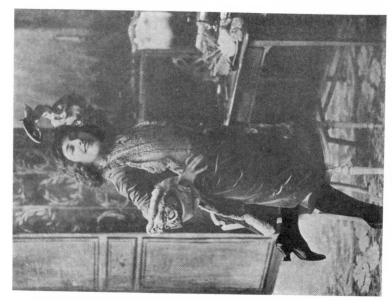

MIGNON

NEDDA IN *Pagliacci*

of the highest order. And rarest gift of all, she has individuality. She did not walk through her part with the accustomed somnambulism of singers who tread operatic boards for the first time. She was a living, loving, suffering Margarethe, not merely a singing automaton. A number of original touches in the most hackneyed situations testified eloquently to Miss Farrar's exceptional histrionic gifts. If all this came from her teacher, then all honor to such a receptive pupil. I wish that the singer had displayed in her costumes the same taste that marked her stage deportment. (Or were the costumes furnished by the management?)

As has been stated, the success was unequivocal. Curtain calls and resounding bravos, mean much in a city that is overfed with music. The newspapers find fault with Miss Farrar's high tones, and they advise the Royal Opera not to make her engagement permanent until she has mastered some roles in German.

Miss Farrar sang in Italian, the chorus in German, and the other principals, with one exception, in execrable style. The exception was Frau Gradl, who did Siebel. Herr Gruening, the tenor, is always a strutting Lohengrin. His use of the falsetto voice was a pitiable performance for so bold a hero. Poor old Mödlinger was a tottering but painstaking Mephistopheles.

Human nature being what it is, I should not have been surprised at rumors and gossip that placed Geraldine's success at the door of a palace intrigue. Actually, it needed an emphatic prodding of the red-tape officialdom to take note of her right to further hearing, and a second role for her appearance; and I could hardly blame the excellent, if slightly over-ripe, native prima donnas for their bitter reflections anent the prerogatives of royal favorites, seeing my radiant daughter. Yet this kind of chatter hurt me to the quick; however, it never seemed to touch Geraldine, who had a rich humor and amazing ability to turn such items into exciting assets of

45

interest and publicity value. Taken to their loyal hearts, the Berliners nodded approval at everything she did and said. With her pretty dresses, her gay manner and easy approach in the halting German she was taking such pains to learn and speak, she seemed indeed a child of good fortune.

Traviata offered her occasion for appearance in modern dress, and a more varied outline of vocal and character delineation than Marguerite.

The pathetic story of *Camille*, as American theatre-goers know the original play, is rich meat for an actress and singer. Though Geraldine is no real coloratura, the flexibility of her voice permits its excursion into the florid cadenzas of the first act with easy grace; and the growing drama of the later scenes lies well, vocally, for a richer timbre of the medium scale, which I think will always be her most expressive asset. It has a haunting quality, very individual in her use and coloring of the phrases she makes peculiarly her own. It is not a big voice and she must be careful not to urge it injudiciously to volume. Intensity of accent will convey a deeper meaning, and not harm its texture. Restraint must be her watchword, not expansion, always.

Her Parisian dresses were exquisite and original. She dressed her own dark hair in the prevailing mode, and played her part with surprising maturity in the difficult third act. She was slender as a birch, and a mania for freedom of throat and shoulders kept me constantly alert for misplacement of tulle and ribbons which she would toss carelessly aside as if no flesh were thus exposed. When I remonstrated, she eyed me with surprise—and said, naively, "But mother, can't you understand I am *not* your daughter on the stage, but an *artist* who is playing *Violetta*. She has nothing to do with me, as Geral-

46

dine. I must act as I think *she*, not I, would act!" I still did not agree with this reasoning, but my hands were tied. I couldn't rush out on the stage and pin up a shoulder-strap in full view of the audience.

I must say, they sat on the edge of their chairs, keen for any daring innovation she might give their admiring eyes— and there were many departures already from tradition; hence a rapidly growing suspicion that the American girl was a tiny bit *verrückt*. Spicy tales and conjectures filtered even to royal portals, where an impetuous heir-presumptive was being groomed for his high office.

So now there came a real worry on my heart's horizon, for the young and very attractive Crown Prince began calling upon Geraldine. Oh, there was no secrecy about his coming! Heralded by fanfares, and preceded by equerries, in his scarlet hunting coat, the slim and bashful lad—my daughter's age exactly—would knock timidly at our salon door at the Adlon. A blushing face with two brilliant blue eyes would peer over the traditional German nosegay—a click of the heels, a hand-kiss—and the careless, happy children engaged in conversation. I could hear merry laughter and the strains of familiar music as both gravitated eventually to the piano. A sweet romance it was—to remain just that all their lives.

Ridiculous gossip and shameful observations ripened into the screaming headlines of scandal and libelous affirmations. Little by little the stream began to assume the unmanageable turbulence of a swiftly flowing, destructive river. The American Press took up the back-wash in comments, lengthy if not always accurate, on the situation that was the feverish talk of the Prussian Capitol. A Boston friend sent me a copy of the following:

47

BOYCOTTING HER

Prima Donnas of the Berlin Opera Jealous of American Singers in General and of Miss Farrar in Particular.

Berlin, Nov. 22.—At the Royal Opera House the latest German enterprise is a protest against the American peril, by resenting the hit recently made by Miss Geraldine Farrar, an 18-year-old Massachusetts girl, which resulted in her securing a three-year contract. Several jealous prima donnas, foreseeing the possibility of their superannuation, proceeded to make Miss Farrar's position among them untenable.

One middle aged Margarita announced that she will not sing on the same stage with American upstarts. Miss Farrar is endeavoring to be oblivious to her detractors, but the latter are influential and may undermine her with the management.

The incident recalls the experiences encountered by another American, Mrs. Webster Powell, last year. Despite her successful debut, the singer was subjected to systematic persecution by her confrères, resulting in her paying the management 12,000 marks ($3,000) for the privilege of canceling her contract.

Another alarmed Puritan forwarded this lively résumé:

GERMAN CROWN PRINCE LOVES MELROSE GIRL

Despite Semi-Official Ridicule Stories of the Infatuation of Kaiser's Heir Continue to Grow.

Berlin, Jan. 2.—For the second time in one short fortnight official and court society is again in a ferment over what is now

48

generally conceded to be the infatuation of the Crown Prince Frederick William for Miss Geraldine Farrar, the beautiful American opera singer.

The report has just been revived as a subject of heated society gossip by the assault a few days ago upon Herr Kohn, editor of *Die Welt am Montag*, by Miss Farrar's father.

SEMI-OFFICIAL LIBELS

Last week the newspapers of the capitol began to comment upon the rumor of the Crown Prince's infatuation. As a method of denying it and attempting to prove its absurdity, articles were published containing the most insulting libels upon Miss Farrar's character. *Die Welt am Montag* distinguished itself by its malicious screeds.

It so happens that Miss Farrar's father is a former baseball player of some renown upon the American diamond, and he determined to avenge his daughter in the old-fashioned American way.

FATHER TROUNCES EDITOR

Forcing his way into Herr Kohn's residence, he dragged that distinguished molder of public opinion out of bed and kicked him about the apartment until he begged for mercy. Kohn finally agreed to retract all of his libelous allegations in the next issue of his paper. He failed to keep his promise, however, and the story of the chastisement became public property today when Mr. Farrar announced that he would appeal to Emperor William unless Kohn printed a full and public apology.

RUMOR WILL NOT DOWN

So it is that the rumor of the Crown Prince's infatuation will not down in spite of semi-official efforts to cast ridicule upon it.

The rumor became current gossip about a fortnight ago, when the Crown Prince put in an appearance at the dedication of an American church in the capitol. Much surprise was expressed at the interest the heir to the German throne was taking in American affairs. Then came the explanation that it was probably

49

Miss Farrar's presence which had brought about a visit from the Crown Prince.

Miss Farrar's home is in Melrose. She has recently been singing in the Royal Opera House, and has taken the musical centers of Germany by storm.

It now seems probable that to dispose of the rumor effectually the Crown Prince will be sent on a tour of the world by his imperial father. The young man seems to have a particular yearning for American beauty. He was reported as devotedly attached to Miss Gladys Deacon only a few months ago.

The post brought volumes of the same to keep us constantly disturbed. And then the American Women's Club of Berlin rose in wrath to defend Geraldine, as here set forth, duly cabled from the scene of all the excitement.

WOMEN VINDICATE MISS FARRAR'S NAME

———

Americans in Germany find Melrose Highlands Singer Guilty of No Indiscretions with Kaiser William's Son.

———

Berlin, Jan. 26.—Officers of the American Women's Club of Berlin have sent to the press a copy of a statement which the Women's Club and the Ladies' Union of the American Church have signed and presented to Miss Geraldine Farrar, the American singer, containing an expression of their utter disbelief in the story of an alleged intrigue with the Crown Prince Frederick William, which has been repeated in many variations.

Miss Farrar, who comes from Melrose Highlands, Mass., and who is now engaged at the Royal Opera House, saw the Crown

Prince once for ten minutes in the presence of the Empress and Mrs. Farrar. Since then an ever-growing story has been related of intimacy between the singer and the Crown Prince, which was published again a few days ago, with scandalous details, in a weekly paper. The police suppressed the edition and Sidney Farrar, father of Miss Farrar, has prosecuted the paper for libel.

The written statement presented to Miss Farrar by the American women, among other things, says:

"We have examined every possible source of the calumny and find there is absolutely no grounds for its existence. Attended as Miss Farrar has been during her life here by her parents, and being herself a young woman of rare purity and honor, we are unable to find the slightest proof of any delinquency, or even imprudence on her part. We make this avowal voluntarily and in the sole interest of right and justice."

These were experiences I had not foreseen in connection with my daughter's career and her honorable activities to obtain recognition by reason of her talent and industry. I should have known, perhaps, the manner of human interest and the reactions of a curious outside world. My husband was far from convinced that a career under these circumstances was so pleasant a result of our ambitious undertaking. It was not easy to mould a parental wrath to philosophical acceptance of these ugly stories, as belonging to a public character, not a private individual.

Eventually, the stormy clouds dispersed, and we settled to a more agreeable existence of routine, and tried to put the memory of such a nightmare behind us. The aftermath was a feeble attempt to discredit Geraldine professionally, which was denied by the American press, as follows:

VOICE IS PERFECT

Geraldine Farrar Has Not Lost
Her Voice.

The report circulated in this country that Geraldine Farrar of Melrose, the now famous singer, had lost her voice, is now proved false. This paper stated that Miss Farrar's friends did not give credit to the report.

Geraldine Farrar, the young American prima donna in Berlin, has not lost her voice as has been reported, and it is said her voice is in the best condition that it has ever been.

An explanation of how the rumor started is this:

She is one of the few prima donnas who have had the honor of being commanded to sing before the Emperor, and so captivated was he with the young woman's genius that he has ordered the company with her to study in Italian some of the best Italian operas, for which Miss Farrar's voice is particularly adapted. Naturally this has created some feeling in the German capitol among the musical set, and the report was discreetly spread about that she had lost her voice.

My heart was torn! But this amazing girl of mine was not at all confounded by the wretched episode. She was devoted to her art, and had no thought of unduly dividing her attention and energy for whatever sentimental reason. Serious heart affairs formed no part in the outline of hard work and ambition that now actuated her. I had every reason to believe her quiet assertion to this effect.

There never was a more charming or idyllic friendship than this one between the Crown Prince and Geraldine; it has so continued, despite the wildest stories, to this very day. It was indeed an unusual attachment in the life of a popular

Crown Princess Cecile

Crown Prince Wilhelm of Prussia

THE CROWN PRINCESS, WITH HER
SONS PRINCE FREDERICK WILHELM
AND PRINCE LOUIS FERDINAND

THE KAISER WITH HIS GRANDSON,
PRINCE FREDERICK WILHELM

HERR AND FRAU VOM RATH

young Prince, where court gaieties offer every inducement to easy conquest. When the Crown Prince married the lovely Grand Duchess Cécile, the gossips could not fathom how it was that Geraldine's popularity even extended to the Marmor Palast in Potsdam. There the young royal couple had set up housekeeping, and she was their favorite singer and a frequent and informal guest on many a happy occasion. Who could foresee that after the horrible events of the World War, and the agonizing procedure of setting Germany to rights once more, that their second son, a personable youth whom Geraldine recalls almost in his cradle, would one day be her house-guest, in Ridgefield, after an enthusiastic and democratic apprenticeship in the Ford factory?

And so these shadows gradually ceased to cloud my sky. My girl was not afraid of work, or criticism—of which she had plenty.

Her next role was Juliette—and what a vision she was! She had compelling ways and powers of persuasion, for these were powerful factors in obtaining permission to wear her own costumes. No one who is unfamiliar with the "stock" wardrobe can possibly conceive the misery of last minute adjustments to various figures. As the predominant girth was usually a mountainous one, to attempt an arrangement for Geraldine in her adolescent slenderness was like sinking her in a sea of stiff satins and brocades! Her Parisian confections were the delight even of the Crown Princess. Later, their designer, Madame Paquin, was invited to Potsdam to confer on the lovely frocks of the royal lady herself. Both she and Geraldine were criticized in the press for this action, and I have no doubt the charming chatelaine of Potsdam envied the freedom of my democratic daughter in matters of such feminine interest.

I recall our consternation once after a successful season, when Geraldine presented me with a sable scarf and muff, and herself chose the same model in ermine. For wearing this latter and having been noticed in making her curtsy to the Empress, by that august lady's Mistress of the Robes, Geraldine was subjected to a reprimand by an opera official. Ermine and sable, it appeared, were royalty's furs! My spirited daughter replied that they were anybody's furs in *her* country, anybody's who could afford to buy them! I heard later that much laughter ensued when the young couple in Potsdam heard this tale, and pert defense!

All young women have a natural feminine predilection for pretty clothes, whether they be of royal status or commoners. And the charming Crown Princess was no exception to this generality.

Frequently, at performances, a page would be dispatched from the royal loge, to Geraldine's dressing room, with the request that she come to greet Their Imperial Highnesses during the entr'acte. These little distractions were discreetly whispered about, and the audience nodded and smiled, quite patiently waiting for the impromptu visits to end, and the opera to go on. Much gossip of course ensued, and the youthful Crown Princess herself came in for reprimand, the three-cornered party not exactly conforming to the stiff rules of etiquette, nor pleasing to a sharp-eyed Mistress of the Robes, in her difficult and responsible position. Nonetheless, the adoring Berliners loved the romantic implication. And it is true that, remarking a notable absence of Geraldine's records from her Red Seal collection, proffered by a leading music house, the Crown Princess requested the firm to send all her recordings at once to Potsdam.

If all ladies—of royal birth or otherwise—were as sensible and free from the prejudices of petty gossip, what confusion would result for the tattle-mongers and the envious! The Crown Prince and the Crown Princess both greatly fancied *Traviata* and *Juliette,* but conceded *Manon* to be their preferred opera choice, not only because of the exquisite music drama, but the handsome costumes Geraldine wore, as well. On some of the visits in their private loge the Crown Princess would softly touch the superb brocades and laces, remarking what a pity it was the ladies no longer dressed in such bewitching fashion. She opined, however, even a present day modern princess' purse could scarcely furnish a privy purse large enough to sustain a wardrobe of such lavish extravagance. Geraldine told me afterwards she understood the frugality of the Kaiser's routine was public knowledge, and his shrewd business sense worthy of any watchful Rotarian husband.

One evening after a concert before their Majesties, Geraldine had lingered over-long in the dressing room where the Crown Prince had dismissed the lackey, himself adjusting her carriage boots and escorting her to her carriage. If there was a warm handclasp and a few furtive kisses, no one should be the wiser. But the Intendant of the opera—a martial Gatti-Casazza of his time—was moved to chide Geraldine verbally for so natural, but so unusual and free a departure from Court etiquette. Quite rightly, perhaps, he felt it was the woman's business to check these youthful indiscretions, which always leaked out later in elaborated whispers over Berlin. Geraldine, however, told him it was all a part of the successful prima donna's role—nor did she seem unduly impressed by his chiding or the breeze of gossip. On another occasion, the poor man met an adamant refusal to wear the prescribed long gloves at a very formal diplomatic dinner-concert at the palace. Geraldine not only hated gloves, but was the first *Kammer-sängerin* in many moons to look like a seductive vision on these occasions, rather than an animated sarcophagus covered with medals. I confess I could have wished her décolletage to have been a trifle less startling—but upon my feeble remonstrances she would airily wave me aside, and remark that we were not in Melrose and she was, in these instances, not my daughter, but an opera star expected to astonish.

I was hard put to realize a great transformation in this facile explanation, and somehow I could not accept without a little qualm seeing her pretty flesh gleaming so very unashamedly from silken straps that apparently began, and ended, nowhere. By way of consolation she would wave a huge ostrich fan and remark, "This will do for covering, if need be, during the concert!" Afterwards she would tell me, with a wicked twinkle in her sparkling eyes, "The fan was laid on the piano during a good part of the program!" And then add, "How could the Crown Prince otherwise pin his rose on my shoulder?"

She was an audacious flirt—and I began to wonder at times if I knew her as well as I thought. Where did she get all this temperament and love of display, certainly not natural to her father or myself? She was extremely self-willed in expressing herself, and not inclined always to follow my counsel. Sweet tempered as she was, I sensed her determination to follow her own dictates, and accepted the consequences of such a decision. Meanwhile, she was not frivolous, and was a glutton for work. Perhaps she was playing a role off the stage, as well as on it. I saw no inclination to bring into her private life the various charming young cavaliers who met her at official and social functions, which was some comfort.

However, at the several concerts presided over by the Kaiser and Kaiserin, I was present and touched as well as put at ease by the gentle inquiry and interest on the part of the Empress. I understood from Geraldine, that she was well aware of her favorite son's sentimental interest in my daughter. Well, of it would come no harm, indeed; so neither mother had undue cause for alarm.

II

THE DAUGHTER

1901 - 1906

HOW remote was Boston!

The good ship Mayflower, fragile little pioneer of Colonial pretensions, was a frequent recommendation for the background of many snobbish New Englanders. To judge from the widespread affirmations, solemnly averred by descendants, the quarters must have accommodated a vast and elegant assembly that would have reasonably taxed the latest sea-going palace! At any rate, interested friends, distrusting the freedom and élan of an artist's life, felt that I needed the indisputable assurance of a bourgeois pedigree to counterbalance the colorful existence of the theatre wherein I yearned to shine. Even at this time of my early youth, there was drawn a line of sharp distinction, and professionals before the fascinating footlights were endowed with all the godless attributes but few of the home-spun virtues, as understood in a conservative New England town. The theatre had not then become a clearing house for bored society women or impulsive young debutantes. The "movies" were yet to invite to celluloid immortality the marble profile and vacuous brow. The opera singer was an exotic—and usually an alien, imported to add lustre to the social structure gradually assuming old world manners with its new-found riches.

The Metropolitan Opera House was such an organization of wealthy patrons. Two notable American singers, Lillian Nordica and Emma Eames, boasted a New England background. Much stress was laid upon the refinements of their Puritan ancestry, and the fact that they were "nice" women endeared them to audiences prone to snobbish sentiment, if not quite boasting the discriminating taste of more sophisticated listeners. That they later confounded their social friends by divorce and its ever unpleasant attendant publicity always seemed to be so peculiar, since both ladies continued as beautiful as before and thrilled with their accustomed art irrespective of marital tangles.

However, to revert to my own genealogy . . . . let it be said, the family tree was traced to its early Norman roots. The name—Farrar—is said to derive from the Latin and French word signifying iron. It was probably used to designate a locality where this metal was found. As a family name, it was first known in England from Gualkeline or Walkeline

To my dearest child
Geraldine Farrar
with all my love
Lilli Lehmann.

LILLI LEHMANN

JULES MASSENET

TWO SCENES FROM *Manon*

de Ferrariis, a Norman of disinction attached to William, Duke of Normandy, before the invasion of 1066. From him all of the name, in England and America, have descended. His son, Henry de Ferriers, is on the Roll-call of Battle in Westminster Abbey, which numbers a list of the Principal-Commanders and Companions-in-Arms of William the Conqueror. He bore for his arms—"Argent, six horseshoes, pierced sable," surmounted by upturned wings and a wreath. The horseshoe is a well-known emblem of luck, a safeguard against malign influences; it was also used as a feudal tribute. Wings are hieroglyphs of celebrity. When wings are borne, they pertain to the eagle. Tips upward are called elevated. The wreath was composed of two rolls of silk, or leather, of different colors entwined. It encircled the helmet and supported the crest. The crest was borne upon helmets, to distinguish military leaders and knights when engaged in battle. And from this aggressive and valiant line, a piping robin emerged, longing to express herself in a world where battle-axes also might not come amiss, 19th Century style! How much more exciting to have this logical line of forbears, than the airy phantoms conjured up by the many who professed to find in me certain supernatural evidences of musical reincarnation.

Besides sponsoring the finest symphony orchestra of its time in our country, Boston, as well, delved deeply into the occult; there was scarcely a drawing-room in which I sang where I did not confront some good-looking young Swami at whose feet sat many a bewildered but enraptured lady, hanging on his honeyed words of charming but indefinite philosophy. It irritated my intense individualism to be pointed out as a musi-

59

cal spirit possessed by a voice from the ether, or a magnetized automaton controlled from other spheres. This pretended guidance by East Indian devices and precepts infuriated me. I had a well-rooted prejudice—often fear—against inviting great and unknown forces to participate in playful tricks and parlor performances, to excite credulous and hysterical on-lookers avid for excitement and the mystery of a social conjuror. That certain feeling persists to this day. I have tremendous respect for any form of research, religion, faith—call it what you will, but the Occidental brand of Oriental philosophy is enjoyed by me, personally, when printed and bound for leisurely and thoughtful reading between the covers of a book. From its contents I can apply what my particular mental and spiritual boundaries will allow.

There were comments enough when my confident mother pulled up stakes and our small family trio started on the sing-ing adventure across the seas. The frowns of mistrust and disapproval would only clear if genuine success crowned the surprising departure from small-town activities and their aims. It isn't given, more's the pity, for every girl to choose a mother of such independence and foresight, but I have often thought how precious to her must have been the growing years she could shape and foster with the practical sense and clear head she owned. Scarcely eighteen years my senior, I shall never know how she must have viewed her early preg-nancy; what professional hopes she may have entertained for herself before my intrusion changed her own scheme of things. That she was no usual creature, her decided character and courage attested all her life. My father, bless him, trusted her judgment implicitly, and opposed no word to any plan she made feasible in our small household.

In the light of today's modern young wives, I wonder how she managed to accomplish all she did, when the mechanics that make our present life of easy idleness were not yet conceived. A young married woman of her modest means cooked, sewed, kept her house, read and studied, brought up her children, was house physician, nurse, companion to them and her husband. She managed to save a few pennies, and the "hired help," in our case, was a precious old Irish soul who took over the heavier duties of laundry, scrubbing, and the spring and fall house-cleaning. How my mother found time to watch over my early musical studies, take me to chosen places for educational advantage, and perform her many home rituals without breaking completely, is all the more mystifying in the light of the radical changes of today, but I was like a member of her body and upon my achievement she had set her heart—or, I should better say, *our* hearts. Nothing could stay her determination,—as witness our surprising Odyssey, and the efforts she made to effect it. So, hard upon the heels of her decision, here we were in Berlin, where dreams were coming true.

Shortly after *Juliette*, I received the precious word that Lilli Lehmann had returned to her home in Grunewald and would receive me. Now, indeed, I was to be put to the test before this great woman. A regal figure met me at the door and a cool hand extended a none too ardent welcome. I sang arias from *Traviata, Faust* and *Juliette,*—not very well, so great was my quaking emotion. As in an earlier day, I was subjected to inquiry and rigorous vocal trial, and accepted— with no great show of praise or enthusiasm. That was not the Lehmann way. Unless a beautiful voice were paired with intelligence and a careful handling of musical resources, she rated the pupil as untalented, lazy, or uninteresting. She was evidently waiting to catalogue me properly.

She was a hard taskmaster and demanded the ultimate; but found in me an energy equal to her own, if not quite to her physical resistance. I earned her respect much later. We argued frequently, for she often urged upon my vocal apparatus measures ill-suited to its particular reaction; where she would force obedience, I would obtain results by less strenuous efforts. Technical control to her meant everything, while emotional color was my natural asset and delight. We had to effect compromises, which in the course of time became my necessary response to her lofty ambitions for the art of song.

Having evolved from her own light vocal endowment a repertoire that ran the gamut from dizzy coloratura to the noble sweep of Donna Anna, Norma and Isolde, she could not understand the more limited and very sensitive instrument that lay in my own throat. With her, Will was Power; in me, she was obliged to acknowledge the particular asset of adaptability to careful choice of roles and lieder. Thus, though no true dramatic soprano, I could so manipulate as to convey the accent of drama in my phrases. I early realized that for my own best result, the power of suggestion rather than actual tone volume could operate to the advantage of vocal resources never to become over-strong.

In a little nook, high up over the Luxembourg Gardens in Paris, lived Massenet—gentle, retiring, and at this time so busy with compositions for librettos contracted over a period of years that an appointment with him was an exceptional favor. The Royal Opera had decided to give his *Manon* especially for me, and I went that spring to consult him for the coming autumn premiere.

Sybil Sanderson, the beautiful Californian, and creator of several of his operas, had just died in Paris. When I was announced, I found him in tears, having just come from her funeral services. The musical world knew of their long and tender attachment, and I felt somewhat embarrassed that this particular moment should find me an observer of his grief. However, perhaps a sorrowful heart had its consolation in reviewing *Manon*—one of her own successful roles at the Opera Comique—for the long consulation embraced as much the topic of Sybil as it did his operatic heroine.

Several later visits gave me a fair idea of his wishes in the outline of this exquisite heroine of the lyric stage. Like most reasonable composers, he allowed an individual leeway, and took into consideration the talent of the performer. Of course, I studied it with him in its original French; but upon my return to Berlin and my summer's study with Lilli, at Scharfling near Salzburg, where she had her country house, it was necessary to revise it all in German. Both she and I worked nobly to voice this Gallic daintiness in the least ponderous Teutonic translation, but it was not an easy task; and no French person could hear the clumsy effort without a shudder, I am sure. Just so do I react, when I hear Wagner reduced to any less vigorous utterance of a tongue alien to its own particular construction and color. The dramatic accents do not fall in place.

The burning question of operas reduced to the vernacular will, I suppose, always be one of dissension among artists and listeners. Personally, I prefer to sing opera in its original tongue. I shall not soon forget once hearing *Faust* in Czech, at Prague, and a Polish rendition of *Carmen!* And, begging the consideration of the zealots in my own country who constantly raise the cry for opera in English, I should like to suggest the desirable combination of a proper lyric text, and singers who enunciate with clarity and understanding to encourage such a movement. English is not the most musical of singing tongues, perhaps, but it is shamefully abused by the careless treatment accorded it, beginning in the early years of school, both in speech and in song.

However, this particular *Manon* in German roused the Berliners to frenzy, and became my own property, together with the later *Butterfly*, till the World War severed my connection automatically with the opera there. Dr. Karl Muck carefully prepared the musical score, and I have sung the role under many conductors, notably unforgettable performances with Toscanini. Dr. Muck, a lean Mephisto-like figure, seldom in expansive humor, was second to none in his leadership of both the French and Italian repertoire. Franz Navāl, a delightful and romantic tenor from Vienna, was engaged to second me, and we were paired constantly in *Romeo, Mignon, Faust, Manon*, and *Black Domino*. At the time of our *Manon* premiere, Vienna was offering it with Van Dyck and, I think, Selma Kurz; while at Dresden, Erika Wedekind and a tenor whose name I do not recall were the protagonists under von Schuch. In all three cities the acclaim was instantaneous. As I have never kept a diary (in these days of prying press agents and blackmailing secretaries—how fortunate!), my memory may be at fault in naming the casts.

One particularly hideous experience was a sole performance of Leonora in *Trovatore*. Insistence from high places was responsible. Vocally I was as adequate as a cricket. Pictorially, a handsome apparition. This was barely enough recommenda-

64

Dr. Holbrook Curtis

Leo Slezak as Otello

Nellie Melba

Lillian Nordica

tion to continue in a part the critics quite properly rated at zero, with a tart reprimand to the management for such poor judgment in casting.

Next came an ambitious attempt at my first Wagner role— Elizabeth in *Tannhauser*. The successful outcome was to be even more unusual since the subject matter was far afield from the *Manon* material that fitted me perfectly.

The preparation for such an undertaking was a painstaking affair indeed. I had always longed to include Elsa, Eva, and Elizabeth, all lovely youthful characters in my repertoire. I prepared them with care under Lilli, and Elizabeth was the first chosen, as the opera was to stage a revival of *Tannhauser* and present not only me in it, but Emmy Destinn as Venus; the combination aroused great interest in the opera-going public. Destinn's engagement had preceded mine by a few seasons, and her fine soprano voice and musicianship made her notable asset to the company. Though she had sung many of the Wagnerian lyric roles, this was her premiere as Venus.

I shall never forget the first fitting with the royal tailors for this costume of tradition. With praiseworthy economy, the seams were of such reserve dimensions as to allow for larger waistlines and more generous bosoms, since several excellent Elizabeths of various sizes and vintage would naturally share the role in later performances.

I was accustomed to the flattering cut, and clinging effects of soft crepe and velvet from my Paris dressmaker, at that time Marie Muelle, whose costumes were miracles of beauty even in Paris, which was noted for its taste and originality in stage costumes. This particular heavy dress was of stiff white broadcloth, besprinkled with huge pieces of colored glass sewn in with the gold braid that outlined bodice and sleeves. A long brass girdle swung about my waist. I was like an imprisoned doll. The cape alone weighted down my slender shoulders, the apparition gained nothing in charm with the addition of a tiny crown perched precariously on top of my head, like a gilt pincushion floating on a sea of muslin drapery that partially hid blonde tresses.

Destinn was swathed in voluminous folds of a particularly horrendous shade of pink satin, a red wig rose from her forehead, coiled in the classic Greek doughnut of museum style, further burdened by a wreath of violent red roses. We managed, even so, to present ourselves with dignity and effect, and the revival signaled for me a definite acclaim from the Press as well, with especial praise for my German diction, and the simplicity I brought to the role—so unexpected was the modification from the temperamental display of earlier heroines.

Lilli Lehmann had her hour of triumph as teacher, too. The Kaiser was pleased to summon her to the royal loge and, proud as she was, I know the accolade touched and pleased her. It is, from my point of view, a pity I was not allowed a further incursion into the other Wagnerian roles I had prepared with her so very conscientiously; but the management had a plethora of dramatic vocalists, and was less fortunate in the lyric repertoire for which my especial type was best suited.

My successes were now being noised about, with such a general word of praise that Covent Garden made inquiry for some guest performances. I should have loved to have sung in London, at any time. The impresario, Harry Higgins, however, wanted me then only for German roles, and added to Elsa, Eva, and Elizabeth, the part of Sieglinde! I spoke with Lilli about this, and my regret that there was no possibility of *Traviata, Faust, Manon,* or *Juliette* to be included in his proposal. Had this been the case, I would have ventured with Elsa and Eva, even if it would have been a first performance outside the study room; but to have no opportunity to display my versatility would have been suicidal in this early stage of my career, nor did I then want to appear solely as a Wagnerian singer before a critical London audience.

When I spoke of Sieglinde, Lilli threw back her head and laughed heartily. Laying her hand affectionately on my slim shoulders, she remarked upon the modest rise of youthful breasts and opined I would have to have "more meat" on my frame before I could—if ever—effectively represent any of the voluptuous heroines in the Ring. I weighed about one hundred and twenty pounds and desperately rubbed cocoa butter on my obvious bones, every night upon retiring. As it was, when my stalwart partners enfolded me, I disappeared almost completely beneath their sweeping capes, lost in the amorphous shadow of bulbous silhouettes.

There was also talk of an early revival of *Otello* for which I would be scheduled to sing Desdemona. I worked out the role in German, very desirous to add it to my repertoire. Paul Kalisch, Lilli's husband, was a favorite heroic tenor, whose permanent engagement at the Royal Theatre in Wiesbaden permitted him the usual guest performances elsewhere in Germany. Lilli thought it would be an excellent idea—certainly one helpful to me—if Paul and I prepared our scenes at her home, before the actual stage rehearsals were called.

67

He was all that was agreeable despite his own many perform-ances of the name part, in which he excelled. A handsome fig-ure, with a more mellow Southern timbre to his voice than is usual in German tenors, he was quite the right choice for the Moor, and temperamentally most effective.

Alas, however, for good intentions. Lilli, once embarked upon the affair, assumed the teacher attitude of invincible authority, which did not promise well for our ensemble re-sults. Broad hints from her developed into sharp corrections and disparagement toward everything he attempted. He bore it all with gentlemanly good humor, for some time; but the constant stream of unflattering criticism upon an artist of worth in his own right, wore him down eventually. I was mortified long before he took his coat and hat, packed a bag, and left for Wiesbaden never to reconsider *Otello* in Berlin.

There was no available Otello, the project fell through, and I never did sing the role of the hapless Desdemona anywhere. The giant Slezak was paired with another prima donna of secondary importance in a later Metropolitan revival, under the leadership of Toscanini. Martinelli, then hardly known in this country, and a young debutant of successful years to come, has undertaken the difficult role with splendid fervor as singer and actor these latter seasons.

I had been singing for some time in German, after unre-mitting labor with my diction teacher. In such roles as Zerlina, Black Domino, and Mignon, where much dialogue was em-ployed, I enjoyed immensely the thrill of speaking on the stage, as well.

Now began the advances from booking agents for musical excursions outside Berlin, on the Continent. I had dear friends,

68

MATA HARI

ISADORA DUNCAN

VIOLETTA IN *Traviata*, ACT IV

QUEEN ELIZABETH IN *Don Carlos*

too, who were influential in Paris. That meant appearances at the Opera and Opera-Comique.

Monte Carlo was fascinating, and during its season all the big European singing stars appeared there. It was there I met Caruso for the first time. We were both to debut in *Bohème*. Never shall I forget the apparition that walked into the first rehearsal. Clad in shrieking checks, topped by a grey fedora, yellow gloves grasping a gold-headed cane, he jauntily walked onto the stage. A happy smile illumined a jolly face, which was punctuated by the two largest black eyes I had ever seen. Fresh from South American triumphs, this young phenomenon was affable and pleasant to us all.

I was a newcomer, from Berlin; and Prussia being a locality not overliked by the predominant French colony, I felt a little out of things and wondered if I had done well to accept the liberal terms that might carry with them no very ardent response from a pleasure-loving public. However, events proved to be of happy augury. Caruso was lavish with his prodigal gift, his triumph assured, and I was most happily welcomed as well, though I almost forgot to sing, so thrilling was that voice! We sang often, but to houses that faded into thin air after the first act. We were all puzzled. Later, we learned the more potent attraction was the gaming tables; but as our salaries suffered no decrease, the company gradually became accustomed to the vacant seats, while our spirits were not unduly cast down.

It was here in the ballet of a lovely Indian opera—Massenet's *Le Roi de Lahore*, in which I sang a pictorial role similar to *Lakme*—that the celebrated Mata Hari first danced. She was a lovely figure of voluptuous grace, poor girl, a

69

charmer indeed; tragic was to be her end, but courageous, too. She proudly faced the French firing squad, and even they—patriotism notwithstanding—felt a quiver of remorse at killing so lovely a creature, despite her unenviable record as a spy in the World War.

Her background seemed to have been one of mystery, a combination of Dutch father and Javanese mother, so the press reports ran. Perhaps the gossip was more spicy than truth warranted, but in appearance she fully qualified for it all. Most unusual in her dancing act in the opera—and engaged for this special ballet act as having herself been dedicated to her native Temple rituals—she swayed and postured, an exotic figure of incomparable grace and appeal, in our first rehearsal.

It was the first time I or any other observer had seen a dancer appear in public without the silken covering of limbs and body, traditionally associated with the ballet as we knew it in Italy and France. At that time, we had not been astonished and amazed at the marvelous Russians and a new form of dance-drama they were so soon to exhibit before the dazzled Parisian eyes.

Mata Hari had no prescribed and intricate ballet technique; she moved slowly with much emphasis on the graceful movement of arms and torso, not unlike our own superb exponent of East Indian pantomime, Ruth St. Denis. Breast and abdomen were naked, and slender limbs lightly veiled, which but enhanced their effect. The startled Massenet could hardly contain himself at the unusual spectacle; the ballet company chattered in undertones, and the wily impresario, Gunsbourg, deemed the exquisite creature a bit too sensational perhaps for even the jaded Grand Dukes' eyes. Mata Hari was taken in hand by a diplomatic wardrobe woman, and further rehearsals and performances saw her chastely poured into a coffee-colored maillot.

There was, despite this concession to modesty, Massenet, and mobile Grand Dukes, plenty to excite the senses when she made her brief appearance as Queen of Heaven; an Indian Heaven, be it understood, whose dominant figure was no placid Christian, blue-eyed Madonna, but a sloe-eyed beauty of carnal and exciting appeal. Once removed from the spotlight, I found her gentle and retiring, with only her unusual carriage and appearance to distinguish her from any other attractive feminine figure to be seen on the Promenade.

A most notable attraction was Chaliapin—great blond cherub of a man, and one of the most astonishing artists it has been my privilege to meet. Of superb physique, he had an uncanny gift for cosmetic metamorphosis, and adding to dramatic gifts a magnificent voice that rolled out like melodious thunder, it was easy for him to equal the triumphs of even Caruso those days! And what a fellow with the ladies!

He had married an Italian dancer—as we were informed— and even then he was awaiting her arrival and a troupe of children and nurses. I am sure he was a kind if sometimes forgetful husband, and an affectionate father, in spite of having a brilliant reputation as conquistador in the domain of Amor. This was not difficult, given his tremendous artistic endowment, and the undeniable attractions of a singularly elemental male.

In this motley crowd of surfeited Grand Dukes, wearied Kings incognito, phlegmatic John Bulls, American millionaires

71

new to this international playground, and sophisticated Parisian elegants, it was not easy to overlook this fascinating barbarian whose sentimental attacks were along lines quite unusual to the traditions of over-polite society, and so, eminently successful. I recall a Russian house where I was frequently a guest, whose brilliant hostess never included her more conventional friends whenever "her Russian bears" as she called them, were invited. She frankly said the reversion to type would be sadly misunderstood. I think I sensed then the great difference in the Occidental and Oriental—or Asiatic—reactions, and personally was not unhappy to be included in the more civilized musicales her refined taste and caution inspired.

Chaliapin could be a wonderful opera partner, with just a little management unsuspected by him, but one had to be watchful for sudden departures from the rehearsed plan, and touches of originality favorable only for the aggrandisement of Chaliapin. I got on well with him, humored his little idiocyncrasies, and did not too seriously consider his many and transparent attempts to "bluff." He was a law unto himself, which I respected, and a pretty woman, after all, had better equipment to mold the performance, than a rival of the same sex. Such a competitor he did meet in that fine artist, Maurice Renaud, whose ability was no less than his own for superb characterization of a role. He was a handsome fellow, too, and took no back seat for the Russian. The women were mad about both of them, and I, for one, understood why.

It was a gay world of froth and frivol. The salaries, good fat fees, were guaranteed by the Casino gaming tables, and almost all our contracts were made verbally or by telegram. Mine was. There was never an argument about money matters in our lyric world, though one would hear and read of

72

dreadful gambling losses and suicides—hushed up by police and press, that cast a momentary cloud on this lively scene. I used to pass a hat shop on my way to rehearsals, and would buy the headgear before I won its price at the Casino! It was a fever that proved infectious, and often for fun I picked up a bit of money in roulette. It was a pastime for which I had little aptitude, however; not like several singers who were so persuaded of their "infallible system" they would even put up their contract as collateral for play—invariably to lose. This crazy procedure opened my cautious New England eyes very wide, a lesson I remembered long and well.

At the close of the season, the Casino gave each of the soloists a very handsome bonus, which greatly surprised my mother and me. We were still naive enough to wonder if there might not be some questionable string attached to so munificent a gesture; but we need not have worried. Nobody had designs upon me in this very large garden where lovely ladies of easy virtue were the rule, not the exception.

A galaxy of beautiful women also contributed to the gaiety of the scene. There was Lina Cavalieri, exquisitely lovely, no mean vocalist either, in our troupe. She later came to the Metropolitan. And nightly parading in the Casino, the glittering, dark-haired dancer, Otero, known to the jeunesse dorée of half Europe. Liane dePougy, another celebrity of fragile grace whose associates boasted crowns, then quite secure, and bursting purses.

The story is told of Otero and dePougy, who agreed to submit their gorgeous jewels to public inspection one night at the Casino, to settle a wager as to which lady owned the unrivaled collection.

Otero, a glowing picture of Spanish beauty, was first to

73

enter to the thunder of applause. She glittered from diadem on ebony locks to the buckles and heels of tiny slippers, moving down the hall like a beam of blinding light. Arrogant and supremely conscious of her own personal allure and the fabulous gems that literally covered her, she was a spectacle rare to behold.

After this brief moment of triumph, the door opened for the second contestant, and Liane de Pougy stood, ready to enter. A slender, aristocratic figure, she was groomed in simple black chiffon, hat, gloves, and purse of the same sable hue to accent her delicate features, and focus a hushed audience upon the unusual vision. Not a jewel gleamed on her; but, close behind, trod her personal maid, aflame like an illuminated Eiffel Tower. The observers broke into a frenzied applause at the ruse, while, with a cry of rage, the exasperated Otero hurled herself in feline fury toward the challenging quiet figure. With difficulty, she was restrained from actual assault, as the gallant attendants withdrew her to their supper party, at a cafe across the way.

This was quite a surprise event that no mere opera singer could hope to emulate in its repercussion of widespread and sensational report. Perhaps it is as well that this social world, half-world, royalty, and outstanding class distinctions, are now an order of the past, while the so-called democratic spirit prevails with no such picturesque exterior appeal. It may be that the sack suit and sport blouse entitle their wearers to even more respect for genuine appreciation of the arts, and theatre offerings in particular. I shall not quarrel with such a premise. Nonetheless, one misses the glittering audiences that were in themselves so much a part of the gorgeous spectacle.

74

There was indeed a snobbish indifference to less fortunate mortals, and it was then not so easy for the fabulous American millions to obtain their present respect in the aristocratic circles on the Continent. Several American heiresses knew this, to their sorrow, despite the huge fortunes their marriages brought to the decaying scions of old families. The bright dollars could hardly refurbish the tarnished European blazons that have since invited holocaust and oblivion. Yet, pageantry belongs to the urge for human expression, in any century, and no matter how eloquently the democratic note is howled from the roof, when occasion demands, there is the ever-old attempt for grandiose display, mass formation of the populace to loud music, and bunting aloft in the breezes. The Russian Grand Duke might toss his barber a hundred franc tip with a graceful gesture; the American set up drinks at the bar with the lavish gesture "All join in." It is still the same bravado of good-humored camaraderie and display.

At this time, I made the acquaintance of a pretty little singer in the theatre. Her vocal exertions were few and far between, and of little éclat on such infrequent occasions. Her sumptuous mode of living, horses and jewels, pointed obviously to other contributions than those won in the coulisses of the opera house. It was my first intimate experience with a recognized demi-mondaine. I bothered my head very little about the distinguished elderly gentleman who figured in her entourage as "uncle"; but my mother was horrified at the thought of any association—which was only at the theatre and which I enjoyed thoroughly—and cautioned me with every known proverb that the good little New Englander is supposed to know and observe. Such as:—"One is known by the

75

company one keeps," "Fine feathers make fine birds," and so on.

She need not have worried. Myrtille—such was her pretty name, like herself, young and fresh as a field daisy—was charming and discreet in manner. To be sure, she would often look at me, shake her head, and say—"Oh, Farrar, how can you let your youth slip away in the drudgery of scales and the uncertainty of an opera career? With your eyes and smile, you could have anybody at your feet, a happy existence and freedom from care!" Poor little moth! So like hundreds, whose gay wings flutter too often and too near the candle that consumes them. I was genuinely sorry when I learned of her death the following year in Paris.

Stars from the Paris theatres also performed in dramatic offerings, in the illustrious personages of Réjane, Coquelin, Mounet-Sully, Lucien Guitry and Segurd-Weber, who exercised their undisputed sway in elegant classics. I often saw a lady of uncertain age, dressed in a fashion of long ago—a little bonnet set on a head still nobly carried. It was Christine Nilsson, the "Swedish Nightingale" of a past decade, intent only upon the one remaining interest her retired life offered— the excitement of the gaming tables. I thought at the time, how pathetic and futile a way to spend one's latter years, after having given so much to the world in song and beauty. The dynamic Mary Garden was a striking figure in the gay assembly, fresh from her Paris success in *Louise* and *Melisande.*

Later, I journeyed to Stockholm and the North in spring. A charming public made guest appearances there a great pleasure. My leading tenor was a well-known figure, despite venerable years, whose clear tenor voice and handsome legs

76

still made more than credible the illusion of a youthful Faust and Romeo. He had sung with Jenny Lind in his youth and had some interesting stories to tell of her disinclination to the operatic stage, and a distressing air of piety that probably irked the lady-killer in him!

Stockholm is a lovely city, and its opera audiences are cultured and appreciative. The Swedish language is not easy for a travelling prima donna, so I alternated in the French and Italian tongue, according to the original text of the work performed.

King Oscar was then the reigning monarch, passionately fond of opera and theatre, and honored me by his presence at every performance. The Swedish company boasted a roster of fine singers and an excellent orchestra; my guest visit was entirely pleasant and successful. I made friendships that have endured over the years, and treasure particularly the Order of Merit that the King was graciously moved to bestow upon me. I believed Nilsson and Melba were previously so distinguished, while our popular Americans Grace Moore and Lawrence Tibbett have been the most recently honored with this tribute.

The hotel was quite lively with the presence of other intriguing professional personalities. Isadora Duncan occupied a suite next to mine; it would take volumes to note her successful progress all over Europe, for she was, at last, coming into her own after the lean years of unsuccessful activity in dance preliminaries at home. Today, her theories are accepted and her freedom of movement, the acknowledged foundation for most all the rhythmic classes, whether designed for health purposes or pantomime entertainment in the theatre. At the time, however, New York had no conception of what she wanted to

77

accomplish, and little interest in the encouragement of her efforts.

Isadora had quite as many revolutionary ideas about love in her artistic life, as the development of her particular dance art; and she was aggressively frank in their exhibition. There was no need to be unduly concerned when the cavaliers succeeded each other with startling rapidity, however. The cherished companion of the moment was Ellen Terry's gifted son, Gordon Craig; himself quite an iconoclast of the theatre, carrying his own eloquent megaphone to reason out his pet theories and plans for innovations.

Isadora wanted me to take charge of an exquisite little statue that had been made of her by a local artist; as it was still in plaster and fragile, she consigned it to me as some friends of mine were leaving direct for Berlin and she still had a lengthy tour before her in the North. They were glad to be of service, and this friendly commission brought us in communication with her more often. I never heard her express an opinion about opera, so I fancy she had no particular interest in that direction. She had, however, amusing details to relate of her invitation to Bayreuth, where the appearance of the Three Graces in the Venusberg Bacchanale—which she was invited to supervise and in which, as well, to appear—brought about quite a sharp clash with the autocratic Cosima. I gathered from Isadora—and having been an eye-witness myself to a superb performance—that the dancer had her say in the end.

Quite alien to this extravagant and fantastic figure was a petite little vaudevillian, Saharet. With her husband, she sat near my table daily in the hotel restaurant. One would never

78

have associated the quiet couple with the professional world, and most assuredly not recognized in her modest appearance the sprightly, whirling figure of many lace petticoats, in the rage for the "Can-Can" as made popular in the open-air pleasure gardens.

There was still another dancing celebrity in the person of the very demure Cléo de Mérode. Known to the Parisian boulevards as a protégé of that gay old dog and bewhiskered "Cleópold,"—otherwise His Most Hated Majesty, Leopold of the Belgians—an indifferent potentate to Congo horrors— Mlle. de Mérode's professional accomplishments were a kindergarten series of traditional ballet pirouettes; but a reputation for "galanterie" under a nun-like exterior was sufficient attraction for quite a few music hall engagements outside her native France.

It gave me pleasure to note these interesting women during my own season.

At a farewell party given me after my last performance, I was introduced to the potent effects of Swedish Punch for the first time. This bland amber liquid is an insidious beverage! It was not too late, after a first sip, to realize I had better let it alone. It may be nectar for the Gods, but much too "heady" for an unaccustomed New England palate!

Then, on to Poland, where the Italian season in Warsaw was a mélange of polyglot types and temperaments from various climes. A delightful city—under Russian supervision and Polish resentment of it—there were many bloody clashes in the streets, even penetrating to my rooms in the Hotel Bristol.

This was an entirely new milieu. I could speak German, French, and Italian, where my native English failed; as a rule,

79

however, the French and German tongues were employed, and even in Sweden I had had no difficulty in feeling free to go anywhere without an interpreter's aid. But Warsaw was another story. The hotel manager spoke halting French, and the porter a polyglot German; in the main, however, the Slav prevailed, unintelligible to me.

Now, in my earlier days in Paris, I had made the happy acquaintance of a Russian and a Pole, students there like myself. Their interest was to serve me here in good stead, in the following manner: The former, a woman my own age and a talented sculptress, was housed near by. Russian Tola Certowicz was all that was generous and hospitable. Hers were the first flowers and note of greeting that awaited me in the hotel drawing room, a most cheerful welcome on a bitter, dark, winter day. The Polish Madeline Wodak was visiting her at the time, fair as an Icelandic beauty, while Tola was like a brunette odalisque.

Owing to their kind efforts, mother and I saw in Warsaw all the strange and Oriental beauty of that interesting city, usually ignored by the casual tourist. Oddly enough, the Russian Government operated the royal theatres, while a Polish faction managed the Philharmonic; and again I found Isadora across the corridor of my hotel engaged to dance with this latter organization. Her success was immense with the Poles, especially as she illustrated much with Chopin's music. Wishing to honor them with a speech of thanks in the native tongue, I arranged with Madeline for her to learn by rote a few chosen phrases to that effect. She received wild acclaim on the occasion, delivering them with aplomb and a most winning manner. When she carried an enormous wreath to

Farewell Concert, Berlin, 1906

MISS FARRAR AND HER MOTHER, NEW YORK, 1906

honor Chopin's grave, the enthusiastic crowds acclaimed her like an Empress.

Meanwhile, my opera experience was wholly charming. I sang in French and Italian, the rest of the native cast in Polish—which sounded even more strange to my ears than the Swedish vernacular. Even then, I recognized also that no matter how good the translation, fitting a musical accent and word to alien intentions can never give the same complete satisfaction of a performance as in its native tongue. Whether or not the listener understands the words, he is bound to comprehend the action and situation involved.

I was to have proceeded to Moscow and St. Petersburg later, but one of the many revolutions was set in progress, so that I not only did not visit these cities, but could not even return to Berlin for an extended period. I was conducted to the opera house for performances that the Russian regime insisted on giving by Cossacks and foot soldiers. It was a safeguard from the rioting crowds and excited mobs, but I can well do without so close an affinity with Mars. It was my first experience with the power of the militia against civil rebellion and not a pretty sight.

Eventually, quiet was restored, and it came time for a gala farewell, acclaimed by a vociferous public. These charming people spent a great deal of time at tables groaning with viands and drink and the artists were required often to grace the occasions, one of the few disagreeable features of a Continental career, as compared to the more democratic homecoming to bed and sleep from the Metropolitan fatigues and worries.

It was Isadora's farewell, so she was also present. Her supper partner was a handsome young student, and mine was a retired ambassador of more elderly charm. The language employed was an elegant French in which one can unblushingly make the most extraordinary assertions, and ask the most impertinent questions. Isadora in her flowing white robes, bared feet purple on the cold marble floor of the dining room, was animated and at her best. The student was obviously enchanted, and his eyes never fell below her own; but my sophisticated Prince, doubtless from long acquaintance with boudoir secrets, was highly curious to know, upon glancing at her frozen toes, if she kept warm above with red flannel undergarments. I naturally disclaimed any knowledge of her particular lingerie, but suggested he apply for information at the source. He assured me later that he did! I did not press him for details.

Her original and superb gifts continued to startle the dancing world for some years, and had a reasonable balance kept pace with her great talent we should not have witnessed the sad close of her later years and so tragic an end. Germany paid her the homage of enthusiasm and understanding. It was there she made her home for some time, and began that early and unique organization, with small children, that was to present them later in a group of beautiful plastic expression, comparable to the friezes of the classic Greeks. The latter years of her unfortunate immolation in Red Russia, the perverted discard of all wholesome expression, shocked and saddened those who admired her—and I count myself among the many. What a wanton waste of great beauty and inspiration.

Isadora's own story is one of interest and fascination. Among the many illustrations, my favorite is a photograph taken in the Paris studio by Otto, about 1911. Here, the semi-recumbent draped figure is like sculptured marble in its incomparable grace and ease.

Her friend, Mary Desti, in additional biographical detail, completes the poignant tale. Its last chapter is tragically eloquent as it leads up to the finale of the fatal motor ride. Seated in a high-powered racing car, Isadora's silken shawl caught in its flying wheels, and, in a hideous instant before the car could be stopped, the end had come. Her neck broken, the jugular vien severed by the brutal twist of the dragging fringes, it is to be hoped she never was conscious of the moment. It stunned the world at large, and left friends and admirers in shuddering sorrow.

Meanwhile, the constant travel to new lands and to other audiences than the devotedly loyal Berliners, was sharpening my theatre perceptions and broadening them. By now I was fairly proficient in three languages—Italian, French and German—and could change from one to another in a few hours of concentrated study. In fact, it was a frequent experience to sing *Faust* in German in one evening, board the midnight express and sing it in French the next night in Paris—or, two evenings later, in Italian in Poland.

My Berlin contract had been renewed without a quibble. The salary was small but the benefits were great, and I worked like an army mule with the indefatigable Lilli Lehmann.

One speaks of the Salzburg of yesterday with bated breath; (it was laden with the aroma of cocktails all too frequently). But in those first days of Lilli Lehmann's direction, with the Archduke Eugene as generous patron, we were offered the most adorable rococo performances one would wish to hear.

Dr. Muck of Berlin and Mahler of Vienna led a perfect orchestra to suit the requirements of the Bijou Opera House, still standing, wherein we performed. It was for her and for Mozart that all artists were glad to come for gala seasons without recompense. It was she who laid the cornerstone of the Mozarteum, she whose noble aim was to make Salzburg a center for outstanding performances that would breathe the true Mozartian spirit.

What real devotion to art, and what fun, our Don Giovanni; the elegant Scotti dressed in his hotel and rode proudly through the streets in a decrepit cab, still every inch the grand seigneur, bowing right and left! The chorus found themselves scattered anywhere, under the trees in the Mirabell gardens or at neighboring cafes in case of rain. Great Lilli minded nothing of the inconvenience for herself, and dressed at a friend's house, close by; while a corner of the tiny stage, behind a stairway, served my purpose as a loge. The one small room, leading from it, was bestowed upon Gadski who had many handsome dresses and a plethora of plumed hats to grace her vocal outpourings. Scenery was a simple matter of two hangings—accessories non est—but with what verve, and beauty, noble singing was performed.

Now, when I think of the transformation of the erstwhile stables, to a so-called auditorium—the cocktail bar of the *Europe* where too many loud-voiced Americans scream to horrendous jazz, the masquerading tourists dressed à la Dirndl—the mobs that flock, not for music but because the publicized statements announce the magic name of Toscanini—and Mozart? Salzburg's intimate charm and rococo fragrance? Oh no—it had a sickening reek of Broadway commercialism to my mind, for I know and remember sweeter

84

and more tender whispers than the hub-bub of the busy magpies it fostered.

The last time I was there, it was to hear the voice of memory more insistent than ever of a past beauty. I am proud it was so. On a great bronze plaque, in the foyer of the Mozarteum, there are engraved names that made those first years of Salzburg's festival possible by their loving services to Art. I am proud mine stands out boldly among them. It was Lilli's superb gesture.

Since the recent Anschluss of Austria with Germany— whether a willing ally or not, is beside the mark here—Salzburg may well undergo another transformation, with the Nazi regime in command. Aside from the undoubted loss and absence of a few splendid non-Aryan artists, I am not discouraged to believe this quaint little town will suffer eclipse. I have seen and heard too many fine performances in recent years, in Berlin, Dresden, Munich and Bayreuth, to sustain such an opinion. However, the repercussion of Nazi intentions has moved many a musician to hysterical reaction from the safe confines of these United States shores. Crawling to popular acclaim under the cloak of adopted citizenship is hardly a gesture I would care to applaud.

At the recent concerts by that superbly gifted singer, Marian Anderson, I was struck by the quiet deference paid this colored woman by an audience composed of all nationalities, classes and races. And I wondered why it was, that musicians insisted upon furthering grimy politics and questionable partisanships when the world of their choosing is the real sphere for harmony and understanding. Especially so, in our own great land of opportunity where the old world barriers of caste and racial frontiers do not prevail.

Why must this country become the nursery for subversive activities and propaganda, too readily fomented by those very ones most eager to promote it, in their migration to these friendly shores? I often wonder if our promised and cherished freedom has not become one of such destructive license as will eventually demand a stiff payment from us in the sorry moment of its collection.

My next interesting engagement was an invitation to sing at the Prinz Regenten Theatre in Munich, Elizabeth in *Tannhauser*. I was very proud to accept, as friendly comrades surrounded me and Dr. Richard Strauss was at the helm. When he is in an amiable mood, he can be an inspiration and, very fortunately, such was the case. And thereby hangs a tale of one of my many encounters with him, since he was on the regular music staff in Berlin and conducted often for me.

By his request, I had journeyed to the premiere of *Salome* in Dresden. I was later to know the reason for it. I was impressed enormously by the work, the superb vocalists who were indeed indefatigable in the intricate beauties of the score, but I was more intrigued by the dramatic and pictorial probabilities of the role. By no means did the weighty protagoniste realize the acting values, or present an Oriental picture of savage grace! Knowing this work was to be on the Berlin opera's roster, once Dresden's premiere had been given, I had gone with Maurice Renaud in Paris (a good friend and comrade in Monte Carlo and Paris), to view the feverish and beautiful decadent scenes as depicted by Gustave Moreau, in a private collection of this artist's work. The slim, young Salome, her lascivious postures, her costumes, her wide-eyed air of perverse naiveté were far and away a different conception from the massive figure of the German prima

86

donna; this latter was a typical Brunnhilde, heaving a ponderous bosom under her glistening breast-plates, with an extended
arm bereft of spear. A twirling ballerina hopped onto the
scene to "double" for the dance, and all illusion was shat-
tered, of course, as the routine steps beat out the turgid,
sensual music in a conventional one-two-three toe-tapping.

But, alas for my own particular hopes; vocally, the demands
were quite impossible for me to encompass. And when Dr.
Strauss bluntly asked me to take on the part—which was, of
course, the reason for his invitation to the Dresden premiere—
I was obliged to regret. He offered to make changes suitable
to my voice, and candidly added: "You, Farrar, have such
dramatic possibilities, can act and dance half-naked, so no one
will care if you sing or not."

It was no temptation, for the meaty structure of the score
could not for one instant be transcribed for my lyric endowment. After all, I was a singer, and a voiceless apparition on
the stage of the Royal Opera, no matter how seductive, would
soon—and rightly—have drawn forth fire and ire! and dis-
missal! Incidentally, the mighty Richard, for all his superb
gifts and the glorious passion that saturates his pages, has a
sharp eye for royalties. Acceptance would not endanger my
virtue, in this instance, but certainly would have cost me a
precious vocal possession I had no mind to risk. So the indefatigable Destinn sang it superbly in Berlin—and looked, as
her predecessor, like a misplaced *Walküre*.

But to return to Munich. The Bavarian capitol is one of the
most beautiful in the world, as well as the coziest. Its citizens,
genial and informal, with something of the responsive Latin
nature, patronize opera and theatre with appreciation and
enthusiasm.

87

At this time, the lovely Berta Morena was an unforgettable artist at the Royal Opera, then under the leadership of Felix Mottl, together with the soprano Fassbender and the contralto Matzenauer, (the latter to become a feature in American circles later) with an outstanding tenor, Heinrich Knote. A notable addition to the operatic roster was the Californian Maude Fay, whose name was coupled also with that of a local royal personage. It was the moment for such glamorous gossip wherever a crown was linked with the lyre!

I was staying at the Hotel Russischer Hof, to which pleasant hostelry I had been recommended by Nordica, until the World War transformed it into a commercial office; since when I make my headquarters at the Continental. Above my apartment, and brought to town by the summer festival performances at the Prinz Regenten theatre, were domiciled three lovely royal sisters. They were visions of beauty when they appeared, and an inseparable trio, in the foyer. The late Dowager Queen of Roumania, the Grand Duchess Cyril of Russia, the Princess Beatrice, now married to some Spanish royalty whose name escapes me. The royal families of Europe were so closely allied, it was pretty safe to classify them as near or distant kin of the fabulous Victoria of sacred English memory.

Familiar sights too in the park and on the broad streets, were members of the Bavarian reigning house, headed by the democratic and highly respected Prinz Regent, with those ladies of immediate connection, so plain of feature, it was difficult to realize they shared the hot blood that had coursed through the veins of the Apollonian and erratic King Ludwig, the friend of Wagner and sponsor of the glorious castles that dot the hills and broad meadows of his fairy-like land, as well as the tragic Empress of Austria, that cousin Elizabeth, who had fallen a victim to a crazed assassin's bullet not so many years before. Happily in this idyllic moment, we were spared a later vision of a gay, cheering crowd that, in the twinkling of an eye, became a roaring mob of brutality and destruction, pursuing this hapless family like wolves after frightened deer, in the bloody uprising of the Revolution, the hideous aftermath of Germany's defeat in the Great War.

Aside from musical events of the moment, there was much going on of an experimental and novel nature in the world of Spiritualism. Baron Schrenk von Notzing is a name known to all who interest themselves in psychic research and phenomena. A delightful cosmopolitan, he was eager to engage upon this favorite topic at any time or place. One experiment considered very unusual, and viewed with absorption by invited guests, was a dance program provided by a woman who went by the name of Magdalena. The Baron claimed she knew nothing of music or the dance, nor was there any preconceived program before her actual performance. It was somewhat in the nature of a slow pantomime, and might have been inspired by the graceful attitudes of Isadora Duncan—without that artist's flame of genius. Once put into a trance by the Baron, she became, at any rate, a creditable and charming figure of Terpsichore. I fear I gave small thought to the means of her so-called "inspirations," despite the diverting entertainment.

I was also sitting to the great portrait painter, von Kaulbach. His father had been the creator of those superb Wagnerian illustrations, as well as other recognized scenes of Teutonic valor; the son was equally gifted in portraiture, sharing with the local von Lenbach, and Franz Stuck, the

89

homage from far and near which their great names brought to their studios.

It was a torture for me to be inactive for the posing. The artist placed me as often as consistent with his work, at his superb Bechstein piano, where I let off steam and my pent-up nervous activity. He painted half a dozen most beautiful canvases which I humbly acknowledge to be far more arresting than ever were my own human attributes; but in so doing, he will leave to posterity such impressions as will inspire the beholder to believe in all the romantic and fixed legends that attain splendor and credence with the passing of time.

I owned a beautiful example of his work, but made a present of it to a close friend whose great music room provides the proper setting for it, in my immediate neighborhood. I am not one to count my silver hairs and years in such close proximity to an imperishable counterpart of exuberant youth and beauty. The others are distributed in museums and private collections. As in many instances where I had been favored with unusual connections, the vom Rath family were again responsible for my association with the great painter, a friend of their own circle. Many Americans, attendant meanwhile at the festival, were loud in pride and acclaim. It was the August of 1906, and I was to make my debut at the Metropolitan the following November.

It was owing to the continued interest of Maurice Grau and his wife that I had gone to the opera at Monte Carlo. It was also his belief in me that had inspired the visit of Conried one spring day in Berlin.

Mr. Conried was to have inherited Caruso's contract, upon Grau's resignation because of poor health, and had been primed about certain other artists in Europe likely to prove

90

good Metropolitan material. At any rate, I received a telephone call at my apartment that Mr. Conried would like me to call upon him at his hotel. With the unthinking impertinence of youth, I extended the invitation for him to call on me. Which this pleasant gentleman did.

It seemed he wanted to engage me for New York, but was some what taken aback at my well-defined outline of a contract there, its scale of emoluments, and certain concessions regarding my choice of repertoire. He listened and departed—with no assurance that my presence was particularly necessary to his operatic company. I telegraphed Maurice Grau, who was in Paris, this negligible result and he, knowing all the tricks of the trade, replied: "Don't worry. He'll be back." If he did not come in person, he sent his agent the following month, while I was taking the cure at Franzensbad.

This clever man, however, ran up against a snag with all his arguments; for both mother and I were fully prepared to defend our prerogatives, knowing (with Grau's counsel) we were not making excessive demands for this particular and important engagement that was to crown our sacrifices. And now that it was actually at hand, we wished it to go through with every success that forethought could devise. The theatre world is a queer one, and no verbal statement or affirmation after a pleasant social dinner, quite offers the same premise for argument as a witnessed black and white document. I could take some things on faith, but not assertions where rival sopranos had prior claims based on popular local preferences. It was therefore most important that I have the proper opportunity to appear before the public. Its judgment is the conclusive opinion by which the artist must abide.

It matters little if a Board member favors a pretty singer,

a critic is enamored of an artist's special interpretation, or a social hostess pushes a protégé toward the limelight. In the end, willy-nilly, the public decides what is the real accolade for the performer. No more dramatic instance of this can be cited, than that performance of *Falstaff*, of not so many years ago, when the hysterical audience shouted itself hoarse for a young American, Lawrence Tibbett, to accept, solo, the curtain calls hitherto accorded Scotti alone in this stellar role. It was the beginning of Tibbett's career in his native land, a beginning encouraged by his countrymen, who have not wavered in their support.

I had faith in myself, once before the public; but politics are another thing again. I hoped I had the proper public field for exploits, for in the opera arena I owned a good weapon for the vocal combat, and I was not afraid to exploit it.

But each time I thought of it, I shivered with apprehension at the ordeal, and almost regretted I had signed a contract. For there was one, at last; so iron-clad in its agreement that the genial Mr. Conried probably thought he had to do with a lawyer-shrew, rather than a song-bird! He said I knew more about protective paragraphs than any other star performer since the vigilant Adelina Patti. But it was no accident that my dear mother had informed herself privately upon such matters. To be sure, we were returning to our native land, but it was a new and strange field for us, all the same, so all plans were in her capable hands. I had only to keep to my work and watch my health. Hers was the arduous, less inspiring task to safeguard our interests, advance my prestige, and see that our family unit was not disturbed in the process of this career making.

CHAPTER FOUR

I

THE MOTHER

1906-1907

MR. CONRIED and his agent have come and gone! And we have each a contract in our pockets, at last.

It is a good engagement for Geraldine, and I do not believe the Metropolitan will be the loser, either, but it has been a wary and involved process. I do not understand why. I detest bargaining. Frank-speaking creates more confidence, saves time, and is a more dignified proceeding than so much distrustful haggling. We never had to do this in Berlin. There the attitude was one of willingness to engage the singer at a stipulated fee which she could accept or not, but these agents wish to create the impression that they confer a favor. As a fat percentage is their part of it all, this attitude strikes me as ridiculous. It doesn't hoodwink me, at any rate. Twice we have seen the present representative of Mr. Conried come and go, after futile argument and now, after the third essay, we have signed on the dotted line exactly as proposed some months ago. A stupid and obvious waste of time.

Geraldine has already obtained the necessary permission from the Royal Opera for a leave of absence. She can wangle almost anything, it seems, when she sets her heart on it.

It appears when she spoke of the matter to the Intendant, he flatly refused to mention the matter to the Kaiser. He said His Majesty had repeatedly asked for certain performers, to find they were mostly guesting out of his capitol. He said he wasn't pleased at this, and hereafter his artists would have to remain home at least part of the time! Geraldine said, with the Intendant's permission, she herself would take up the matter with His Majesty at a forthcoming private concert at the palace, which she did. She frankly spoke to His Majesty of the pride she felt in her return to her native land, the goodly sums mentioned in the contract, the liquidation of the large loan that was still looming upon her horizon; in short, a most understandable longing to essay the home adventure. This fascinating monarch could be kind, and granted the desired leave of absence from November until the following April— to be extended for three years provided New York set its seal of approval on her. For that favor, however, she was to return each spring to her duties in Berlin, and remain there; no skipping off to neighboring cities, and no surcease in hard work, and public appearances. It was a fair enough proposition to which she gladly consented.

I was trifle anxious whether her strength would withstand this exhausting and emotional routine; but that we had to chance, and she was all eagerness to do so. There were demonstrations at every performance, once the news was given to

MISS FARRAR'S AMERICAN DEBUT
AS JULIETTE

Metropolitan Opera House
Lessee CONRIED METROPOLITAN OPERA CO.

GRAND OPERA

SEASON 1906-1907.

Under the Direction of MR. HEINRICH CONRIED.

OPENING NIGHT

MONDAY EVENING, NOVEMBER 26, 1906,
at 8 o'clock.

Roméo et Juliette

OPERA IN FIVE ACTS
AND SIX SCENES.

(Preceded by a Prologue.)

MUSIC by GOUNOD

Book by Jules Barbier and Michel Carré.

(IN FRENCH.)

JULIETTE ....MISS GERALDINE FARRAR
(Her first appearance.)

STEPHANO....... ....MME. JACOBY

GERTRUDE ....MME. NEUENDORFF

ROMÉO.......... ....MR. ROUSSELIÈRE
(His first appearance.)

FRÈRE LAURENT........ MR. POL PLANÇON

CAPULET ....MR. JOURNET

TYBALT ... .MR. BARS

DEBUT PROGRAM,
METROPOLITAN OPERA HOUSE

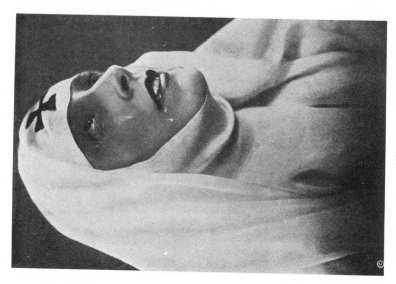

THAÏS

MARGUERITE IN *Faust*, PRISON SCENE

the press, and the last weeks of great excitement culminated in a most beautiful concert she gave for a pet charity of the Crown Princess. The Court was present and a huge audience wildly enthusiastic.

Every detail of Geraldine's activities was now cabled to America. Speculation about her was rife from every angle. No planned demonstration could have surpassed the effect of the farewell crowds, and their cheers that lingered long in our grateful ears after we had left Berlin to embark at Bremen. Geraldine, with it all, had a sensible head on her shoulders and accepted it as the tribute to a public character. She was never out of this role when under observation.

Once alone, two happy New Englanders laid aside the glamorous trappings evoked by fevered imaginations. Soberly and calmly, we began to plan for her further career. As on a voyage into a strange country, we took careful bearings and endeavored to keep cool under exciting circumstances. The barrage of questions we knew would be fired upon landing in New York must be answered with tact, yet with pleasant and apparent frankness. I could trust my girl to carry off the situation.

From that first day, romance and glamor were to be synonymous with her name. Once arrived, she was eager to talk of music, her hopes, her teacher, her opera experiences, the musical situation. The gentlemen of the press were not interested at all. They wanted to know point blank why she hadn't married the Crown Prince?—or vice versa, now he was married, did she visit the Crown Princess? Was it true that she had been requested to leave Prussia at one time? That officers had quarreled over her? That young Lieutenants broke champagne glasses once her lips had touched them? That the pearls she wore were a gift from royalty after a particular soirée at the Palace?

I was heartened to see my child parry it all with spirit and good humor. She disclaimed regimental disorders, was modest about her agreeable visits in Potsdam, discreet as to personal triumphs, and begged only to be judged by the coming debut which she confessed was the highlight of her career to date. On a frosty November morning, no place in the world is as dreary as a shipping dock; but so lively was this scene we did not feel cold or fatigue till eventually released from hectic questioning and allowed to go to our hotel.

Our rooms were a bower of flowers from old friends and unknown well-wishers. The telephone and press were unceasing in their search for news. Geraldine held herself in readiness for the first rehearsals and encounters with the members of the opera company.

She prepared herself carefully for what was to be our most difficult task thus far. Nerves took possession of her, insomnia ruined her sleep, and I had never seen her so restless and apprehensive. She said the opera house frightened her by its size, after the more intimate frame in Berlin. The climate was trying, also. Then there were always self-invited listeners at the rehearsals, which bothered her somewhat, though she did enjoy meeting Emma Eames, a noted member of the company and a favorite New York artist. (They later became fast friends.) Geraldine was accustomed to long, painstaking rehearsals where stage business was meticulously worked out for every member of the company; and now she was greatly irritated at the airy indifference of those comrades who hardly bothered to sing in half-voice, and hatted and gloved, paraded to and fro as if the occasion were a social tea, and time for the rehearsal begrudged. She had new "business" which perhaps was resented by the older members, but her fresh young enthusiasm prevailed and eventually she did obtain her own results.

Then and there the "boys" backstage, those indispensable, if unseen Gods that make or break a performance, took her to their hearts, and for all the years to come never faltered in their loyal devotion and aid. They may have been often surprised at the requests she made, the accessories and stage furnishings, the introduction (later) of live geese in *Koenigskinder*, the readjustment of Marguerite's spinning wheel, or Tosca's crucifix, but they were always willing to do their important bit toward novel touches and ideas for a new stage picture and interpretation.

Romeo and Juliette had been chosen by Mr. Conried for Geraldine's debut, and the opening night of the season. This selection was not as satisfactory as she would have wished. Despite her recent success in Berlin and Munich as Elizabeth— which till then she considered her finest role—it availed nothing against Mr. Conried's preference for a French offering of gaiety, lovely costumes, and a more traditional adherence to the popular standard repertoire.

In previous years, the opening had been chosen from the Italian and French list, perhaps because of the overwhelming popularity of the redoubtable Jean de Reszke, and the galaxy of sopranos such as Melba, Calvé, Nordica, and Eames. It would be hard to match that distinguished company of singers at any time. Rousséliére, her Romeo, had been a familiar

97

partner in Monte Carlo, so they were agreed upon the stage pictures with little difficulty. Pol Plançon, the great basso, was a tremendous favorite already, and the others in the cast were the usual well-trained support.

Geraldine and I drove to the opera house with excited hearts; the emotion was agonizing. I looked at her pale face and closed eyes, while a certain measure of pity vied with my triumphant joy in the certitude of the acclaim I knew was to be hers once she entered upon the fever of the performance. For this supreme moment I had labored, planned, economized, and prayed. We could not fail.

Her devoted maid had laid out the shimmering silks and chiffons in the afternoon, for at that time the star dressing-room was shared by all the soprano soloists. This I noted, and already had stored in my mind a plan by which Geraldine might own a corner to herself in which to house her gorgeous wardrobe and accessories. For the present, however, the big draughty room would have to do, though its impersonal walls and scant furnishings were scarcely inspiring.

Geraldine sat before the mirror and began the make-up process by which she became the heroine of the evening, a transformation I always viewed with astonishment, and a slightly uneasy feeling that my daughter had slipped away from me. I was confronting a stranger, vaguely resembling her in looks and manner. With the jewels sparkling in her hair, the flowing draperies gave her quite the air of an Italian beauty come to life from a Renaissance painting. Mr. Conried passed by to wish her God-speed—the call-boy cried out the last warning—the orchestra began its haunting overture, and

THE GOOSEGIRL IN *Koenigskinder*, WHEN LIVE GEESE WERE USED

my girl sprang to her task, like the race-horse she was and always would be, in this arena of quivering emotions.

Her entrance was greeted by a welcome of stormy applause—which almost unnerved her—but she recovered herself quickly, and broke into the measures of the waltz. Knowing herself no competitor to the dazzling coloratura effects of a Melba, she swayed ever so slightly into a dreamy intention of this first solo, a half-whispered mood of insinuating and mellow vocal daydreaming. The tempo was slow and novel, but it suited her style perfectly. In the meeting with Romeo, and the subsequent balcony scene, mounting to a passionate flow of melody and irresistible ardor, the audience was touched by her flame. I watched from the wings and realized my child was at her best, and spurred on to effects I had never heard before. There was no denying her genuine impulse and originality throughout the opera.

Thus, in this Juliette, there was no stiff-necked, brocaded prima donna sitting upright in a conventional chair, center stage, to vocalize upon the delirious delights of a bridal night; but a lovely, languorous figure, in flowing draperies, reclining on a couch locked in Romeo's arms. The passion in this duet lost nothing by its seductive visual appeal, and her abandon. Many such original touches she worked into the whole traditional opera pattern, to give it life by dramatic interpretation. With the close of a brilliant performance, which ended in a warm and generous accolade from a brilliant audience, New York was ready to welcome a new and glowing personality.

The *Evening Sun* of November 27, 1906, in two columns commenting upon the event, remarks as follows regarding Geraldine:

99

FIRST OPERA'S FARRAR FUROR IS
GROWING YET.

———

SUCH LOVEMAKING NOT SEEN SINCE AUNTY
CALVE, SUCH JOYOUS GRACE SINCE
GRANDMOTHER SARAH.

———

HER WHISPERED WALTZ A DREAM.

———

METROPOLITAN BOX ENLARGED FOR THE
OCCASION.

———

THE LITTLE STAR DROPS GERMAN COURT
"CURTSIES" IN A TANGLE OF AMERICAN
BEAUTY BOUQUETS AND A TROOPING
OF FOREIGN COLORS.

———

FRERE LAURENT PLANCON ON STAGE, AND
FATHER SID FARRAR AMONG THOSE
PRESENT—BUT STANDING.

———

Let truth be told. The Farrar furor which startled 4,000 New Yorkers out of any desire to fall asleep during the mere music of last night's annual meeting of society at the Metropolitan Opera House, was still growing today.

That woman's voice in a girlish body had the haunting effect of forgotten impressions from one's early years.

Last night's Juliette is the first this generation has seen who looks the 14-year-old Verona girl, the youngest of operatic roles.

Here was an actress who enters the American stage, exhibits the manners of a court, whispers a worn-out old waltz song pensively, as if she were thinking aloud, and suddenly finds the coldest audience in the world taking her to its heart in a storm of applause that could not, would not end.

Half terrified, half pleased, she dropped little German court curtsies, bowed herself down to the stage, but firmly declined an encore.

More praise for that, too.

The voice is curiously rich in what sound experts call "color," especially of the "darker" hues that a Ternina mixes with brains.

The utterance is a free, full-hearted outpouring of rippling tone, a natural touch of what Sembrich does by sheer skill.

What may this girl not do? When Farrar twisted her little form into its turquoise wrapping, as she spun out the waltz's final trill, she could have wound that audience around her little finger.

Such serpentine grace has not been observed since the Carters and the Bernhardts, nor such love-making as last night's tropical garden scene since the age of Calvé.

It was the picture of Beardsley's Salome or Rosetti's Lilith, old Adam's "first wife!"

Two laurel wreaths bore a joint trouping of the colors of Germany and France, while Juliette yet curtesying, tore her laces in a thorny forest of American Beauty roses.

Miss Farrar's immediate future is to be French, because later Mr. Rouselliere must leave for Monte Carlo.

It is not till she sings the German Elizabeth that the last word on her voice can be spoken.

She sang the fourth scene last evening lying down. It may do queer things to the voice, but there is evidently a fearless originality in this youngest of the newest stars.

Already on Broadway today you heard the famous canonical jest: "She might go Farrar and fare worse."

She was, however, to learn further that the organization was not conducted along the routine lines of the Berlin Royal Opera. There were other stars in the company, and prime favorites by right of precedence and artistry. The question of repertoire was the stumbling block, primarily. Several outstanding prima donnas for *Faust, Bohème, Traviata, Tosca,* and so on through the standard repertoire, had to be reckoned with. Mr. Conried, like any astute impresario who has his eye on the box office as well as the excellence of his aviary, probably thought the novelty of *Salome* would be a second focal point of interest, and begged her to consider it for a New York premiere; but Geraldine had the good sense to refuse him, as she had refused Dr. Strauss, and for identical reasons.

The opera was to be given at all costs, and later Olive Fremstad played it in superb fashion—but for one performance only. The Board of Directors felt it incumbent to withdraw so curious and decadent a subject matter from their chaste boards. Manhattan, however, flocked to see and applaud Mary Garden's later assumption of the naughty dancer, when Oscar Hammerstein gave the city something to admire, and the Metropolitan considerable anxiety, so fine a company was his rival organization.

Meanwhile, Geraldine was busy with Puccini's *Butterfly*—which preliminaries involved her in an expenditure of enthusiasm and research. She had a co-worker, a delightful little Japanese actress, Madame Fu-ji-Ko, whose dainty personality and grace were her model for authentic gesture and carriage.

Those cold winter days, when the bitter winds howled around our corner apartment at the old Hotel Netherlands, Geraldine padded about our rooms in gay silk kimonos, the heavy wig elaborately dressed, her feet in the little one-toed canvas shoes used by the Japanese. She shuffled, posed, danced and gesticulated under the watchful eye of the Japanese artist, herself in native costume. A mighty pretty picture they made.

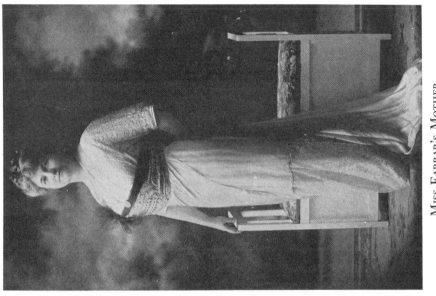

Miss Farrar's Mother

Kate Douglas Wiggin

MADAME BUTTERFLY

These two were so eager and intent upon their work, I had their luncheon and tea brought to them on trays, insisting they stop long enough to have some nourishment. What the waiters thought of these exotic goings-on, I could well imagine!

To conform to the correct physiognomy, Geraldine had shaved her own eyebrows, and drawn the thin arches of substitutes well above their natural place. This was as it should be in costume à la Japonaise, but when the inevitable hour came to cease play-acting and resume Occidental dress, the effect was very strange indeed. It was many years later that the plucked eyebrow effect was to become a decided fad for the screen professional, with no special indication in courteous acknowledgment to its Oriental source.

Ricordi and Puccini also had their particular views to impart, and were kind enough to add their personal visits to the hotel, as well as being the high irritants of those scheduled meetings for general company rehearsal at the opera house. The chief difficulty, from Geraldine's report of the little undercurrents of friction, seemed to be a different method employed by Italians in rehearsals. Naturally endowed with resilient vocal material, their mellifluous speech aids a beautiful singing production. Delighting in their own superb crescendo, they never spared themselves in a spontaneous outpour, but sang full voice at every rehearsal—apparently impervious to fatigue. Geraldine had been schooled, in Germany, to the use in preliminaries of the half-voice, saving the full power of expression for a public performance, and thus modify the consequent fatigue and unavoidable reaction. She was so highly responsive to the emotional side of a role, this was a wise measure to preserve as long as possible, the peculiar melting quality of her own organ. She had never had an overstrong larynx, and had to work very carefully and softly on her daily scales, coaxing them rather than urging to force. It was only upon the stage itself that she flung caution to the winds, and allowed herself the full and dynamic combination of voice and action. However, the dissent and arguments were not such as to invite open combat, for which everyone was grateful.

Caruso and Scotti had been the London favorites to support Destinn as the Japanese bride, so their presence at these rehearsals was more of a friendly act of co-operation than otherwise. The important dress rehearsal drew an invited audience which brought sandwiches, and the new fad then on the market for keeping liquids warm, the Thermos flask. Out of this ingenious cylinder, I fed my excited daughter hot bouillon between the acts; she had no time or taste for food. Louise Homer's preoccupation of the moment, aside from the contralto role she sang so beautifully, was her anxiety about her young pair of twin babies, wondering if their meals at home were being capably administered while she was at the theatre!

The actual performance came at last—and Geraldine scored another great triumph.

The picturesque Belasco, the genius of our theatre who was responsible for the play in which Blanche Bates had one of her most poignant roles, rewarded her dramatic interpretation with warm praise. For many years he was to be her friend and admirer, and often voice a tempting plan to induce her to a dramatic career under his expert guidance.

And another charming gentleman of wide travel and culture, Mr. Burton Holmes, was moved to genuine admiration of Geraldine's assumption of the little geisha maiden. He supplemented his compliments by presenting her, after one of his tours, with a complete wardrobe of lovely kimonos including all the pretty toys which Butterfly must withdraw from her voluminous kimono sleeves in the first act with Pinkerton. And among them was the beautiful blade for the final *hari-kari*, sheathed in an exquisite lacquered case, embellished with her monogram in Japanese, signifying Butterfly.

Clyde Fitch, our outstanding dramatist, greatly admired the beauty and appeal of Geraldine's very unusual personality, and at an exquisite dinner in her honor, she formed a firm friendship with the favorite authoress, Kate Douglas Wiggin who composed the following verses for the occasion and read them to the enthusiastic response of the applauding guests:

A Toast

Here is a toast to Geraldine!
The bird that lights on a bough to preen
His soft little breast with a satin sheen,
None of his notes are so sweet, I ween,
As those in the throat of Geraldine!

Here is a toast to Geraldine!
Her heart's as warm as her wit is keen,
She's a rosebud, still in its sheath of green,
In the singing garden of girls, the Queen!

Passionate Juliette, scarce sixteen,
Grave-eyed Elizabeth, stately in mien,
Marguerite, innocent, crystalline,
Loveliest Butterfly ever was seen
Drink to the future of Geraldine!

When the emotion evoked by these lines threatened to overcome the gathering, Mrs. Wiggin rose to add this postscript, on a higher note:

> *In the poem just repeated*
> *I've struggled to glean*
> *All practical rhymes for Geraldine!*
> *It's lucky for me that the girl I mean*
> *Wasn't born twins, or a "philopene,"*
> *Then had my muse still wearier been;*
> *For nothing is left me but atropine,*
> *Listerine, vaseline, glycerine,*
> *All most unworthy of Geraldine!*

It was not until *Butterfly,* with its overwhelming appeal, was produced in February, 1907, that Geraldine's success became an established fact. This charming and pathetic figure of the deserted Japanese bride fitted her like a glove; no one else seems to have usurped the memory. And with this creation, her place was definitely accorded as a stellar feature in the New York operatic world, where she was to have only Caruso as a friendly rival in box-office attraction.

II

The Daughter

1906-1914

THE nervous excitement of the debut out of the way, I went on to the *Damnation of Faust.* This work, then recently expanded to the scenic grandeur of the opera stage by the

106

resourceful Gunsbourg at Monte Carlo, offered me a beautiful but brief appearance as Marguerite. Despite the noblevoiced Plançon, who covered himself with glory, the box office was not besieged. It was a succés d'estime only, and performed but a few times.

I had occasion to present my version of the more popular *Faust* heroine a few weeks later, followed by a momentous occasion that earned me indisputable laurels, as that sainted Elizabeth I had begged to have serve me at my debut. I might add, it was the one and only performance of so lovely a role that I was permitted to sing at the Metropolitan in all my career there; but of that we shall speak later.

The *Butterfly* premiere had been an arduous business in its exciting preparation. First of all, Henry Savage, a successful Boston realtor, had realized the financial possibilities in an English singing company, and, among the many artists he engaged was Florence Easton, who presented a *Butterfly* at the Garden Theatre before our own Metropolitan production. I could wholeheartedly admire her rendition, particularly the crystalline entrance of the first act, which she delivered in flawless fashion. Later, we became friends and comrades at the Royal Opera in Berlin, as well as at the Metropolitan. Not unlike the great Lilli Lehmann, she proved herself in both lyric and dramatic roles.

Caruso and Scotti had created *Butterfly* the preceding summer, with Destinn, in London. She was a superlative singer, also a member of the Berlin Opera, but, for the moment, disinclined to listen to American dollars. I was thus chosen. Louise Homer, our native contralto, abetted me on the distaff side. Puccini came over to grace the occasion, with his editor Tito Ricordi. The composer may or may not have approved

107

the Metropolitan's choice of protagonists; I have been told of acrid letters of that time, where his anguish was voiced frankly in my disfavor. Ricordi, also, accustomed to control musical matters in Milan by autocratic ukase, was none too happy that such supervision was definitely out of place in Manhattan. One heard rumblings of protest, but, as nothing came out in the open, rehearsals were never unpleasant as far as I was concerned.

In my first *Bohème* performance with Caruso and Scotti, Puccini shared our curtain calls and was all that was agreeable, as well he might be, seeing the royalties that came his way from our efforts.

I was particularly happy on my twenty-fifth birthday when Mr. Conried allowed me to sing Violetta, a role that had been one of my most popular offerings on the Continent.

Pagliacci, with Caruso, was my next opera. I had sung it on a last minute call in Berlin. Here, it kept me before the public eye—which was important with so many stellar competitors; and then, before we realized it, the first New York season was over and the road tour begun.

It had been the Metropolitan's policy to lengthen the New York program by several weeks of spring performances in the larger cities.

The horrors of the earthquake in San Francisco, of a previous season, had interrupted a coast-to-coast tour; so Mr. Conried ventured nearer home, beginning with a week in my native Boston. I was announced for four of the eight performances, including the honor of the opening night in *Faust*, shrewdly presented for box-office reasons. Eames followed in *Tosca*, with Caruso. She too was on home soil and a great

(To the most intelligent artist, Miss Geraldine Farrar, this remembrance of her incomparable Butterfly at the Metropolitan offers Giacomo Puccini.)

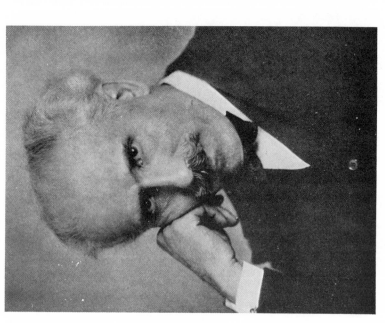

ANTONIO SCOTTI AS SCARPIA IN *Tosca*

ARTURO TOSCANINI

favorite. Then came my *Butterfly* with Andreas Dippel, that serviceable tenor who was to cause so much controversy later, in which everybody was, willy-nilly, involved. Gadski carried nobly the German wing, as Isolde. Winsome Bessie Abbott, making her local debut as well, was a charming Martha, sandwiched in between queenly Fremstad and myself sharing honors in *Tannhauser*. A second Eames performance in *Aida* was companioned again by Caruso. I accepted *Pagliacci* at the request of Mr. Conried, who saw his closing Saturday evening otherwise bereft of any stellar attraction. If I had not been so young and eager to please both management and public, I would have demurred and left as a last memory *Tannhauser* with its indelible impression of beauty. For, aside from *Butterfly*, it was at that moment the most revealing role I had sung. The company continued through several of the Eastern cities, my particular activities comprising these two roles as well as *Mignon* and *Bohème*.

Meanwhile, I had made some records in Berlin that had achieved European popularity. It had remained for Caruso to be the first to lift the Gramophone Company to unheard of success with thrilling records of his incomparable voice. Later, we all joined forces at the Camden studio where was born that fine Red Seal Series that has not since been equalled. Sembrich, Eames, Gadski, Schumann-Heink, Tetrazzini, Melba, Calvè, Caruso, Amato, Ruffo, Bonci, McCormack, Plançon—to mention a few of those earlier giants.

Our good friend, Calvin Child, in charge of the artists' department, said his earliest recollections of me were two—and quite disappointing. The first was when he drifted into the Royal Opera at the sole performance I gave in *Trovatore*.

He said he heard a gentle murmur of mellifluous Italian pitted against an heroic tenor and barytone, both of whom outclassed me in noise and girth. The sword of the barytone (Rudolf Berger, whose fine barytone eventually became a serviceable Wagnerian tenor, for an all too brief season later at the Metropolitan) was so much taller than myself, he feared I would be impaled upon it in full view of the audience. In the darkness of the dungeon scene, my black robes obscured my slender figure almost to the point of invisibility. The effect was somewhat of a small mouse squeaking from a dark corner. And his second indifferent impression was caused by that early, innocuous record of *Cherry Ripe*, at which he still chuckles today. If he had not visited another performance and, later, paid assiduous attention to my Metropolitan appearances, I might never had had the opportunity to convince him I was Red Seal material. *Butterfly*, of course, was the answer, and other selections were gleaned from succeeding operas.

Emilio de Gogorza was delegated to be Victor's genial intermediary with the artists. Superb artist himself and a fluent linguist, he could and did successfully approach temperamental songsters, not only in their own vernacular but according to their particular psychology as well.

These recordings went out over the country and served a wonderful purpose as advance réclame for later opera and concert tours, not to mention the generous royalties that accrued from their popular sales.

I had good reason to be happy with my American activities and departed for Europe with a light heart.

My new role for the second season at the Metropolitan was

110

a third version of Marguerite; that one in Boïto's *Mefistofele*. It had charming opportunities, but was mainly chosen to exploit Chaliapin; and what a magnificent and compelling performance he gave. The success, however, did not measure up to the European hysteria to which he had long been accustomed. He was displeased, out of sorts, and dissolved in a huge Russian pout all winter.

This humor did nothing to effect harmony in a revival of *Don Giovanni*, in which he was cast as Leporello, under the electrical baton of Mahler. Mahler was very ill—a doomed man; highly sensitive, irascible and difficult, but not unreasonable if the singer was serious and attentive. Chaliapin, however, was completely oblivious to rehearsal obligations. Mahler was sorely tried. The beautiful Emma Eames and the reliable Gadski, with Scotti, Bonci and myself, did our best to avert clashes. As I had sung Zerlina in Berlin under Strauss—under Muck in Salzburg—this training earned me Mahler's pleasant commendation; but we were, nonetheless, on pins and needles at every meeting. Happily, no overt act marred the performances, though it was a trifle disconcerting, to Scotti particularly, to have Chaliapin make a studied departure into Russian recitative where the fluent Italian text offered cues none too facile at any time; but this was purveyed with such bland impertinence, it was impossible to resist or chide this naughty giant!

Mignon was a lovely role soon after. The tenor hero, Bonci, was diminutive of stature, but not of voice. Together with a charming American friend and comrade, Bessie Abbott, the whole performance pleased our large audiences.

These two seasons were proving very successful. I was in

passable health and good spirits, adapting myself happily to the routine of the Metropolitan, and making friends with my growing American public.

Butterfly was rapidly becoming my personal property, by reason of box-office acclaim; but I was hoping gradually to be allowed an extension of my repertoire. This was not easy. Sembrich was still preeminent in *Bohème* and *Traviata*, while I had no desire to invite comparison with her in *Rigoletto*. The role of Gilda I had undertaken in Berlin (in Italian), in order that Caruso might include the Duke in his guest visits. Miss Hempel had not then effected her successful debut, so I was a logical choice. It was a favor only, and never my real vocal meat. When he first came there, he had sung at the Theatre des Westens, creating a furor. Then came the offer from the Royal Opera—after all, the terrain proper for this phenomenal attraction. I may add, also, that owing to my warm praise of Scotti to the authorities, he, too, later was invited to a combined trio in *Pagliacci* and *Bohème* that literally tore the roof off the opera house. Both Neapolitans were wildly cheered; while, being "at home" so to speak, I, too, had my hour, with them!

Berlin, contrary to frequent assertion, can be as uproarious as any Latin country in approval and reaction to fine performers. I have been witness to such receptions accorded Sembrich, when she brought her own company in the spring seasons at Kroll; to Coquelin, who aside from enchanting a splendid public, was an intimate and favored breakfast guest at the Kaiser's table. I don't wonder at his choice of this dear old friend of mine; such rare wit and manner are seldom found. He was a gentleman of an elegant school. He often boasted to me that he was the ugliest man in Paris—yet could,

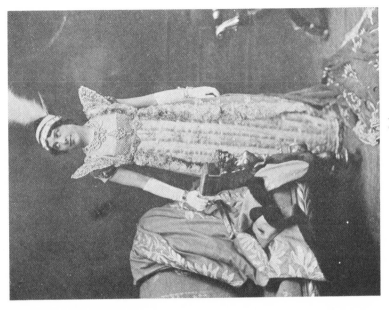

Mme. Sans-Gêne

In Franz Lehar's *Romany Love*

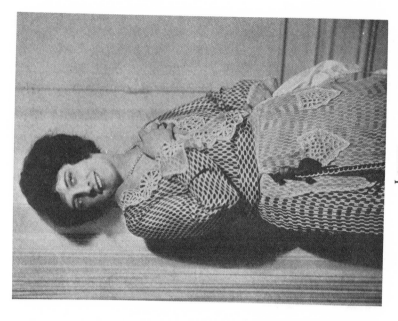

LOUISE

TOSCA

and did count his conquests! That I willingly believed! Though hardly the prescribed ideal of Don Giovanni, he was indeed not the ugliest man in the world. So entirely the charmer, aside from his superlative gifts as actor, what woman wouldn't have succumbed to this eloquent Cyrano? Sarah, the divine, never had more fervent tribute—nor the sad-eyed Duse—than in Germany. While Melba, our beautiful country-woman, Nordica, and a host of others could count upon discriminating and enthusiastic audiences.

However, to return to the Metropolitan and my problems. Emma Eames was still a favorite, and beauteous as Marguerite, Juliette, and Elizabeth. While I was human enough to enjoy the furor *Butterfly* created, I visualized the danger of too close association with one role. I had others in my repertoire that I had sung in Monte Carlo, Stockholm, Warsaw, and Paris; but they were not on the Metropolitan's list. Mr. Conried was always agreeable and understood my ambitions, even though he was constrained to smother them with good advice for patient waiting, for various reasons besides real managerial necessity. The critics bore down heavily on my youth, with caution to develop slowly.

Meanwhile, Mr. Conried's ill-health was a subject of grave concern, and, on the advice of his physicians, he resigned that spring. Of course, much buzzing speculation ensued as to his successor. Many names were proposed—among them, business men, as well as those engaged in theatrical enterprise—all Americans. Even our good friend Scotti nurtured a hope! Eventually, the press confirmed the engagement of two gentlemen from Milan, Mr. Gatti-Casazza as Managerial Impresario and Mr. Arturo Toscanini as Musical Director.

The public at large had never heard these names, and many

were the caustic prognostications—not always favorable to the introduction of alien control. I can see now how the Italians might have found it no easy sledding here at the beginning. A new post in unfamiliar surroundings. An institution saddled with unknown quantities in the shape of old contracts, labor unions, as well as established artists who had firmly entrenched themselves in local esteem. Our opera routine had its primary roots established in catering to the social seasons. Preferences were voiced in no uncertain terms from the parterre boxes.

For the sake of the record, let me throw the light of veracity upon the oft-quoted insolences with which I am credited toward the new arrivals, Gatti-Casazza and Toscanini. We shall begin by accenting a dual control that could not fail to be embarrassing to all.

Andreas Dippel, a personable tenor member of the company over a period of years, was chosen to share the responsibilities of the Metropolitan with the newcomers, at Mr. Conried's retirement. He was empowered to make new contracts, and many of the older members felt their interests would be best protected dealing with him, rather than waiting for the arrival of the Italians. Dippel knew the New York terrain and the artists already established. Many startling stories had been advanced about the regime from Milan; it was understood they were introducing new singers, favored importations consecrated at La Scala, and a horde of minor attractions to supplement those already on hand. It was also the time when I was to sign another contract. Mr. Dippel arrived in good faith and pleasant humor to do so; but I met him with two definite suggestions—a yearly increase in salary and extension of a guaranteed repertoire, which was a surprise he had not anticipated.

It is never to be supposed that a clear statement from the artist meets with like frankness and approval from the impresario. There is always the preliminary hem and haw of wearing argument, whereby the singer is made to feel either overbearing and obdurate if he persists in his theory that "Life is short and Art is fleeting" and therefore his material wants must be satisfied; or a cloak of suspicious gratitude is wrapped about his shoulders, if he supinely accepts the terms of the party of the managerial part. That was never my way. Arguments ensued, of course. The press introduced an acrimonious embroidery—the impasse occurred; and I sailed for Paris in May, with no engagement at the Metropolitan after that coming fall season.

I was guesting at the Opera Comique when Dippel arrived one evening, between the acts, to urge me to reconsider my refusal. Never the most tactful person, he drew forth a cable from Otto Kahn which advised me to accept the old terms as being an excellent offer no other opera house would make me. I flared up, and again refused. The gentle intimation that I could not better myself was not very flattering; and I did not forget the Berlin Royal Opera where I was mightily at home for an indefinite period, as a base for operations. Dippel left, crestfallen. I returned later to my usual happy duties in Germany.

Plans for seasons in Europe and South America were under way when Dippel reappeared, ready to sign the contract as I had previously outlined; but the delay had given me time to make inquiries anent the Milan organization, and put new ideas into my head as well. Having had to wait my turn to sing various roles of my repertoire, as youngest member of the Metropolitan, I was now minded to secure prior rights to subscription performances in New York. Otherwise, who knows? I might be shifted in and out of popular-priced offerings, sent out of town, used in Sunday concerts, or at private musicales; all these naturally would count as contracted appearances. I did not fear comparisons once I had the opportunity to appear, but if appearances were so rare that I could not establish myself with the public, there was no sense in a Metropolitan career. Besides, there were already many singers for the same roles; how could the repertoire be stretched to accommodate an added roster?

Also, I thought it wise to incorporate a clause whereby there were no agent's commissions due anybody, or any organization, for phonograph recordings, or tournées before or after the opera season closed. Further, that I would have the right to refuse the usual spring opera tour by notice to such effect in early February; this was to clear the way for my return to Berlin, as I was dependent upon the Kaiser's orders. And there was the matter of a private dressing-room, with a key, to which I alone would have access. A miserable, airless little box then used for odd articles, and stage properties, was my choice. No one could envy me its possession, yet it would allow me a much desired privacy.

Dippel read those typewritten suggestions, clutched his hair and dashed out of the room. He must have kept wires busy; for back he came, and the agreements were eventually made. I set sail after a fall season in Berlin. Constant travel, study and singing were beginning to take their toll of my strength. Insomnia, an unreliable stomach and the handicap of a delicate throat made my health no robust guarantee. I arrived in New York not overstrong, and saw Mr. Gatti for the first time at the opera house.

He presented himself, behind a jet-black beard; a heavy-set and pleasant mannered gentleman, with a tightly buttoned lip and appraising glance. It took me some years to relish his capacity for infectious humor and easy flow of conversation when the mood invited.

"The Maestro" (so now known to idolatrous millions of the air audiences), was a bundle of concentrated quicksilver. Neatly compressed into his black jacket, he wore a broad-brimmed fedora crammed over deep-set burning eyes. Portentous silence was broken by an occasional and solemn raven's croak. This was the result of long assault upon protesting vocal cords. We were to experience later—and often—the amazing crescendi to screams and expletives that rose to unparalleled dynamics in rehearsals. However, these tempests became less terrifying by reason of their frequency. We recognized the lightning's play, sure to be followed by disarming—if unstable—serenity.

I felt sure the newcomers were no more comfortable in making their first survey than the older personnel confronting them for inspection. The first error made, despite good intentions toward all, was ever to suppose a third party could enter an effective wedge into the necessary readjustment of the opera organization. Mr. Gatti and Mr. Toscanini had given ample proof of their joint ability to bring La Scala to a high point of perfection. Even judged by the best Italian standards, they needed no co-operation. But perhaps for local counterbalance and acquaintance with certain new departures here, Andreas Dippel had been selected for an executive post that was to prove no enviable distinction. The Italian wing accepted him with an outward show of cordiality. Good friends sustained him, among them, naturally, his colleagues who trusted and liked him. Just what his duties and authority were to be, however, gave us singers much cause for concern, so that eventually five of us signed a round robin on his behalf, as well as our own.

It is amusing to recall that Caruso and Scotti were the most agitated over the control allowed their compatriots. Due to much heated surmise, the following letter was drafted and sent:

New York, Nov. 25th, '08.

To the Chairman of the Board of Directors:

Dear Sir:

We, the undersigned artists of the Metropolitan Opera Company, hearing of a movement to grant Mr. Gatti-Casazza, the General Manager, and Mr. Toscanini, Conductor, a three years' binding contract, do hereby express our desire, in the protection of our artistic interests and the welfare of the Metropolitan Opera House, that Mr. Dippel be granted the same privileges under contract that may be accorded to the above-named gentlemen. Our confidence in the managerial and artistic capabilities of Mr. Dippel gives us sufficient reason to associate ourselves firmly with his ideas, which have been, always will be, and are for the best of the Metropolitan Opera House.

Therefore, we heartily indorse Mr. Dippel in whatever measures he may be obliged to take.

(Signed)

Enrico Caruso
Emma Eames
Geraldine Farrar
Marcella Sembrich
Antonio Scotti

Miss Farrar listening to her first recording

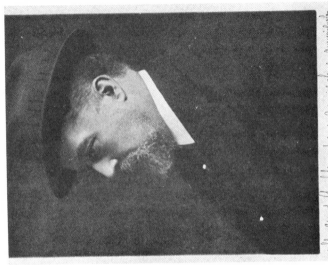

GIULIO GATTI-CASAZZA

ENRICO CARUSO

It brought this later reply:

Ladies and Gentlemen:

We beg to acknowledge receipt of your communication of November 25th, to which we have given due consideration, with particular reference to your expression as to the protection of your own artistic interests. We fully realize to how great an extent the prestige of the Metropolitan Opera House is due to the great artists, like yourselves, who have given it, and are giving it the service and renown of their splendid gifts. The Board and the Management are grateful to you, and sincerely appreciate that you are entitled to every consideration and courtesy. Your interests and theirs are identical, namely, to achieve for the performances at the Metropolitan Opera House the highest possible level of artistic excellence. While we know well that, to accomplish the best results, it is necessary that you be happy in your work and contented and that you have the assured feeling that your great accomplishments are recognized and respected, as they deserve—on the other hand we are entirely convinced that your own experience and intelligent appreciation of the facts must lead you to realize that, however great the individual artists, the greatest artistic success can only be accomplished if there exists a spirit of willing co-operation with, and submission to the Management, and a recognition of the necessity of centralized authority, together with mutual confidence and good will. It is not possible to administer an organization like the Metropolitan Opera under two heads, and it was never intended that it should be so administered. We do full justice to the excellent qualities of the Administrative Manager, Mr. Dippel, and to his intelligent and zealous labors. We desire to show him every fairness and to accord him every consideration and opportunity consistent with our conception of the paramount interests of the organization; but there can be no divided artistic authority, and, while there remains a large and important field for Mr. Dippel's valuable capacities, his functions are and must be subordinate to those of the General Manager, Mr. Gatti-Casazza, who is the supreme executive head of the organization.

It is but natural that under a new management there will arise at the beginning occasional misunderstandings, which call for mutual forbearance, and patience, but you may rest assured that the Board, as well as the Management and the conductors are animated toward you by no other feelings but those of good will and high regard, and we trust and believe that we may always rely upon your wholehearted and harmonious co-operation in our common aim, to make the Metropolitan Opera, in every respect, the very best and greatest amongst operatic art institutions.

Very truly yours,

(*Signed*)

Otto H. Kahn
M. E. Vanderbilt
F. Gray Griswold
Executive Directors

Messrs. Enrico Caruso and Antonio Scotti
Mesdames Eames, Farrar and Sembrich.

The *Sun's* correspondent precipitated the news. It seems Caruso—perhaps with foresight—had not his copy of the first letter with him, so the press asked for mine, and got it. I see no disfavor in either, really. Much publicity was given to the incident. In the excitement, we all talked too freely. The opera house was a hot-bed of partisanships. In any case, Caruso and Scotti offered persuasive and soothing extenuation of their part in the letter, to their irritated countrymen. Under pressure and inquiry, it was a natural thing to do. Scotti, bland and childlike, added that he had signed because I asked him! With fervor, both Neapolitans disclaimed offense. They ended by almost giving it. In the afterglow, Sembrich remained tactful and silent. Eames stood pat—and never bent the knee. Why should she? She was always quite frank in her disapproval of the new regime. I assumed all responsibility for the letter, and whatever results were to be forthcoming.

It speaks volumes for Mr. Gatti's patience and philosophy, and greatly facilitated our later friendly relations, that he took notice of the affair in the manner of the traditional opera intrigue. It was never meant to be so intended. The frankness of the letters should attest it. But Gatti never could quite forget this first sign of rebellion, which I always regretted in view of the general esteem he subsequently and properly merited. Whatever his thoughts, however, at the time he was consistently courteous under circumstances trying for all. Quite naturally, the moment was ripe for further distrust and its repercussions.

It began while the redoubtable Toscanini was at the desk, to conduct *Butterfly*. We clashed immediately. I have never seen Vesuvius in eruption, but probably no more inflammable combustion takes place in its venerable interior than in the person of this musical Napoleon, when the wild mood is upon him. We carried our differences to Mr. Gatti's office. There ensued an exchange of heated words and retaliation—Italia versus New England—which Mr. Gatti vainly tried to stem. My particular personality, it seemed, in no way pleased the illustrious one. I made no move toward propitiation. We were both wrong to plunge into such enmity—perfect strangers as we were—but it was a hot and unrelenting one that season. Press and theatre gossip kept it alive, with malice and glee. And then, one day, Destinn fell ill upon her first *Butterfly* performance. Gatti phoned, with a certain constraint—would I take over the *Butterfly* that evening, at such short notice, with Toscanini conducting? It would be almost impossible to change the opera.

I think he was mightily surprised at my immediate acceptance. It happened to be a popular Saturday night performance. The house was half-full; and while I never gloat, this circumstance was an obvious reminder to both Gatti and Toscanini of what I had said at the moment of our earlier arguments. There were indeed stars in Heaven—and I did not disagree with the Maestro's observation to this effect, but there was also a human constellation that trod the Metropolitan's boards to the renown of that institution and the gratification of the public; not to mention the box-office.

It all seems so childish now—these feverish reactions to the say-so of those whose idle tongues wag constantly about our opera world and people. But the theatre is like that. Emotions, atmosphere highly charged, intrigue and gossip—all take on a particular flavor of the illusive, artificial world wherein the artist lives and has his being. The whirl of creative effort and super-sensitive nerves. At any rate, Toscanini allowed himself the shadow of a smile as he took up that baton. He conducted with every delicate consideration, so that it was a joy. As I had no interpretation to offer different from the earlier one that incurred his withering disapproval, I gathered that his periodic upheavals were without peril to a truly artistic association, nor likely to be of enduring or personal resentment.

However, the season was not easy for anybody. I was harassed and out of humor. So before we set forth on the spring tour, I begged Mr. Kahn to cancel my contract. The discord in the company seemed insurmountable and the monetary consideration less desirable to me under these circumstances. His position was doubtless no sinecure; he counselled patience and refused to free me.

In Chicago, an exciting *Butterfly* performance brought the Maestro before the curtain with the artists. I knew by this and his warm hand-clasp, that our sad differences were at an end. And so they were—for all the inspiring years he was to stand as the incomparable fountain-head of our organization.

Carmen had long been a favorite offering in New York, which had applauded several eminent luminaries in the name part.

It should be a matter of pride for us Americans to realize that a native prima donna, Minnie Hauk, was the first to make a popular success of this opera. Outside Paris, the initial performance of the opera took place in London in June, 1878, with our American Carmen following close upon the French prima donna Galli-Marie, who had created it on her local heath. After successful performances in the English capital where Minnie Hauk garnered merited laurels, the company gave the Bizet work in Dublin, Cork and Glasgow prior to their New York season. This occurred that same fall at the Academy of Music, and in October Minnie Hauk quite definitely established herself not only as a prima donna of parts and temperament, but an original Carmen of merit and popularity, in her own country. Her Carmen became so popular in fact that she declined a later American season—1883-1884—because the manager at the time, Mapleson, refused to allow her to enlarge a repertoire in which he candidly confessed no interest since "*Carmen* fills the house." How often have I heard this statement, too!

Evidently there must have been a later amiable agreement,

for history records her spirited introduction of Massenet's *Manon* at the Academy in 1885. I was just three years old at the time. Oddly enough, she sang only in a few performances of *Carmen* and *L'Africaine* at the Metropolitan in 1890-1891. It seems to have been entirely a German company and one notes the name of Dippel as a leading tenor, with young Walter Damrosch at the conductor's desk. A performance of *Carmen* in April 1891 was her last appearance there. Her career was colorful, of pioneer vigor and initiative, while the industrious scribes presented her in the same sort of headlines of operatic gossip as were prevalent in my own era of prima donna glamour, satisfying the curiosity of the opera public. She acquired a nobleman for a husband, and unlike the latter day procedure, seems to have been happy till his death and her old age, saddened by blindness and poverty, overtook her. In 1924, some of us were agitated by her tragic situation and, with other sympathetic contributors, we were able to make her declining years more comfortable. Her death occurred in February, 1929.

A later New York contestant for *Carmen* laurels was the sprightly Zelie de Lussau, Manhattan born, and a popular standard-bearer of the Bizet opera. She made her debut at the Metropolitan as the gypsy girl in November, 1894—Nellie Melba being the phenomenal voiced Micaela. I believe her performances numbered some 600 of *Carmen* in her successful career, at home and abroad.

It is interesting to know that though great artists are often tormented by ambitions and desires to essay a role particularly appealing to them in fancy, their actual embodiment can be a disappointing and sometimes humiliating experience. Such was

124

the error in judgment of my great Lilli Lehmann. Her debut at the Metropolitan in November, 1886, was made as the Spanish wanton—a performance sung in German with spoken dialogue! The handsome Siegfried of the moment—Max Alvary—was the Don José, and Anton Seidl descended from the magnificent halls of Valhalla to conduct this sparkling score of Iberian derivation. This statuesque Donna Anna, the incomparable Isolde of supreme tragedy, the Norma of classic beauty, was in no wise suited for any of the gypsy's requirements and high animal spirits. But Lilli never ceased to berate the critics for their lack of appreciation and the public's cool response, to efforts that she considered of superlative appeal. Brunnhilde with castanets, Isolde in a Spanish comb? But she seemed obstinately more sensitive to this *Carmen* episode than jubilant over subsequent triumphs in her rightful domain of Wagner and Mozart.

The one unforgettable gypsy was yet to burst upon the scene. If Emma Calvè made a pleasing, if not spectacular, debut as Santuzza in November, 1893, she fired the New York public instantaneously with her Carmen a month later, the first time the opera was given in its Gallic original in New York. It was my own first hearing of this prima donna and this opera on the company's spring tour that included Boston. The impression is still vivid in my mind—what a personality, and a memory erased by no one, worthy of every superlative granted by public and press.

A great artist like Olive Fremstad was not at her best in a *Carmen* of March, 1906, which offered Caruso as Don José for his local debut in this part—and was probably the reason for the opera's presentation. The moderate praise of this

125

Nordic interpretation rose to a triumphant acclaim for her assumption of the Wagner heroines, notably Kundry and Venus.

And now a native Spanish artist was to come forward in the roly-poly Maria Gay, of sparkling eye and flashing smile. For her, Mr. Gatti entertained justifiable hopes for enduring success in this particular role. He surrounded her with the best his house afforded—Caruso, Note, a new French Toreador, myself as Micaela, and Toscanini inspiring us all with his leadership—or shall I say domination? At this period, the great Italian was becoming better acquainted with his singers, who tried to please him; and we, in turn, were less irritated and astonished by the superficial thunder-heads of temper that generally blew themselves off our musical horizon in the breezes of artistic co-operation.

I fear as Micaela, I made a less passive character than was the usual pattern, for in the tussle of the third act, I recall I, too, had a hand in the rough-and-tumble between Carmen and her infuriated Don José.

In view of later lurid reports of my own assault on Caruso, when I assumed the title role (in 1914), the busy scribes would do well to refer to the records of that year for true reports of the tempestuous daughter of Iberia and grant me the justice of a composition far less extravagant in action. She kicked and spat, till even the blasé New York dowagers were moved to raise their fans to shocked faces, to screen some of her more frank and realistic attempts at seduction. A shower of orange juice precipitated with accuracy toward the unfortunate hero surprised not only him, but the audience in general, to general protest. Other studied bits of realism made an

126

SARAH BERNHARDT

MISS FARRAR IN 1912

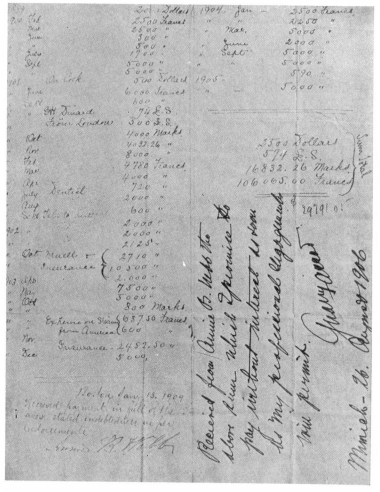

ITEMIZED STATEMENT OF INDEBTEDNESS TO MRS. ANNIE B. WEBB,
PAID IN FULL BY MISS FARRAR IN 1909

unfortunate impression on the aristocratic Metropolitan stage, quite as objectionable, in their frank vulgarity, apparently, to the powers-that-be, as was the *Salome* episode of previous heated discussion and ban.

Maria Gay, however, is nonetheless a singer of experience and interest, and if New York now welcomes her as an impresario-teacher in these later years, she has enjoyed an excellent professional reputation in other lands less critical of elementary physical display.

A most beautiful *Figaro* remains a precious memory. Two superlative women, Sembrich and Eames, with Scotti as the most elegant of noblemen, myself as Cherubino, were inspired under the magical Mahler. This time, there were no Russian cloudbursts, as in a previous *Don Giovanni,* to disturb the serenity of a well-nigh perfect tribute to Mozart.

That Manon who had captured Berlin appeared here a month later. Caruso and Scotti completed the seduction of an enraptured New York public.

To add to my well-being, before sailing I had the joyful feeling of release from a tremendous responsibility. I was able to liquidate my entire obligation—nearly $30,000—to the generous Mrs. A. B. Webb.

My methodical mother who had handled these loans with care and scrupulous regard for their future repayment, was minded to take no chances of losing the precious original, as receipted by Mrs. Webb. She had known of other loans effected so carelessly that, come pay-day, neither party to the transaction was agreed as to sum and manner of obligation.

Again my homecoming to Berlin, as always, was signalized by warm welcome and plenty of work.

Middle-summer, and need for change, found us ready to adventure. Motoring has always been a passion with me, so we planned a trip. No more heavenly route can be imagined than that leading from Munich through the Tyrol (then old Austria), to Italy and the South. It was just outside Milan that our huge Mercedes turned turtle. Luckily, the damage of the spill was centered on the car. It cracked up. And while repairs were in progress, we found ourselves at the Villa Serbelloni, in Como, enchanted to pursue our work in fairy-like surroundings. It is owing to our insistence there that the first bathtub was installed for our family use. I hope the present guests are properly grateful for such American initiative!

Who couldn't sing with nightingales to respond and magnolias so fragrant as to keep one flower-intoxicated a good bit of the time? It was here I worked on *Tosca* and *Werther*. Our good friend Scotti was of the party at the moment. To his Italian taste, I was not material for this melodramatic heroine. His ear was accustomed—in Italy—to the dynamic vocal surge of a ponderous female, whose bulk prevented too sudden an onslaught on his fastidious person! But I saw the fine Latin hand in these silky objections, and coaxed him to help me all the same. He did so—graciously enough.

When it came time to sing it, I was almost paralyzed. The feature comment from a leading critic was evoked by a Paradise plume I wore on my bonnet in the first act. I had to compete with several lovely predecessors—the memory of Ternina, and the actuality of Emma Eames, Olive Fremstad and Lina Cavalieri. Somehow we all managed to sing the role off and on—and no bloodshed, either! There was never, however, but one Scarpia—and he was the peerless one, Scotti.

128

Emma Calvè

Two Great Carmens

Minnie Hauk

MISS FARRAR IN HER METROPOLITAN OPERA *Carmen*

As for the placid Charlotte to the romantic Werther of Edmond Clément—an artist of the most exquisite taste and dramatic elegance—the opera served us both fairly well; but a gorgeous new theatre on the West Side—more like a Babylonian seraglio—completely foiled every attempt at operatic success. One could neither hear, nor see. It was not the house for opera comique—not even for Ziegfield's Follies. And when a pretty girl can't entice the tired business man, it is a poor show place, indeed.

Werther was, aside from the debut of Clément, also memorable for the first appearance on any stage of a radiant personality and most lovely voice. Alma Gluck's entree into our musical circles was thus made, and with enduring success.

The spring of 1910, before returning to my Berlin duties, I had been invited, with Scotti, to give some guest performances of *Tosca* at the Opera Comique. We would be allowed to sing in Italian, the while others employed the French text. The Metropolitan, meanwhile, was taking the entire company there under Toscanini. The Maestro was eager to give Puccini's *Manon Lescaut*—a truly beautiful opera, too—and wished me to accept the role. I had to decline. First, I had never sung it in public, though I could have managed it in a pinch, I suppose. Secondly, and more important, it would take the cream off the *Tosca*, already contracted, and I did not think it fair to ask Carré, the manager of the Comique, to consider giving me such a favor as might embarrass him with his superiors! For in Europe, boudoir whispering frequently involves officials and foreign countries, even, over the precise "pas seul" of a fascinating ballerina or a pretty stage favorite's whim. Paris was alive with noble incogniti backstage, who were the real Czars of the opera world.

Under the circumstances, and need for a requisite star, it was not surprising that a young Spanish singer thus proved her right to join, later, the Metropolitan's family, after a thoroughly brilliant debut here. She has been a shining light in New York for many years. You have doubtless guessed her name? It is Lucrezia Bori.

It is fitting to peer a little into the future here, as regards this delightful artist and friendly comrade. The goodwill and affection of the public was given to her as an artist, and when she ceased to adorn the stage, as a woman.

Her debut had been effected in the Puccini *Manon Lescaut*, the same that had earned her the plaudits of a discerning French press. Much gossip ensued—about the two Manons, the two Mimis, and a later Iris, that could well be considered a rival sister to Cio-Cio-San. If the busybodies had any intention of fomenting a feeling of ill-will, they reckoned without the decent qualities of sportsmanship. The Spanish lady and the New Englander were not so stupid as to afford the reporters a Roman holiday, nor so lacking in appreciation of each other's professional qualities. No reports of disputes or hair-pulling, therefore, splashed into print. I have contended that *Iris* suffered less general acclaim because of its libretto, a Japanese tragedy of realism set to beautiful music; it lacked, for our American audiences, the obvious appeal of Puccini's forsaken child-bride, the canny Belasco touch, and the heartbreaking introduction of the baby, Trouble, that stimulated the tear-glands of audiences all over the country.

Lucrezia pursued the even and successful tenor of her way for several years, until the strain and fatigue of professional activity caused her temporary retirement from the local scene. Happily she overcame her troubles to make a triumphant return in *Bohème* some five years later, and graced the scene of her earlier successes, till self-elected resignation from the opera, at a recent date.

With Mr. Gatti's retirement, and the appointment of new members to the Metropolitan's Board of Directors, she was proposed and accepted as one of that governing body. My opinion is that she honors the group who try to carry on the glory of the house and its noble traditions—not an easy task.

But let us return to that gay spring in the French capitol. So many musical stars singing for this and that, as is their wont in a busy season. Paris can be exhausting in her kindness. It was time for quiet, study, and a return to Germany on my part.

Tears come to my eyes every time I think of that most poetic of fairy tales, the *Koenigskinder!* How I wish it could be revived with a young, lovely talent, and made vivid once more! It would take patience to train the live geese, but results would amply repay such effort. Oh, why wouldn't Mr. Gatti let me sing this sweetest of roles, and Elizabeth, before the great, golden curtains closed on me forever! I shall never know. But all his objections seemed stupid and inconsistent, at the time.

I can dismiss the vocal mathematics of *Ariane* with short praise. At best, it was a test in memory and rhythm. Toscanini may have obtained his pleasure in the intricate score. I had nothing but fatigue and misery. And he was a demon at painstaking rehearsals!

More in the fanciful Mozart style and wholly agreeable to my feeling was *Donne Curiose* and the same composer's facile and melodious *Segreto di Susanna*. In both works, I felt at home.

Now, and for the last time I had waived aside Scotti's matrimonial intentions, but since this latter opera employed us both in delicate sentimental allusions, the occasions were not without a strain of absurdity. He chose to glower. In a Neapolitan, it is not at all frightening—simply the fierce frown of a child denied. The curtain call manners were amusing—frigidly polite!

Mr. Gatti was disinclined to invite concurrence with Mary Garden's *Louise;* she was eminently successful in the Hammerstein company, nearby. So he hit upon the sequel to it, as embodied in a wild and confusing hodge-podge called *Julien,* my next novelty. Caruso had extremely difficult and taxing measures to sing. No merit for the singer.

Charpentier had been kind enough to come and speak with me about the whole work the previous spring while I was in Paris, but I dreaded these descents from Mt. Parnassus, as the hours were late, long, and completely futile. Also vain were the attempts to have him lend his personality to the premiere, in New York. He feared the ocean. Albert Wolff, our genial conductor, related that, really desirous to come to the Metropolitan, Charpentier had taken, by way of introduction to the waves, a fifteen minute boatride on the Seine. He became so violently ill that, pea-green, he set foot on terra firma never to leave it again. He cabled his regrets.

In this precursor to the "movies," one might say, I had five roles, sang about two phrases in each, and undressed more and more until the degradation of the last act. This final apparition of a lost soul, in a drunken unsteadiness, gave birth to most surprising recommendations for a later *Carmen* assumption! I never understood why. Some critics must have peculiar fancies as to operatic conceptions!

132

CHAPTER FIVE

I

THE DAUGHTER

1914-1916

WHO could have dreamed of the terrible castastrophe that was about to involve the major civilized countries during this summer?

The usual spring concert tour went off here, as pleasurably and successfully as usual, and I set sail for Paris, and a gay interim, before returning to my duties in Berlin. Caruso had expatiated upon the excellent results obtained from the waters at Salsomaggiore, the iodine properties particularly favorable to singers' throats. So—once my vacation earned, and armed with a recommendation to his own physician, I motored there for rest and treatment, but was properly confused, once arrived, to have him pronounce me suffering from a mean attack of the measles! A young friend, an ardent Gerry-flapper it seems, had passed me the germ with her other more welcome attentions a few weeks before!

133

After a brief quarantine, I was allowed to proceed with the cure; not disagreeable, but boring in the prolonged seances of the vapor room where the thick mist prevented any activity or distraction. Part of the treatment was the complete rest of the vocal cords—so even whispers to neighboring patients were discouraged. But I was to be discomfited by more than the temporary irritation of measles—for my ever sensitive digestive organ completely failed me and I retraced my route, over the Alps by motor, to my good doctor's sanitarium in Munich, where I had vainly tried, each summer, to repair the ravages that emotional reactions and hard work over a period of years had entailed. I lay very ill indeed, with no perceptible improvement of a stomach that refused to act in a normal way.

And that August saw the flames of war ignite. I was counselled by my American friends to depart for America at all costs, and at once. That was not possible for the moment. I was unable to get out of bed, nor did I share the panic that now seized upon the summer visitors. I was at home in Germany, and unless the United States became involved—which seemed highly improbable—I was not worried about vacating the premises in haste. I was concerned only with recovering strength for my musical duties later. My French maid and Belgian chauffeur were courteously placed aboard the train that conveyed all foreigners belonging to the fighting countries to their respective frontiers at a given date. They were to sail from France and join me in New York.

I occupied myself with the mental preparation of *Sans Gêne* and *Carmen*, while waiting for my needed strength to return. When the day of my departure eventually came, I made ready to sail from Rotterdam—the Dutch boats being neutral and still in service. With the impedimenta of much luggage, chiefly costumes and theatre belongings, my companion and I left our good Munich physician, and our friends there. Troop trains were speeding to the battle areas, so our progress was slow but not uncomfortable. At the German-Dutch frontier I bade farewell to a young officer whom I had known in Berlin, whose tact and kindly courtesy effected the disposition of my all-too-prominent baggage easily. I little realized that this same route would later serve the flight of the unhappy Kaiser who had been so kind to me, and the further immolation of my friend, the Crown Prince, at Wieringen.

Once at Amsterdam, crowds and excitement announced the fall of Antwerp. The refugees were swarming into Holland. A dreadful confusion. Plucky little country—I wonder, with the rest of the world in flames, how she managed to keep disentangled through the years of horror!

At Amsterdam began the arrival of telegrams from Gatti, from Milan. Arrangements had been made for most of our Metropolitan troupe to sail from Naples, and I was urged to join him there. At this point, the Dutch boats were held up in the channel, the English authorities claiming contraband practice. At any rate, sailing from Holland's shores was now out of the question; but to return again by train through Munich, Switzerland, via the Alps to Southern Italy, seemed wholly impossible to my wearied body. However, repeated wires had their effect. I picked up a Dutch courier to handle my luggage and the visa necessities, and off we started. The same charming officer, somewhat surprised, nonetheless made our re-entrance into Germany as pleasant as he could. Soon

135

we were on the slow-moving freight toward Switzerland. Curiously enough, the Swiss conductors were the most meticulous in passport inspection. It took many gold francs to convince them that I was, as indicated, an harassed opera singer, and not royalty, incognito, bent on strange errands.

Once in Naples, where a few days respite allowed drives in the sun and beauty of this fascinating city, the company reunited and Mr. Gatti's large family of song birds was ready to sail. As testimony of his welcome, he presented me with a large, (but obviously moribund) bouquet of carnations; I was touched, as he was notoriously averse to pulling his hand out of pocket.

That voyage was amusing, and sometimes quite exciting. The English officers were calm, the service agreeable. Mr. Gatti was bellicose about submarines (and there were plenty in the Mediterranean waters) during the daytime, but at dusk, when the tiniest illumination was all that was permitted in dark corridors, he would plaintively remark to me that if we did meet one of these sea monsters, he relied upon my Berlin connections for a pleasant recommendation to considerate treatment! Facetiously uttered, perhaps, but I detected agitation. The fact, as well, that he had tripped more than once in these murky passageways did not contribute to his good humor or optimism after sundown.

A beautiful moon rode high on waters that happily remained tranquil. Let us subscribe to her witchery, the happy dementia that invited general tête-à-têtes, and the maximum of pleasant society on the upper decks. The moment was also propitious for work; a routine that I welcomed, for I did not like the ennui of the boat, nor its idleness. We set to it with

136

vigor, for Mr. Gatti decided that *Carmen* would be our revival novelty.

I was now eager to play this fascinating role that I had, for some years previous, refused to consider. A tiny piano served Toscanini for his orchestral effects; the important male cast was present in Caruso and Amato, and the other members would join us in New York, having sailed earlier from Paris. Time passed quickly and agreeably. We landed in Boston, after eleven uneventful days, and plunged into routine. That November performance was a most gratifying success— happily quite different from the previous one wherein I had figured as Micaela.

I had always wanted to go to Spain for local color and a study of the gypsy type there, before I presented my idea of Carmen. Then, too, Emilio de Gogorza had spoken enthusiastically of certain native dancers to study, and places where the atmosphere would lend an authentic note, particularly in the second act. I was eager to have our revival on other than the prescribed traditional lines, even as to costumes and décors.

Well I never did have time nor strength to get to Spain but my imagination was lively and I had a certain definite and natural feeling for this role, so grateful in its dramatic impulse, so physically animated in song and movement. Familiar with the music since childhood, I knew the medium scale of the vocal effort was one for no dazzling display; but rhythm, clear diction and character tone-color must not be lacking, no matter what caliber the timbre of the instrument. Oddly enough, the sopranos have proved themselves triumphant over the more opulent-voiced contraltos for this successful delineation. Perhaps because with the vocal intensity, there was too much girth and heaviness of foot to be entirely convincing for the wild-cat portrayal of this restless feline.

Banal though this explanation may read, I always felt that when Carmen dashes onto the stage, her appearance alone must be so exciting and magnetic that every man will edge forward on his chair and scheme how to venture past the stage-door Minotaur with his orchids! She is so frankly physical, so insouciante, careless and cruel in the natural pursuit of her quarry and subsequent gratification of her senses to satiety, it should give no one a headache to compose a mental composition of so elemental a creature. But I have heard some eminent prima donnas remark the need of cerebral application to the study of this ardent gypsy, hence I offer the observation.

Rehearsals at the opera house were pleasant and painstaking —and Toscanini continued in angelic humor to lift us all above ourselves. In later years I was to tour the country with my own company, under the management of C. A. Ellis, and reduce it as well, on a second tour, to miniature proportions that invited large audiences and big returns.

Margaret Matzenauer was a Carmen who "took over" several times when I was indisposed; one performance, I understand, being particularly notable for the unexpected behavior of the last-act equines introduced, and necessitating much leaping about the stage on the part of the distracted lovers. Accidents will happen. I heard as a young girl, of the contretemps of Calvé, whose generous waist unexpectedly strained at a button and resulted in the fall of ruffled lingerie, unmistakably bifurcated objects. It seems that, not at all abashed, she

138

had the nonchalance to claim them then and there. And why not?

I regret American audiences had too little occasion to admire a truly beautiful little Carmen, in Conchita Supervia. There were excellent performances offered also by Alice Gentle and Marguerite Sylva in other companies than the Metropolitan.

The next protagonist at our Temple of Music was to be the Viennese "thunderbolt," as the press referred to Maria Jeritza. Highly successful in the Wagnerian repertoire, as well as certain more dramatic Italian roles, she began to prove a gratifying box-office attraction in a sensational *Tosca*, that first burst upon an amazed public during the latter seasons of my membership in the company. Little note was taken of her handsome presence and brilliant soprano rendition of the role; the "clou" of the performance lay in a pose of unashamed abandon on the floor during the famous *Vissi d'arte*. From my seat, however, I obtained no view of any expressive pantomime on her pretty face, while I was surprised by the questionable flaunting of a well-cushioned and obvious posterior.

For the first time in his career, the wary Scotti was non-plussed by this act that completely spoiled his previous conception of attack upon the defenseless heroine. With the lady writhing on the floor, there was nothing for him to do but stand, guardedly, against the back wall, until she resumed an upright position.

Duly recorded in flaming headlines, this innovation drew the crowd. Mr. Gatti had cause to smile, and perhaps concluded such bold display would guarantee certain returns in *Carmen*. It is, however, difficult to duplicate so startling an

139

innovation as carried this *Tosca* to acclaim; and a later *Carmen* and *Thais* failed to sustain the cherished hope. Every singer has roles that suit her less than others, and the statuesque Jeritza was no exception to the rule.

I am sure it will make no difference to Mary Garden when I say I did not care for her Carmen, but she had her own ways and a devoted public, and it was probably a pleasant change for her from the pale Melisande and the touching little Jongleur, not to mention her incomparable Thais that was the talk of the town.

And since from the pinnacle of memory we are able to survey the future horizon, it does not come amiss to remark that Rosa Ponselle has been one of our best recent Carmens. That phenomenal voice had within its velvet splendor all the necessary fire and color; she studied her part well, and if she made that easily rectified mistake of all novices, in perhaps too many enthusiastic innovations, the promise was apparent. In person and temperament a credible Latin figure of frank vivacity, if not very subtle allure. Save for an unbecoming last act costume, the three acts were effective in dress and action. With my card of good wishes and roses for the occasion, however, I begged her to "tune up" with Norma, Gioconda, or Donna Anna whose splendid vocal line demands a routine, which the all-too-easy vocalism of Carmen tends to displace unless religiously offset by extended scale work.

Unfortunately, for her admirers at large, she confines her public appearances to the less spectacular effects of the concert programs.

The New Year of 1915 brought forth Sans Gêne—a role I greatly enjoyed for its acting comedy. Amato was superb as the Corsican and Martinelli scored as Lefebre.

The season was a busy one despite the dreadful war activities abroad. Although the United States was officially neutral, the sentiments of the public were generally admitted to be in favor of the Allies. Because of my loyalty to Germany, and those German friends of long standing, highly spiced stories began to bear fantastic fruit and a certain number of suspicious reproaches were directed toward me. Wherever the National Anthem was heard, at the first blare of a cornet, or squeak of a fiddle, everyone stood at rigid attention. I recall an incident at a theatre one evening, where in a potpourri of *Butterfly* where several phrases sound a few notes of the hymn, I was cut dead by some associates because I did not jump to my feet, among other stragglers. Between the urge from hoarse-voiced orators to buy Liberty Bonds and the constant din of the Star Spangled Banner that pervaded every place of entertainment, one really had to forego much enjoyment, so hysterically did the super-patriot bedevil us all in places of public patronage. Bored society women took up the sweet cause of (their pet) charity; the singers were hounded to appear for this and that; the public exhorted to disgorge in auditoriums, churches, stores, or street corners. An exhausting business.

Tales of atrocities and espionage were so eagerly put before public and private gatherings that the narrators began to believe themselves eye-witnesses, lost in impressive oratory and booming denunciations. On one occasion, I listened to an excited harangue about Dr. Karl Muck's encounter with authorities, for traitorous observations and actions unbecoming a gentleman, at a certain concert of the Boston Symphony Orchestra. The oh's and ah's had hardly subsided when I rose to my feet—and said that I regretted the necessity of branding the story false and malicious, but truth compelled me to do so. No such outbreak had occurred at this, or any other concert, for I had been the soloist on these several occasions, and the audience, as well as the conductor, had behaved themselves in exemplary fashion with dignified absorption in the musical program. There was no riot.

Dr. Muck was a colleague from my early Berlin days. He was never too genial a character and made few friends by reason of a taciturn nature and sarcastic tongue; but he was at all times a fine musician, a splendid figure of restraint upon the podium, and one of the great names that adorned our page of musical history. I need hardly add that many musicians envied him his high position. The emotions of the time—and matters of a private nature, foolishly made public—provided the weapons for an all too successful effort to discredit him. Later, with others, he was interned at Fort Oglethorpe during the period of our participation in the World War.

One man who had enjoyed long and well-deserved popularity, both as artist and lovable personality, was Fritz Kreisler; but he, too, came under the ban. Friends turned aside when he passed on the street; and because he and his wife were honored guests at a Christmas party in my home, their presence brought me a sheaf of scurrilous—and, of course, anonymous—letters about the occasion. I was taken to task as well, by a recently naturalized citizen, for my loyalty to old friends. I pointed out that this country was not, at the moment, at war with any other. I had too many forbears listed in the accounts of our various wars to preserve this democracy to warrant self-invited criticism offered in the first flush of recently acquired patriotism. And my birthplace, almost at the foot of Bunker Hill, should sufficiently guarantee my own American integrity—as well as my sense of fair play.

A really amusing incident was caused by the withdrawal from several public libraries of my modest little book, in the nature of an autobiographical narrative, first published in the cautious columns of *The Ladies Home Journal!* It had no particular virtue save pleasant reading for those who keep abreast of stellar attractions in our music world; but I felt like some outstanding Nobel Prize winner, at odds with the reigning powers, when it invited elimination from the public shelves. Zealous defenders of the flag were often actuated by motives that smacked of a strongly personal sentiment. I suppose upheavals always entail questionable ardor, often misplaced and hasty in judgment.

There were, unfortunately, German members of our troupe who were lacking in discretion and good taste; these nullified the effects of those who conducted themselves properly. It was not always easy to maintain harmony, and avoid heated discussions; and with many unpleasant encounters, of a private nature, there arose a situation not foreseen with the closing of our opera and concert season.

Automatically, European centers were no longer negotiable territory for the artists of former international activities. I harkened to the voice of the movies, silent in those days of 1915. The year before, in Berlin, I had been asked to consider an appearance in the films. As an example, I had witnessed a few hundred feet devoted to the ample figure of Destinn, in a lion's cage (presumably a double exposure), which had caused an uproar in the august circles that sustained our musical prestige. This circus stunt was awful. Of course, I refused to consider such a peculiar avenue of activity. But in New York, Belasco's son-in-law, Morris Gest, had no such painful idea of flamboyant ballyhoo when he approached me. With Jesse Lasky, a theatre man of taste who had attended the opera to hear me, he was intent upon legitimate work on the screen, if I could be interested.

I was enthusiastic. The opportunity for acting, the charm of summer in California, the vocal repose—all seemed to point to a happy adventure of interest and novelty. I never regretted the experience. That first season we picturized *Maria Rosa, Carmen,* and a special story, the type that has since served anybody who can lay claim to a vocal chirp—how the little home-town girl makes good in grand opera, upon merit and virtue; it was called *Temptation.* In those days that title was thought to have considerable sex-appeal. Wallace Reid, that charming screen-hero—too early dead—was the young lover who rescued me from the plots of the arch-villain, Theodore Roberts, very obvious in crêpe whiskers. I made pleasant friends in the studio and enjoyed every bit of the time. Of that early group, only Cecil B. DeMille remains triumphant in the later field of mechanical marvels, and the sound track of today. Of the movie career, we shall speak in a separate chapter.

Meanwhile, on a near-by stage, in our small Lasky studio, there was a certain fascinating young actor also at work. A tragic interest was to be catapulted into my life in the casual meeting there, with Lou Tellegen.

II

THE MOTHER

1915-1917-1921

GERALDINE was not going to be happy nor have much peace of mind, that I could see. Her stubborn loyalty to her German friends and the royal family, together with her sense of gratitude to that public that had welcomed and loved her as a young unknown, was much criticized and misunderstood. Wilfully, I should say. Patriotism serves so many interests; not all of them objective. The *Lusitania* tragedy gave the signal. A sad instance of Teutonic blundering. The United States joined wholeheartedly on the side of the Allies that April of 1917. For Geraldine, that meant a deep personal loss—in separation from her revered Lehmann and other friends, as well as from the Royal Opera, where the men, of course, were leaving the Muse to follow Mars.

She enjoyed her screen activities—and prepared to continue them during the summer season, while opera and concert tours kept her busy in the spring and fall.

Her health gave me cause for alarm, in pursuit of these three careers that gave her no respite. She was too thin, a victim of insomnia, and developed an apprehension, ever-present, of losing her voice. She worked too hard and played too little for a young woman; but this career and the slippery pinnacle on which it rested were such as to challenge every bit of her nervous energy, at all times devoted to clinging to its precarious elevation.

I rather liked this attractive Tellegen. He had come into our circle of friends, and was very sympathetic and charming in manner. His acting ability was limited, spectacular rather than of stable routine, while an unusual stature and exotic manners contributed to early success on Broadway. Son of a Greek father and Dutch mother, with a record of Parisian training in the company of Sarah Bernhardt, his background gave him a romantic aura to which feminine hearts were very sympathetic.

My husband had become quite desperately ill on our return to New York, and while Geraldine was on tour. As I spent most of the day and night at the hospital to be with him, Tellegen came daily to inquire and keep me company. I was appreciative of the attention. His play was going nicely and he had confided his matrimonial hopes, regarding my daughter. She was then absent and had not made any definite mention to me, up to that time, but I had had a notion how the wind was blowing. I viewed the situation with no great degree of enthusiasm. Time, however, was to tell if such a bond would endure and satisfy both temperamental children of the theatre.

Geraldine had had her romances and passionate attachments, to be expected in one of her vital and emotional disposition. I had, however, never thought she would consider matrimony. She was not brought up to be good material for tandem going, I admit. Constant travel and work—the delicate problem of keeping her vocal resources in order—the daily drudgery of scales she never neglected—all was a routine of concentrated effort that left her depleted at the close of the day, and not always in the humor for carefree family con-

146

ferences or outings. I understood and accepted all this naturally, as the price of our joint endeavors. It was the necessary part of her accommodation to this arduous chosen career, which she served with fidelity and her best effort. Her devotion and affection were always reliable; but more was needed to manipulate the elastic ribbon of a marital tie. I was at the same time apprehensive over two careers under the same roof. One so over-balanced the other, in fame and security—would the gentleman, still somewhat of an unknown quantity, be understanding, and care enough for her to accept graciously her greater renown?

They were married quietly at our home when my husband returned, still too ill to allow the excitement of a big wedding. Geraldine herself was most happy to have a ceremony of such intimacy, with only two of our closest friends present. She wanted desperately to feel the security of family association; to plan for a future, that would not always contain such crucial professional responsibility. Now she confided to me many hopes upon this theme, of which I had never dreamed. She thought marriage based on sympathetic attraction, respect and good comradeship would have better chance to survive, especially in the theatre world, than if it were engendered by an infatuation too intense to endure. Geraldine in a domestic role, I confess, was one so strange to me that I could only hope her ultimate happiness might be the answer to this venture in double harness. At any rate, work for both of them was a safeguard for the moment.

Thais was proposed as her next novelty. Though not keen on it, she accepted for want of a better choice.

Another summer in Hollywood was as pleasant as usual—

147

followed by the concert peregrinations before the opera opened.

Lodoletta was a charming little tid-bit that enlisted her services, with Caruso and Amato. Owing to an attack of bronchitis, at its premiere, she was in wretched health and begged a week's respite before a second performance; but Gatti had his reasons, probably good ones, and would not hold the second performance for her, despite her entreaty. Easton and Martinelli gave it as scheduled. Geraldine flatly refused to pick it up—and held to her word. I couldn't blame her; but the occasion resulted in gossip, as usual. Fortunately, no discord could mar the good camaraderie that for years existed between her and Easton—dating from Berlin days.

Now food conditions, coal shortage and many annoying incidents in every-day life were giving us all some concern. Geraldine shivered in icy wings—as did everyone else—at her performances. She ran a temperature, coughed continually, and was in despair at being so frequently unreliable. At last, our good friend and throat specialist, Dr. Curtis, after painful examination, advised an operation that involved both the throat and vocal cords. It was a delicate affair—through which more than one artist had agonized. He couldn't promise definite results—that was in God's hands—but he warned her she would be voiceless within two years if some drastic and immediate measures were not forthcoming. The verdict was, prolonged rest or the knife. She came home, stunned. Her will-power had carried her so far, she could not realize this grave ultimatum. In broken whispers, she talked over the dire possibilities of unsuccessful results—a nightmare of fears!

Then we called in Mr. Gatti—and explained the perilous situation.

148

Geraldine proposed a year's rest from singing, which would allow complete silence and recovery. She had been approached by Mr. Goldwyn for a longer contract and this sabbatical response might be the answer, in silent and agreeable interests. She also suggested, since the German repertoire and singers were absent, and the question of their replacement somewhat problematical, the accenting of the French repertoire for this time and the engaging of Mary Garden and Muratore in their several splendid roles.

Gratuitous advice.

Mr. Gatti was not minded to increase expenses when Caruso and she could hold down both French and Italian offerings. The conclusion of our conference was her acceptance of the knife at the close of the spring season, hoping that, with good fortune, she would be able to report for her opera duties in the fall.

I pleaded with her to let me accompany her when the time came, but she was adamant, and refused. She said she must get her strength alone. To see me suffer would be worse for her than absence, so she persuaded me to remain home. The last performance concluded, she drove alone to her ordeal. Our small family waited—in my apartment by her request—frantic with sympathy and impatience. Soon she was back, hysterical. She could not master her nerves and the anaesthesia had so excited her Dr. Curtis would not operate until she was more calm. She begged me to leave her alone, after a sad family dinner. That night she must have come to some understanding with herself, for the next morning she telephoned, in cheerful mood, and set off determinedly. She refused anaesthesia, and went through the affair with courage and control, so Dr. Curtis telephoned once it was over. And from that time, she obeyed faithfully his instructions for absolute silence for months. Communications were effected by writing, pad and pencil always at hand. She resolutely cultivated a cheerful spirit—read a great deal—studied her scores mentally—and did not deprive herself of many pleasant social gatherings with friends—with the pad and pencil always at hand.

Meanwhile, the movies were a godsend. Her mind was kept busy, her body active, that summer of imposed silence. A fall concert was to precede the opera season and, aside from several intimates, we had tried to keep news of Geraldine's vocal condition out of public and press domain. This was fairly easy in Hollywood, since the super-subject of all subjects there was exclusively the movies.

An early fall came and it was time to make the first timid attempts to sing. The entire family was on tenter-hooks. Smooth, easy tones happily were immediately forthcoming. The new tissues were healed, but delicate—and would not bear the weight of heavy singing or prolonged work at first. Hence, a program of charming but not obvious dramatic import. The tour was a pleasant and successful preparation for the opera season, and restored Geraldine's confidence in herself. It had been badly jolted.

The Armistice—thank God—was signed and everybody breathed easier.

Suor Angelica and *Fiammette*, the latter chiefly notable for indifferent music and her superb costumes, put no further strain upon a throat now fairly strong.

It was not until the flamboyant *Zaza* came along that Geraldine had occasion for a flare-up of her old time temperamental

LUCREZIA BORI

MISS FARRAR IN *Zaza*

GIOVANNI MARTINELLI

display. Belasco, long a friend and admirer, was co-operative in counsel for this role. He came to the house where her colleagues were good enough to work in unison, to put real drama into this opera the music of which is not particularly remarkable without such underlying intention. It was a sensational success (alas! if far away from Mozart and the classic hopes of Lehmann!); and Belasco's accolade was something precious and worth having. That year she was tempted by him to consider a real theatre role in a piece he had written; but after mature reflection, she had the good sense to realize that the singing phrase was her particular medium of expression.

This *Zaza* went over with great acclaim, and triumphant box-office appeal. She thought it great fun to play, and not too strenuous vocally. The tender emotions of the third act, with the child, amply compensated for the calculated vulgarity of the first act—where the music-hall singer indulged in actions that shocked many a staid Metropolitan listener; yet it was surprising how frequent were the demands for front rows, by those claiming defective vision and poor ears, the better to view the bewildering undress changes that enlivened that first act. Geraldine was undeniably magnetic and effective as she raced through the scenes of daring deshabille and seduction; but I always felt squeamish—while her father would not behold his daughter in any such display. He smoked his cigar outside until this excitement was over. It was never an operatic procedure to him and he hated to hear her criticized! To him she was always his daughter rather than the artist.

And speaking of incidents likely to embarrass an artist on

151

the stage, it was in a highly emotional scene between the vivacious Geraldine and Martinelli that the latter, failing to embrace her at the usual prescribed moment, sat down heavily on the sofa at hand. Geraldine, surprised and fearing a sudden indisposition, leaned over to inquire. In an agonized whisper, however, the genial artist confided the sudden defection of a suspender strap and the consequent possibility of a mishap if he dared to rise. Accordingly, she draped herself over him in the most beguiling fashion, herself taking the initiative properly the tenor's.

Quite a sharp reprimand was administered by the press the following day, remarking Miss Farrar's disposition to submerge her partner in original if dubious innovations in acting—followed by cautious questioning from Mr. Gatti, always very sensitive to the fountain-pen reaction.

Though the story never got out in public domain, the situation of the opera moment was saved, which was the more important for both the artists, while Mr. Gatti had a hearty laugh at the thought of the momentary predicament.

Geraldine rounded out a season more or less routined and the summertime again saw her busy with the screen activities.

The news of Caruso's death affected her greatly. His tragic illness and the manner of its inception was the topic of affectionate concern all over the civilized world. He had been a good comrade and friend since those early Monte Carlo days. It was he who had devised her professional motto:

Farrar farà

with the robin perched atop its buckled wreath that enclosed her initials. Generous of heart and happy in the outpouring

152

of a wonderful voice, God must have specially favored him to take him hence in the splendid prime of his powers. He never grew old or weary—nor faced a retirement desolate to songbirds who have no inner resource of the spirit.

I can see him still, on so many pleasant occasions in and outside the theatre. His kindness was proverbial to his comrades, whether of solo or chorus importance, the "boys" backstage, as well as the house personnel. Marie Savage, the stately duenna of the Metropolitan choristers of present-day activities, herself an ornament to the operatic stage over a period of fifty consecutive years, sang with him in various opera houses. She notes his modesty, and unfailing kindness, his capacity for work, and his own close analysis of the world's most phenomenal tenor voice which was housed in a larynx of fabulous worth.

He called me, affectionately, "Mammina," and, indeed, I had a real fondness for the great boy he sometimes showed himself. In his spectacular career, he was naturally an easy mark for women of all kinds and classes, very susceptible to their flattery. His native shrewdness often saved him from complete disaster, as he was often the target for persons who had hopes of material gain.

There was that disturbing little incident at the Central Park Zoo where an hysterical female accused him of attack in the shape of a sharp pinch near a region then not usually mentioned in general conversation and most modestly hidden under multitudinous pleats in the style of those days. This, while a crowd gathered in front of the cage that housed the chattering and curious monkeys.

The repercussion cost Mr. Conried great anxiety, before

153

the season's *Bohème* brought forth Caruso after Geraldine's opening night. But the audience took the lurid reports with their customary grain of salty dilution and remained faithful in their attendance and frenzied acclaim of the popular idol, on that eventful evening. Which shows their good sense; but we all breathed more easily, I confess, once the tension was so fortunately dissolved. Nothing came of the accusation, but it was impressed upon me that persons much in the public eye have to fight, apparently in more than one arena, to vindicate their personal integrity and maintain their professional honor.

He was a considerate father to two boys born of an earlier association in the artistic world. All his friends were happy when he made a later marriage with a charming American girl, Miss Dorothy Benjamin. The birth of their daughter Gloria was an occasion for his extravagant rejoicing.

Yes, God was kind to see fit that his services on this earth terminated so gloriously. The hysteria at his death has subsided, but all those loyal friends still hold him in abiding memory, as an especially endowed human being, and a great-hearted artist. The loss to the Metropolitan could not be denied. There never was his equal, nor will there be in this generation; but—"the show goes on"—as the seasons change.

Louise was Geraldine's next essay, again a repertoire choice, not her own preference. She had accepted the role with the distinct understanding there would be no shirtwaist-sailor hat-pompadour effect, as at its Parisian inception. An ugly silhouette. She said she wanted to make it a modern picture of grace and vivacity. She carefully chose her wig, a light brown color that favored her. The simple but well-cut little silk frocks lost nothing of charm on a slender and elastic figure.

Miss Farrar in a Liberty Loan Drive pageant

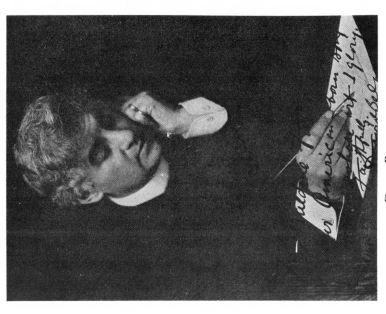

David Belasco

Mr. and Mrs. Sidney Farrar in 1917

Indeed, she did look young and pretty—which was her first intention—despite the easy approach of the forties. Gatti essayed an objection to her costumes, in the roundabout fashion of asking someone else to consult with her. The emissary was kindly received—and one concession made to the get-up by wearing the fur piece of her maid instead of the one shown at the dress rehearsal. It was a luxurious pelt, much more costly than the original, but the masculine eye could not detect the value.

It appeared Gatti had been disturbed by some music critic's unfavorable comment on the dresses. His intention was kind, but my girl never cared about such opinions. Contrary to many singers who disdained press reports, or said they did, she read every word written about her performances, and, being human, was pleased when they were favorable. But if they were not, she did not feel her world had been plunged in darkness. Her real discouragements lay within herself. She was therein honest to her own set standards, in pulling down her own particular star, for she would tolerate no inferior lights along her chosen avenue of endeavor.

The arrival of a handsome blonde prima donna from Vienna was the opera sensation of 1921. Maria Jeritza was quite rightly welcomed with fanfares. The press was moved to foster a campaign, hinting at Geraldine's heart-burnings and chagrin at this artist's gratifying success, culminating in a sensational innovation in *Tosca*.

I suppose it would be asking too much credit for my daughter's sense of fair play and decency, if I were to say that she indulged in no such stupid reaction. This little baiting program had likewise been tried—without avail—in the successive warm welcomes bestowed on Hempel, Bori, and Muzio. She remained steadfastly good comrades with all—and minded her own business. She did, however, feel Mr. Gatti, as previously mentioned, had no valid reason for not allowing her to vary her repertoire with some performances of Elizabeth and the Goosegirl. His reply to this request was that German artists must sing German operas. As Jeritza was busy with Santuzza and Tosca—not to mention a later Thais and Carmen—this still leaves the question open; and how was he also to reconcile the statement with the admirably vocal Rethberg in such Latin parts as Aida, Iris, Leonora, and so on, to remark upon other departures from the German line?

Meanwhile, there were many reasons for my girl's heavy heart and faltering spirit. Health and voice were giving her great concern; and an ill-timed domestic crisis was upon her, as I had feared. She was still too loyal to admit defeat in this particular case; but this time she was dealing in a human, not a vocal problem. She had had no proper experience to handle such a situation; I had not foreseen this, in my love and ambition for her.

My own married existence had been one of harmony, with no complications of temperamental divergence in tastes, ambition or standards of conduct. Perhaps it had thus ill-fitted me for the proper perspective of the situation in which Geraldine now found herself.

It was by no means an unusual situation. Many artists had found the divided combination of duty to their profession and family life none too easy to carry out successfully. Careers demand much in the sacrifice of the individual, and tend to self-centered development, offering their best fruit for the table of public ceremonials.

156

At first, Geraldine was indifferent to the ugly gossip that began to percolate in the printed medium, while the favorite avenue of the evil-minded—anonymous communications—made her daily post a bulky nuisance. The whispers and significant looks exchanged among friends aggravated the situation. Knowing the theatre and the frequency of allegations based on thin air, Geraldine, kept hold of herself commendably for some time. It was her husband's own insulting behavior toward her that cruelly opened her eyes to distressing incidents, too flagrant for denial.

Treason of the body is a sad human failing, but not necessarily sufficient cause for drastic and final renunciation; however, fidelity of the spirit must be present, to insure integrity and respect on both sides, and continued partnership. I grant that a handsome young man of dramatic appeal certainly has no easy problem in the hysteria aroused in the opposite sex. Public adulation must necessarily be fostered and nourished, as part of any professional and successful career. The stage ignites mob worship more spontaneously than other more subtle fields where the personality of the participant is less evident. In the masculine world, the orchestra leader, the tenor of the moment, the writer, and the actor often have difficult times in their encounters with feminine worshippers, and are likely to suffer surprising consequences if these affiliations are carried to great length and imprudent commitments. Their natural ego expands to such inflated importance as to make an otherwise charming and magnetic husband a real problem in behavior at home.

The lady herself, the center spot in the calcium of public acclaim, consecrated to the difficult task of a career demanding every ounce of energy and interest, has no patient Griselda touch for a domicile that of necessity is more a working studio than otherwise, housing two intensely concentrated individuals with little common basis for daily living. There is also the argument and resentment when the material success of one outstrips the other. The husband forgets—or ignores—the wife's earlier years of unremitting labor to merited reward, while she, in turn, despises the lax methods and come-by-chance attitude of the actor's easy acceptance of any good fortune.

Geraldine was tactful and alert in her public relations, punctilious in her professional duties, and directed her entire attention and enthusiasm to the service expected of her, by reason of her stellar position, and numerous contracts that overlapped in the successful whirl of opera, concert and screen activities. Her husband was lazily indifferent to appointments and contracts, arrogant with important professional officials, and endeavored in his screen and Broadway career to conduct it along the pleasant but loose lines of the theatre as he had known it abroad. The following illustration is significant:

When we were all happily engaged in those first Hollywood screen interests, Geraldine would be called for a nine o'clock studio appointment, ready in costume and make-up. The call was for Tellegen, likewise, at the same hour, for work on a nearby set at the head of another unit. Even then, the methods of the movies, to my practical mind, were of a strange order in their overhead charges and waste of time and energy. Morning after morning, Geraldine would depart at seven-thirty for her scheduled outline of scenes, to be ready at the requested time. Sometimes she would wait for hours before working, sometimes the day would not be utilized at

158

all and home she would come to bathe and rest for the same procedure the day after. A few such experiences for Tellegen sufficed; he would turn over to sleep longer, with the remark that a noon hour would still be too soon for his own participation and the easy-going director who favored him. He would be correct, too; but one of the rubs came between them out of this small difference in fundamental integrity of spirit.

Geraldine contended since her time was being scrupulously paid—whether or not employed—she owed it to the company and herself to obey the director's request. At nine o'clock, therefore, she was ready for her call, and employed her time while waiting by memorizing her concert programs and opera scores, designing her costumes or reading some worthwhile book. She disliked idleness. Tellegen laughed at her for a fool and pursued the easy tenor of his way as he understood it.

In the singing season, Geraldine's day began at nine o'clock, with her scales. Lunch was the hour when she saw the sleepy Tellegen, who managed with great effort to attend it. He was—quite naturally, by reason for his calling—a night owl, Geraldine a morning lark. Thus, their lines couldn't be continued in harmony. His metier called him to the theatre every evening; once a play was rehearsed and produced, he had nothing further to do than to lead a gay, carefree existence, provided the box-office behaved with decent enough returns to keep the theatre open. The nights when Geraldine did not sing she was asleep at ten o'clock, storing up all her energy for her delicate and exacting regime. She needed eight good hours' sleep. From this vocal responsibility she was never free during her singing days. Tellegen was a fine athlete, loved all sports, and excelled in fencing and shooting, while dancing divinely to the great joy of his lady partners. Geraldine hated any physical exertion, feared draughts, chills, snow and rain, smoky atmosphere, and the fatigue of loud talking engendered in big social gatherings. At their home parties, it was understood that she would, with rare exception, retire at ten o'clock, leaving her guests to amuse themselves as they wished, with the rich provender of the pantry at their disposition.

There was really no footing on which they could agree, and the passing of time intensified the widening gulf, caused by circumstances and uncongenial temperaments for which neither was to be specially blamed. This would have been a reasonable enough cause for an amiable divorce; but there were more ugly incidents, best left unsaid, that precipitated a long and unhappy lawsuit. Geraldine was entitled to the freedom she won at the cost of much unpleasant publicity, wily maneuvers, and great expense. During it all, she continued to fulfill her engagements to the best of her ability, and put aside her more personal feelings in the hard work she was intelligent enough to invite. It was, in a measure, a soul panacea, but even her determined will asked too much of her failing strength. She was to pay dearly for it all, later. Hurts and humiliation did not encourage inspiration for her last novelty—*La Navarraise*—and it was shortly followed in the early winter of 1922 by the premature and surprising announcement of her definite retirement at the close of that spring season from the Metropolitan.

When she quietly told me of her decision, I thought my world had come to an end. The concert tour of that previous autumn had been the usual successful one, as far as I knew.

160

Lou Tellegen, Geraldine Farrar, Mr. and Mrs. Farrar in Hollywood

ABOVE: FROM THE MOVING PICTURE VERSION OF *Carmen*.
BELOW: FROM *The Woman God Forgot*, WITH THEODORE KOSLOFF, WALLACE REI

Of course, I realized with all her travel and work, she was laboring under emotional disadvantages. The frequent and necessary consultations with her attorneys kept her stirred up continually, and the attacks from her opponent in the divorce action, which were hard to bear, grew to reports of salacious and unbelievable mendacity. Perhaps the object—stupidly enough—was to break her spirit and force her to a dramatic exit from the professional arena, and a settlement out of court. If so, this maneuver failed quite completely. She told me repeatedly, no matter what the cost in strength and money, she intended to fulfill her contracts and see the miserable business through to the bitter end, with no compromise to win the freedom that was her proper due.

As the delinquent husband was then on tour, enterprising managers raised his posters wherever her concerts were announced, for the same locale was often visited by them simultaneously. If this effort was intended to foster undue curiosity and business for Mr. Tellegen's production, Geraldine gave no sign of concern, but lived quietly on her private car, attending strictly to her own business.

And the matter of her professional retirement from the lyric stage was not precipitated by her domestic disagreements. I well recalled those earlier statements of hers to Lilli Lehmann, and her oft-repeated observations about singers who lingered over-long upon the stage, where the smoke of their own incense too often blinded them to the discreet disappearance under the Exit bulb. She had for some time fixed her own opera retirement at the forty-year limit. Like everyone else, however, I did not really believe it. I did not want to believe it.

These long years of my planning and struggle had been

161

the major factor in my own existence, the one exciting pattern I knew, richer in color and experience than any I could ever hope to enjoy as a private individual. I couldn't conceive that Geraldine—the successful medium for all this—could want to renounce it all any more than did I. It never honestly occurred to me that my girl, too, was marching along that avenue where eventually the years accumulate to middle-age and such a decision must eventually be considered.

She was to be wiser than myself in such foresight. True, I had noted in her colleagues slight defections that now and again came to the fore in performances, where an indulgent audience overlooked occasional lapses in voice and action. In Geraldine, while my critical eye and ear observed similar concessions to indisposition and less brilliant effects, I attributed it entirely to a nerve strain of a temporary nature that would shortly adjust itself once the domestic horizon was clear of troublesome dark clouds.

But Geraldine herself saw more clearly. Courageously, she placed herself outside the professional realm, calmly taking stock of the situation. Very few singers of her calibre and artistic stature, I think, would have been so frank in their self-analysis. She was proud and happy in our achievement. Our material as well as artistic ambitions had been gratified. Every penny of our loans for her musical education had been scrupulously repaid long since. We had a large and pleasant social circle. But—the nature of her lyric art did not predispose her for further development along the heroic or classic lines; there was no going forward for her, in a career that at best would continue to repeat itself in a well-worn repertoire of which she was rapidly tiring. After a few years devoted to

162

the eloquent and exquisite Lieder programs, she would thus leave behind her the memory of a radiant figure, still gracious and endearing, with her banner flying high.

Yes, she knew herself better than I did, in this later development of the woman predominating over the artist. Her book of life was opening to new chapters which I could not grasp and for which reading I had to cultivate a new interest when my uneasy surprise allowed a calmer reflection.

Once the news of her retirement was released by the Metropolitan, she was pestered with strange and flattering offers; but the sensational schemes proposed were primarily to exploit her valuable name. The various busy agents were firmly rebuffed as she went about the preparation of programs, in these final years of her proposed concert activity.

That Christmas of 1922 was our last family reunion, and the short prelude to my definite farewell to earth. I had been somewhat invalided over a period of years, but sharing so keenly all of my daughter's joys and sorrows, I laid the cause of a decline in strength to those same emotions that so long had influenced her life. With this new outlook to encourage, I perhaps presumed upon energy that gradually failed me.

Shortly after the New Year, Geraldine came home for a few hours' visit between concert engagements; she spared me all detail of those frequent and painful visits to her lawyers, and I, in turn, never questioned her about them. We tried to be gay, and direct our conversation along lines far afield from that particular heart-ache. As she wrote me every day, I was well aware of the pleasanter side of her singing duties, and the interest of her unceasing efforts in the careful study and handling of a larynx that became yearly more fragile and subject to the slightest temperature variation. As she raced from North to South, East to West, it was not an easy task despite every effort made to keep the private car at a stable temperature. When she embraced me that evening, in farewell after dinner, and jocularly remarked on the perils of the snowbanks that awaited her in Canada, after a tour under southern skies, neither of us realized it was to be our last meeting here. Some days later, I seem to have drowsed to slumber in my husband's arms. . . .

That repose lasted a long time. Then came my awakening to new interests in another realm which is a story in itself, for another pen than Geraldine's. For here I must leave her. I have wanted her to write these agreeable memoirs for some time; but they are not yet of that fuller, more recondite soul-value that I pray will be hers as the years go on, to complete a ripe and constructive womanhood. There is a higher world where I would welcome her; so perhaps some time she, in turn, will know and see my spirit face.

CHAPTER SIX

The Daughter

SCREEN ACTIVITIES

1915

IN 1915, the shining lights of the silver screen were Mary
Pickford of the fabulous golden mane; Marguerite Clark, a
winsome stage recruit; exotic Theda Bara, whose romantic
Egyptian background was played up in the press (I believe
her birthplace is Cincinnati); sinuous Louise Glaum; the dark-
eyed Clara Kimball Young; Dorothy Dalton of the pretty
dimples; the Gish sisters; and a delightful sprite of a come-
dienne, Mabel Normand. Francis X. Bushman and William
Farnum were the pet heroes that stirred the feminine hearts,
Lon Chaney of the "thousand masks" enjoyed a special public
who loved his sinister characterizations, while an ingratiating
little clown was working his way up to extraordinary stardom,
Charles Spencer Chaplin.

As previously noted, Morris Gest had engineered my affiliation with the Lasky Company, of which Jesse Lasky was

President, Samuel Goldwyn (then Goldfish) Vice-President and Treasurer, with Cecil B. DeMille as Director and partner.

I had come to the Coast in my private car with my family and several friends, and was met at the Los Angeles station by a fanfare and crowd, then an innovation there, perhaps only possible for the arrival of an opera star—now become the settled part of a studio's publicity program for outstanding names and persons. A lovely house and a competent staff were placed at my disposal for as long as I was to be at the studio. There, I found a special little house had been erected, with dressing rooms and accommodation for my grand piano, and the indispensable Victrola. It was also the beginning of the "star" bungalow, but not yet portable, which is now, I understand, in vogue for the luxurious stellar beauties. Though every possible comfort and convenience had been provided, I still had to use my legs in a short promenade to and from the various sets.

The real object of my engagement in Hollywood was to film *Carmen*, this having been my triumph of a previous opera season. Whether or not I would prove screen material was an undertaking of small risk, for the Metropolitan prestige and my personal réclame would guarantee one feature picture, while curiosity would do the rest to cover the expense involved.

Fortunately for us all, Mr. DeMille was not minded to launch me at once with *Carmen*, which was to be our star offering, of course. Earlier in the season, Lou Tellegen had enjoyed a spectacular Broadway success in a melodramatic little Spanish play called *Maria Rosa*. In fact, it was because of his part in it, that Lasky engaged him for the movies, though not in this vehicle which had been acquired for me as a

166

screen play. Though he had been a fascinating villain in the dramatic production, the major role was really designed for the woman. In my screen play, Pedro de Cordoba played Tellegen's role, and young Wallace Reid was a handsome hero, shortly to invite stardom under the Lasky banner. Much of our outdoor work was in the beautiful, natural setting of the neighboring countryside, not far from the company's modest studio on Vine Street.

When I view the staff that now follows the stellar luminary about in her studio preparations, I am amazed at the small effort required of the leading ladies. Apparently nothing is demanded of them but easy acquiescence to the hovering helpers. In my early experience, the cosmetics applied were more or less of a white grease paint, with an overlay of Rachel powder, a little eye-shadow, all applied by my own hand. I used no lip rouge. I wore my dark abundant hair which I dressed myself, parted and coiled at the nape of the neck. I needed no seamstress, make-up specialist, consultant or other specialist in my preparations to meet the camera.

I will grant that latter day improvements in the mechanics give stable lighting effects such as we did not know, but it is with so much insistence upon the laboratory marvels that I feel, as in the case of the record-making, that much of an individual's expression has a hard time to make itself felt. Our earlier Klieg lights, burning brightly with intense heat and no glass protection, claimed their victims often when eyes swelled and watered, requiring several days' retirement to dark rooms, bandages, and idleness till the inflammation cleared up.

Maria Rosa's simple peasant dresses were easily donned, scarcely needing my maid's assistance. We had to select those colors best suited to the lens, for the usual white threw off a harsh luminosity; troublesome also was the dazzle of silver or gilt ornaments that had to be smeared with a cream to kill light-reflections. This was particularly desirable for all the armor worn in *Joan the Woman*, production of another season. Thus in costumes, the pastel shades were chosen to absorb the light.

As work progressed, Mr. DeMille evolved many effects to heighten the expression of our drama. It was the day of the close-up innovation, but there was a certain peril in this exaggerated facial display for my features. In the "shot" thus enlarged, my grey eyes, under the glaring Kliegs, faded out so completely that I had the sightless orbs of a Greek statue. When I saw the first studio "rushes" I nearly fainted from the shock! But Mr. DeMille repeated these "close-ups" the following day, with an assistant holding a large square of black velvet just behind the camera on which the pupils of my eyes were focussed intently, the retina expanded and darkened in its usual normal expression. The camera and lights were not always in accord when smiles were in order. Many a scene we repeated for the sake of Kliegs that cast villainous shadows and left some of us quite toothless in what was supposed to be a seductive smile!

Mr. DeMille's long and varied experiences in the legitimate theatre gave him an uncanny reading into his actors' psychology. Thus, with me, he outlined briefly the scenes, their intended length, the climax—and with the minimum expenditure of precious energy in preliminaries, set his cameras at all angles to catch the first enthusiasm of a scene, which spontaneous impulse was always my best interpretation. We were not cautioned to beware of undue emotion, disarranged locks, torn clothing, etc. We were allowed free action as we felt it; so

168

TWO SCENES FROM *Turn of the Wheel*, ABOVE WITH PERCY MARMONT AND VIOLET HEMING; BELOW WITH HASSARD SHORT

Two Scenes from *Maria Rosa*, with Pedro de Cordoba
and Wallace Reid

we acted our parts as if we were engaged in a theatre performance, and I believe, for this reason, we had real expression
and feeling, which I find so often lacking in the beautiful but
monotonous faces of so many of the screen stars today. Publicized legs and profiles must be a complement to something
more stirring than their constant and tiresome illumination,
disposed at strange angles. At any rate, Mr. DeMille understood my enthusiasm and left me free to express natural impulses wherever my feeling prompted them. The experience
was wholly enjoyable, and the gay studio crowds, the departures to the woods and parks for "location" scenes, took
on the delight of a picnic outing. After the responsibility of a
long singing season and anxiety over a troublesome and delicate larynx, this was a carefree heaven indeed for me.

This first picture was concluded in a short time, to everyone's satisfaction. Meanwhile, the playwright and brother of
C. B. DeMille, William DeMille, had completed our special
scenario for *Carmen*, which enjoyed the same cast as *Maria
Rosa*. I was most eager to get to work on it. It was then that
I asked Mr. DeMille if we might have music during our scenes,
as I was so accustomed to orchestral accompaniment for certain tempi and phrasings, I felt I could better pantomime the
rhythm of the effects. A little piano was hastily wheeled on the
set and the talented Melville Ellis, who knew every kind of
music, Broadway jazz as well as the classics, by heart, inspired
all my scenes with his impromptu playing. I believe this
started the habit for music "off stage" for all later aspirants
to emotional appeal. At any rate, from that time on I always
had a musician at my elbow whose soulful throb did more to
start my tears than all the glycerine drops or onions more
frequently employed by other less responsive orbs.

169

This *Carmen* has been a popular subject for many mediums. Prior to the Lasky production, I saw a very good one headed by Marguerite Snow—quite operatic in outline with the blonde Micaela as a foil. Our scenario, however, was based more on the Mérimée novel, and my biggest fighting moment was not the traditional third opera act where the two women claim the bewildered Don José, but a vigorous quarrel in the tobacco factory where the amiable Jeannie Macpherson, Mr. DeMille's right hand scenarist and an actress of no mean ability, loaned herself to my assault in a battle that made screen history.

Here I garnered material for the first act of the Metropolitan's scene, that is usually indicated by a phlegmatic chorus line-up, waiting for a Carmen who seldom looks as if she had done anything more vigorous than drink a glass of orange juice in the wings. As in the movies, therefore, and with her willing connivance, in the opera version I fell upon a chorus girl in the provocative first act, seized and kicked her, and bowled her over in an exciting tussle that entertained even her blasé colleagues, looking on. Much was made of this violent innovation by the music critics, and even Gatti was a little timorous in his objections, while Caruso is said to have given me a sharp reprimand about such tiger-like tactics in my scenes with him, with special emphasis on the unfortunate importation of movie technique! He may have done so—I can't recall in the excitement of the uproar, but I do know he never sang better in his life—nor did I—and we shall let it go at that. For he, too, knew good box-office, and we certainly "had a pip" as one of my devoted stagehands gleefully expressed it. The public continued to flock, hoping for gore and, I think, even murder!

It was at the close of that opera winter that Caruso was approached by Zukor for two pictures, one of which was released under the title of *My Cousin Carus'*. What a shame the talkies were not then invented, when we would have had an imperishable expression of his personality.

Incidentally, I remember Mr. Gatti asking me pointedly, before Caruso signed his contract, if I thought the movies would react unfavorably on his opera prestige? Would his vocal réclame suffer? I assured him solemnly that I had experienced no lack of enthusiasm in my opera and concert audiences, and that an artist should consider every legitimate domain that would encourage his popularity and emolument. This apparently satisfied him.

Also, I want to add that Paolina, the agreeable victim of my rude attacks at the Metropolitan, is still there, and no doubt regrets that subsequent Carmens do not make the kindly gesture of a fat check as recompense for her hearty co-operation in the stormy quarrel, now a feature of the usual performance.

The third picture of this movie season was one in modern dress—*Temptation*—employing the same cast, fairly successful, but no such dashing attraction as the previous two Spanish subjects. The summer was a most pleasant one, and I signed up for another season in Hollywood to begin once my opera duties were over.

1916

Now, though everybody concerned knew when I left Hollywood in October, for my concert tournees, I would be back the following May, all during the winter there was never an effort made to provide me with a story or consult me about a script. I believe this same lack of anticipation still prevails, resulting in needless waste of time, energy, and, above all, incurring overhead and unnecessary expenses—this idle waiting while people in authority try to make up their several minds.

At any rate, it was almost as I boarded the train for the West that the decision to make *Joan the Woman*, a special feature, was agreed upon. I was delighted, for this peerless girl was one of my favorite heroines of history. The influence of the War times suggested a modern prologue and epilogue to introduce an historical and costume play that the producers felt might otherwise lack incentive for popular appeal. They were very well conceived and—at will—could be divorced from the story of the Maid if desired, without undue discrepancy in sequences.

Together with the *Birth of a Nation*, *Joan the Woman* made movie history. The panoply of marching crowds, prancing horses, massed effects of courtiers and soldiers, the glorious cathedral scenes, with the burning at the stake, made a dramatic and splendid impression new to the movie world. The novel lighting effects and superimposed double exposures brought forward in eerie fashion the beauty of Joan's visions and saints. Nobody could have had more enthusiastic support than that offered me by the retinue of young men and women who changed from courtier to peasant, court lady or soldier, in the twinkling of an eye under a watchful wardrobe mistress.

An ordeal for me was to come. From peasant girl, I was to emerge a warrior maid. Now, I am notoriusly afraid of horses. Any equestrian activity leaves me shaking with appre-

172

hension. As Joan the Soldier, the time came all too soon to don heavy armor, sword, gauntlets, with crucifying helmet, and mount a noble white animal that had ten thousand devils in his wicked heart and heels! Hobart Bosworth and Charles Beldert, fine horsemen and good comrades, kept a careful eye on me when a great show of martial valor was demanded, as we dashed before the grinding cameras. To them I owe protection for so closely following, and pressing their own steeds to the flank of my animal whereby he could not buck or throw me, evidently his dearest daily wish. He was no gentleman.

I was practically helpless in my high saddle, being lifted on and off by two men especially designated for this service. Encumbered not only by my armor and huge sword, I carried aloft a heavy banner that floated out for a good three yards on a stiff breeze. This maneuver demands a sturdy right arm! Yet when the bugles shrilled for our charge and maneuvers, I couldn't help thrill, and forgot my fears, my inexpert horsemanship—everything, in fact save that I was actually the Maid bent on her holy errand.

In fact, so high was my reckless courage one day, that my horse kept on dashing far up the meadowlands; I soon realized he was running away, and saw myself a miserable broken thing dangling from his sides, not a pleasant vision—especially in a vice-like iron suit! Like a messenger by the grace of God, a figure came galloping to the rescue—in the person of a charming gentleman and a fine actor whom you all have seen in so many excellent films, Jack Holt. Under his guiding hand, my steed meekly came to order, and I was led back to my armies where Mr. DeMille was frantically holding up a battle till its leader returned! This episode determined him upon a second Joan in a wonderful horse-woman, Pansy Perry, who took over all the hard and fast riding in the long shots, while I was reserved for less dangerous "close-ups." Mr. DeMille laughingly said he had to conclude our picture on schedule time for my concert tour and he was taking no chances of an accident and consequent delay. My face, not my horseman-ship, was his only concern.

The filming of *Joan the Woman* took all summer, and was a thrilling experience. Some of my cowboys were afterwards sent overseas, and their chosen section lay in Joan's country. Later I learned that one of my ablest riders was found dead among five German soldiers, having taken a machine-gun nest alone. An heroic but sad finale. Others returned, and told me of their special interest in that corner of France they learned to revere because of our inspiring story on the screen.

Ray Hatton as the King was like a Maxfield Parrish color-plate—Theodore Roberts a powerful avenging Bishop, and Tully Marshal the fanatic Monk responsible for Joan's torture. Wallace Reid was the English Soldier, a veiled interest of sentiment permitting him a sympathetic contribution and that touching, closing scene of history, at the stake, whereby Joan received at his hands the little cross of twigs to help her brave the flames.

The entire company was obedient and enthusiastic to Mr. DeMille's inspired direction. In the gory fight of the Siege of Orleans moat, and subsequent capture of the towers, we were all immersed in cold water up to our shoulders for hours. The water itself was pleasantly cool, but we nonetheless risked pneumonia, with the August sun blazing down upon us like a furnace. Mr. DeMille was over-solicitous for the welfare of my throat, in consequence, and endeavored to spare me every possible danger of temperature, axe blows, flying arrows, as well as impious hands of opponents on my azure mantle. My task was to rise from the moat, scale the ladder with that accursedly heavy banner held high, and enter a breach in the wall, just opened before my surprised eyes, in a shower of rock! This battle raged for about a week, with retakes and "close-ups." We were granted a few days respite, during which I felt still fresh as a daisy, while Mr. DeMille was speechless with the laryngitis I should rightfully have suffered! A very gallant attitude on his part, even if involuntary by reason of circumstance.

When it came to the coronation scene, it was imposing beyond description. Everybody thrilled to the service and the spell of the great organ. For the climax at the stake, my clothing, skin and hair were treated with a fluid to make scorching impossible. I had cotton, saturated with ammonia, placed in my nostrils and mouth. . . . The flames were truly terrifying, and the experience was not without some danger. For the final immolation, in the long shots a figure of wood was used, cleverly arranged with shrouded, drooping shoulders, and the face well forward, covered with disarranged locks. For the "close-ups," I was placed in the middle of tanks filled with oil; their ignition and spectacular flames together with the clouds of rolling smoke, gave a perfect illusion in the "cut-backs." It was a supremely lovely film—and I never played any screen part that inspired my love and enthusiasm as did this beautiful story.

Joan the Woman was shown as a special feature in New York that autumn—and was subsequently cut to various lengths for the usual chain theatre programs. Shortly after,

Sarah Bernhardt's film of a story of the trenches in which she had actually visited the battlefields under fire—intrepid woman!—incorporated many of our more uplifting visions of the Maid, which the Lasky Company graciously permitted the French producers to use. I felt honored in their kind courtesy, and in the association with this great personality.

1917

The gorgeous settings and costumes employed for the story of Aztec love and adventure made *The Woman God Forgot* a justifiable choice for my third season with the Lasky Company. With Wallace Reid as a soldier lover among the followers of Cortez, who was superbly played by Hobart Bosworth, this scenario treating of the conquest of Mexico by that ruthless hero made a picturesque and dramatic offering.

No idea can be obtained, however, from the mere black and white photography, of the lavish splendor provided by Mr. deMille's taste and imagination. It was the era preceding his golden beds, Swanson fantasia in dress and coiffures, and riotous effects of voluptuous and dazzling surroundings. For more and more opportunity was to be invited by the complicated sex urge in the screen dramas, as the basic of box office appeal. The Western heroes and historical heroines were to make way for the picturization of sinister and questionable events of our national life, as reflected in racketeering, prohibition, war stories, motor, plane, and submarine adventures. Douglas Fairbanks came into the limelight, a dashing figure in fast-moving comedies that caught the public's fancy—and, likewise, Mary Pickford's heart. Theirs was the most publicized romance of the day.

176

Miss Farrar in *Joan the Woman*

ABOVE: FROM *Flame of the Desert*, WITH LOU TELLEGEN AND ALEC B. FRANCIS.
BELOW: WITH MILTON SILLS IN *Shadows*

It would be hard to tell here which of our Aztec scenes was the most beautiful. The feathered attire of the men and women was a great novelty, while even the soft rugs, underfoot, were riotous in exquisite colors blocked and hand-woven in lustrous patterns, copied painstakingly from authentic designs of this picturesque people. In one of my scenes beside a pool, my girl attendants rose from the water like nymphs, while hundreds of gay birds fluttered about us, in sweet song. The whole studio was enclosed in fine wire netting, with lush tropical greens screening the protective walls. In another sequence, my boudoir was hung with ropes of huge fresh magnolias, renewed twice daily. This floral magnificence was in itself an incentive to passionate action. Theodore Kosloff of the Russian Ballet was an exotic figure at the head of the Aztec soldiery. After many stirring scenes, the concluding drama was played actually in Yellowstone Park, where the lofty grandeur of these mighty cliffs gave us fresh impetus.

Meanwhile, Jeannie MacPherson had completed another scenario for my use before the usual departure for fall concerts. This time we utilized the splendid coastline and rocks for *The Devil Stone*—almost like a holiday on the beaches, while filming the entire production.

The picture, though modern had an interesting flash-back to a former incarnation of the heroine, as a Norse Queen of cruelty and vigor. The equipment was the prescribed Valkyrie pattern, and I must say, seated in my high chair with two vicious wolf hounds at my feet, I had somewhat the vicarious thrill of playing Brunnhilde, even if it was a voiceless one with no battle-cry!

A frequent visitor in my studio house was Fannie Ward,

whom we all called the "Wonder Girl." I have never found any professional who knows Fannie's correct age. She herself was so baffling an ingenue that we wondered if she hadn't just drifted down from some pink and white cloud, in no particular century. Dainty and petite, with a laughing face framed in auburn curls, she carried the inevitable parasol to shade her baby-like complexion, which she candidly confessed "took hours to fix up"; Fannie would favor me frequently with a visit from her neighboring set, armed with a tempting ice cream cone, or cooling drink for my thirsty palate. Mr. DeMille regretted we had no use in our scenario for a cherub, since all Fannie needed was a pair of gauze wings to fit the part perfectly!

Mrs. DeMille related an amusing story, too, that those who know Fannie will not find difficult to credit. At one of her tea gatherings, when the social and screen world met in the lovely DeMille gardens, Fannie arrived in a mist of white organdie, for all the world like a sweet girl graduate; but unlike these fledglings, several ropes of her famous pearls hung about her neck. Her pretty manners enchanted everyone, and after bowing herself out, a conservative lady was heard to remark to the hostess: "Such a sweet young thing—but why does she wear all those pearls, at her tender age?"

1918

Tellegen had been having a none too successful career in his screen activities, and Jesse Lasky had suggested that he take over a post as director. To this arrangement he was agreeable, and started auspiciously enough on a scenario. I was busy with

178

my own duties and knew little of what transpired at the studio. At any rate, the picture he directed was not satisfactory to the officials—which is no crime or reflection on either party. However, Tellegen chose to get very upset about the whole matter. Naturally, my interest and support were his, and, whether right or wrong, I did not renew a further engagement with Lasky on his account, though my personal relations were then, and still continue to be, without rancor. In this instance, wifely loyalty prevailed over professional discretion.

Meanwhile, Samuel Goldwyn also became restless and decided to branch out completely on his own, so it was a convenient and immediate stepping-stone for my continued movie activities to sign up with him. He was optimistic enough to contract also for Mary Garden and Maxine Elliott, certainly so outstanding in their theatre popularity as to warrant his venture. From this standpoint, it should have been crowned with unqualified success. If you want to know why it was the reverse, as well as other enlightening details about some great names, read his own narrative in *Behind the Screen.*

Lovely Pauline Frederick had been a successful and highly paid star with Paramount, and he was desirous to add her to his list of artists, as she had been sure-fire box office attraction. Just married to the brilliant playwright and actor, Willard Mack, the couple were newly installed in the house where I also had an apartment. Doubtless for harmony's sake on the distaff side, Goldwyn acted for the best in adding Mack to his company as scenarist and supervisor, as he did in a later proposal to include Tellegen as my leading man.

Our studio was at Fort Lee, not happily equipped for

179

grandiose drama, such as was to be had for the asking in California's favorable climate. The summer months were stifling, the ferry journey, to and from New Jersey, a smelly pilgrimage that wore everyone's nerves to a frazzle, while the choice for extras and second part roles was not at all so wide as in Hollywood where the movies were becoming a recognized industry.

Mary Garden's screen *Thais* and a second picture were not designed to make the singer happy nor encourage the venturesome Goldwyn. It was an error in judgment only for screen values, not in actual theatre standards. Garden got her big salary, while Sam took it on the chin—soon after breathing a little more freely when Mabel Normand and Madge Kennedy added their note of gaiety and monetary return to the studio releases.

Turn of the Wheel was a tale of Monte Carlo that allowed me to walk through many scenes in priceless jewels, furs and bird of Paradise hats. They contributed only a sartorial value, but Goldwyn thought the movie public should know me as I was in modern dress—or undress. Herbert Rawlinson was my handsome lead—and was probably as bored as the rest of the company with a tepid narrative. Reginald Barker was our director in this and subsequent pictures that summer. A charming fellow who became a good friend in the process.

A second feature, *Shadows*, involved me as a singer in an Alaskan music hall, subsequent marriage to a wealthy clubman, fearing always that he would discover her dreadful past, after the birth of an heir and favorite child. (My first role picturing mother-love, which Goldwyn thought would invite interest for its new screen angle; he should have realized that a

180

previous tale of royal affiliation along these maternal lines was already an old rumor to the American public.) Tom Santschi was the "villain who pursued" from the past, and Milton Sills was the all-forgiving hero husband.

Meanwhile, Mack had a brainstorm when he delivered his new story, ready for my immediate use; it was called *The Hell-Cat.*

The workings of such a fecund imagination really bears telling here. One hot summer morning, Mack and Goldwyn met in my library to talk over the preliminaries for this new play, which was to carry us out of Manhattan to a locale to be determined as the story developed. Mack walked briskly to and fro, his brilliant blue eyes snapping, his rich voice reading off each part in a stage exhibition it was a shame to perform solely for so critical and prejudiced a listener as Sam. But he was the producer, and his guess at the probable reactions of the public colored his box-office hopes when judging a script. His objections were well taken, I thought, and saved me voicing any protest for this lunatic fancy to which we listened. Pancha O'Brien, as Mack's Irish-Mexican lassie was to be called, was to invite a *Perils of Pauline* rescue by a squad of United States Cavalry (co-operating of course with Rio Grande officials), death to the villain in a bloodthirsty scene of revenge, knives and guns, ending in a wild ride to the North, with the handsome cavalry rescuer as prospective fiance. One little episode that Mack assured us was a "sure-fire" effect would be Pancha's clever theft of our flag, and, during her flight for help, she would snip it in pieces along the mesa wastes for a series of rescue signals to the oncoming cavalry, swift to avenge pure women and national insult!

Sam kept a cool head—despite the torrid story and sizzling city air—I trembled with fear that he might approve this melodrama. Mack's dramatic fervor, however, had worn off by this time, and he was amenable to suggestions so sweeping as to change all but the title. Eventually, I became the heroine of a Western feud between cattle-men and sh᷉p owners. Without realizing the true import of this age-old disagreement in the Western ranges, the company entrained on the hottest day of the summer for Cody, Wyoming, to film in discomfort and irritation a story that could quite as well have been photographed in Northern New York for all we saw of Western scenery. Milton Sills and Tom Santschi were again my leads.

If you love Western life, horseback existence, camp trails, bathing in icy brooks and hit-or-miss canned cooking (the kind I am told is greatly appreciated by lumber-jacks after toilsome labor) you would doubtless have had your fun in this novel change. Add the questionable excitement of greasepaint and costumes on a rainy cold morning, idling around a fire, or on a corral rail waiting for an obstinate sun; make undesirable acquaintance with the insect world above and below the ground—the pet surprise being the snakes—and when the signal for departure comes for "location" some distance away, stagger to a horse—usually one with an iron jaw—for your locomotion; *The Hell-Cat* was no misnomer. But all things come to an end, even this odd existence, and I was jubilant when I struck home to resume my accustomed effete manner of living.

A fourth picture—*The Stronger Vow*—brought me back into a more congenial Spanish atmosphere, and had the usual cast in pleasant association.

1919

Greatly to everyone's pleasure, Goldwyn had now moved his plant to the beautiful Culver City studios where I worked in the summer of 1919. I was very happy to find myself again in California with the prospect of an interesting screen season; everything was couleur de rose. Goldwyn had engaged Tellegen as my leading man, and while I was greatly pleased, I had not been the one to urge it as a gesture for my personal happiness. Mack, too, was in his important and lucrative position as actor, scenarist, and supervisor. My director was to be a distinguished gentleman who is still making fine and beautiful pictures today, Frank Lloyd.

We started off well with a story of such tragic momentary interest, the Russian Revolution; *The World and Its Women*. I never did understand what the title had to do with the tale, but it was not without vigor and interest. In its release, my billing was, of course, the star's big print. Tellegen was furious. Puzzled, I began to reflect upon his continued petulance and dissatisfaction with the officials, cameramen, his costumes and the progress of things at the studio in general. My sense of loyalty prompted some sharp talk to Goldwyn—in which attitude, I own, I was completely wrong. He was paying me a huge salary for a name that warranted it, and I was mistakenly trying to force him to rate Tellegen's value to that par. The unwise effort toward domestic and professional alliance always results in trouble for the wrong person. I happened to invite myself to be that one, and realized it all much later. Pauline, too, was having the same unpleasant experience with the aggressive Mack. No wonder Goldwyn was uneasy with his stars. One never knows what fools women will make of themselves when they place heart loyalty above pride and monetary interests. Yet, I began a second picture—*The Flame of the Desert*—with Tellegen still as my lead, hoping that good humor would prevail for all. But only in those scenes where he was prominent did he evince any interest in the proceedings. It was not a proper attitude toward anybody—but everyone suffered his bad temper for my sake, as I found out afterwards.

Despite him, it was a jolly time—for the company went to the desert at Oxnard for much of the exterior, and the troupe was friendly and co-operative. The story was laid in modern Egypt—which permitted picturesque streets, buildings, crowds and animals. One particular camel was such an olfactory offense I showered him copiously with a daily Houbigant bath—at what an expense! We used to laugh heartily also to see the artificial palms being disposed in. solo, duo, and trio effect, against a sunset sky, or placed to create an oasis in the burning sands, a few paces beyond our tent habitations, with their hot-dog stands and lemonade buckets. The one least agreeable feature of the story was the inclusion of another horseback episode, where once more I mounted a beautiful but ill-mannered beast at the peril of my soul's tranquility, if not of life and limb.

For all these screen stories, Bendel had created a luxurious wardrobe which intrigued the movie fans as much as it did my concert audiences. I was proud in the possession of a rarely beautiful sable coat, and longed for the occasion to wear it on the screen. When that happy moment came, it was in the middle of August under blazing lights that almost singed my eyebrows; I discarded it at the earliest opportunity, wonder-

MISS FARRAR IN THE SABLE COAT THAT PROVED TOO WARM
FOR DESERT WEAR

ing why I hadn't been fortunate enough to select a winter scenario at Lake Tahoe! We seem never to be satisfied.

Back to Hollywood and a little respite, while waiting for the next feature to be decided. I went one evening to a supper party at Pauline Frederick's. Among the interesting guests was a handsome young gentleman who took a seat beside me, introduced by Julian Eltinge. Very modest, he said he was trying his luck in the movies—but so far nothing very certain had come up, so he was thinking of accepting Eltinge's proposal for an Australian tour, in a dancing act. We conversed in Italian, that being his native tongue. Another young hopeful, recently released from Army service, was the means of their joint wild-fire success, one as hero, the second as director. Rudolf Valentino and Rex Ingram rode to unquestionable fame in *The Four Horsemen of the Apocalypse*, the immediate sensation of the hour. The young Italian continued in a spectacular career until his early death, which engendered hysterical mourning on the part of his fans, all ages and sizes, naturally of the feminine gender.

About this time, Pola Negri was imported in her excellent European version of *Carmen* called *Gypsy Love*, and that lovable, unforgettable, irreplaceable Will Rogers loped into our own Culver City arena to make the day brighter with his pithy observations—which spared nobody, of high or low degree in the movie hierarchy.

I was finally called to work in my third and last picture of the season, and it was to be my final one with the Goldwyn forces—though none of us knew it then.

The French classic was the source of my screen version for *The Woman and the Puppet.* It was cautiously arranged to suit the censors and the general idea of the movie public's morals, the spicy Gallic insinuations and wicked perversity of this fascinating Spanish wanton being ruthlessly expurgated. The model, of course, was *Carmen,* whose fascination every Spanish heroine hopes to duplicate or incorporate. It was, even so, lively, pretty, and pictorial—inoffensive, too.

I left Hollywood with the happy anticipation of returning the following summer to this agreeable vacation interim and the emoluments. As I pulled out of Los Angeles, I could still hear the cheers of farewells and good wishes for a happy opera winter and my return to true and tried comrades of the silver sheet. In fact, Mr. Goldwyn had been eager to make some arrangements that would permit a longer term for work, under less pressure in the scenario department, for my stories, and thus engage me in a longer stay on the Coast. Concert and opera plans were the handicap for such an outline, of course.

1920

It was in mid-winter that I was giving a large and formal luncheon party for Mr. and Mrs. Fritz Kreisler, in my home. Just before dessert, the butler announced that Mr. Goldwyn was calling on a very urgent matter, and wished to see me immediately.

I excused myself from the table and went up to the music-room, wondering what was up. There sat my visitor, eager to deliver his message that, in the nature of it, I could well appreciate was an embarrassing communication he wanted to have over. I, too, like plain speaking, and therefore appreciated his direct approach. It was to say that my pictures were not making the returns desired; my contract had still two

186

years to run, twelve weeks of annual screen activity, with the guarantee of two hundred and fifty thousand dollars. The situation was critical for his company.

Goldwyn himself has often broadcast my simple solution of this difficulty, which was to tear up the contract without further ado. I still do not understand why such a perfectly natural impulse should awaken any wonder, or particular admiration; but it seems to be a feature in his résumé of screen stars and their characteristics, and I appreciate the sincerity of his compliments about the incident.

The following letter from my banker friend and trustee puts its own interpretation on the gesture:

The news that you have concluded your Goldwyn contract arouses conflicting emotions. Nature intended you for a singing actress and the role of movie star has always seemed incompatible with the high place you hold in the operatic world. The redeeming feature in the film business, of course, has been the enormous earnings you were able to command, a not unimportant consideration for one with your positive genius for spending money; but it is not everything, after all, and if you will make your budget conform to your still princely income from music, I am glad you are out of pictures. The applications for your services in concert indicate large amounts from this source. The Victor is also doing splendidly for you. Meanwhile, it may not be too late to congratulate you on your huge success in *Zaza;* a creation which even your enemies (if you have any) must praise. It is as well a credit to "The Temple of Art" which I hope that management appreciates.

Thus wrote my conservative Boston friend.

It was only a few years ago, at the premiere of *Bittersweet* in the Hub, that a cheerful voice greeted me in the orchestra aisles. It was Mr. Goldwyn, apparently not a day older than when I last saw him. This amazing man looked critically at my silver hair, and surprised me indeed by a suggestion. "Why not *now* make a talkie *Carmen?* Thinking perhaps I had misunderstood, he affirmed that it would be a "great show." Undoubtedly—if I were so ridiculous as to believe it—but not in the complimentary sense. I shook my head and disclaimed any movie-talkie intentions after a lapse of twenty years.

In 1920, however, I was again tempted to a movie offer that had every promise of interesting activity, with Pathé—well worth my effort from the financial angle, as well. Two features were to be made that summer. *The Riddle-Woman* was spoiled by poor writing, poor camera-work, and impossible direction. The excellent actors did their best against studio odds, but I refused to go on with any such further irritations. The contract was amiably dissolved, and thus ended my movie experiences for good. I had greatly enjoyed them, and only regret my own era was too early for the combination of the present acting and talking features.

CHAPTER SEVEN

I

The Daughter

1921-1932

THIS decision to leave the opera was not a hasty one. Perhaps unconsciously, it had long been a part of my professional plan.

I recalled vividly my first visit and audition with Lilli Lehmann, as a young enthusiast. She had said: "Learn your métier well and you will sing till you are seventy." And I had replied, with emphasis: "But I do not want to sing till I am seventy—not anywhere near that age!" Some instinct spoke within me then—and now the moment, self-chosen, was upon me. I was laying aside this glamorous cloak of opera—denying the fascinating heroines I had so many years companioned—with little regret. My career had amply repaid all the sacrifice our small family had made for its fulfillment. I was unusually fortunate in the enjoyment of the results of application and devotion. My parents lived in comfort, our obligations were cancelled. But the laurels had become burdensome, and exacted a toll of strength and spirit I no longer cared to spare in that direction. The sign-posts were clearly erected; and I must travel a new road—perhaps a strange one, and alone.

The decision, I knew, wounded and surprised my dear mother. She was more attached to my career as an avenue of our joint expression than I previously realized. It had been her life's work. But I was conscious of a program stupidly repetitious, born of routine and integrity, rather than illumined by inspiration, and magnetic with spontaneity. I was ready indeed to concede a definite farewell to the land of illusion, and my part in it. The distressing vision of prima donnas overstaying their artistic prime and inviting apology gave me the horrors. That sad ego of self-deception was not in my make-up. I was, meanwhile, conscious of tendrils that drew me gently in directions other than the tried avenues of my singing. They had no source in the art, my career, or any earthly loves I had known. Perhaps it was a soul's voice trying to be heard through the glamorous weave of the artist's controlled medium. An inner hunger for understanding of harmony more recondite and rare than the material ear alone would allow.

Contrary to general gossip, I was not forced out by a discipline-minded management intent upon reprisals, nor did I give my congé in pique. At forty, a milestone had been reached. And the misty foresight of earlier youth was a commitment I intended to fulfill, in retirement from this present and particular field.

It was not to be expected that Mr. Gatti would take my decision seriously. The public, likewise aware of the changing humors in temperamental performers, had no more reason to accept the definite conclusion at its face value. But it made daily gossip of interest, and was kept alive by a speculative press. Kept the box office content, too, and evoked a series of demonstrative and affectionate tributes that would gladden any human heart; certainly mine!

The last performance was hectic. It carried itself on a crescendo of frenzy, hysteria, tears and cheers. A nerve-wracking finale that transpired April 22, 1922, at a matinee. The opera was *Zaza*—proposed by the management. I made no demand, no request for alteration of their outlined program for a farewell offering. The public had hoped it might be *Carmen, Butterfly,* or even the bone of contention—*Tosca*. But I wanted all to be correct and without reproach on either side. I only exercised the prerogative of making my own farewell speech, alone on the stage, once the comrades had shared the curtain calls. I refused public eulogies from the Management, or Board of Directors, in the usual routined fashion; no farewell supper and patronizing addresses to follow. I had my own pride and knew quite well what had been my efforts and accomplishments. I desired no gold wreaths, cups, platters, brooch or any mementos which are so often the well-meaning, but—to me—distasteful results of canvassing for public presentation on these occasions. Flowers there were en masse, and such banners and flags as carried in no uncertain terms the sentiment of the public. I had loved them. They had loved me. And to them I wanted to address those last words. And so it was.

The friends of the chorus and those helpmates backstage tendered their gifts—which I prize to this day. Somehow my motor, sunk in gorgeous blooms, drove to the stage door, and, working my way through the crowds, I was soon carried away—more dead than alive. Happy to have been held so dearly, and admired so consistently in an exciting career; grateful to have had a fortunate role in our glamorous opera life. But now, my shoulders were free of responsibility and could straighten to meet new issues. Since early youth, I had lived three lives in this one existence to date. Concentrated, feverish, ever keyed to vivid emotions, but always in a routine of slavery, nonetheless. It had exacted its toll. Rightfully! It was a now closed chapter. There was new reading in the next, for me.

Once home, and with my dear parents happy—if in joyous tears—we sat at a pleasant supper table, this small family so closely bound by its loyalty, pride and affection. It was my mother's crowning achievement; and for the moment we gave ourselves up to the glorious triumph she could so truly call her own.

They soon took leave, for their own home. I was left in mine. A big and beautiful house—fashioned in anticipation and enthusiasm; but never a home. All its beauty and treasures would never make it so.

Slowly I sat before the mirror in my boudoir. I was fagged in body, but alert in mind . . . . self-questioning. How often I had played such a part before a hushed audience. It was quite in the operatic picture, even if I were the lone public. A suggestive touch was supplied incidentally by the masses of flowers, wreaths and banners that had figured in the afternoon's farewell. They lay about me, as if to honor a bier. A dissolution was near, perhaps, but in this sea of fading blossoms

DEPARTURE ON CONCERT TOUR, AFTER METROPOLITAN OPERA
FAREWELL PERFORMANCE

INTERIOR OF MISS FARRAR'S PRIVATE CAR

I could feel no sadness, no regret—only a wonder and curiosity about myself.

The woman who reflected my earnest gaze seemed a vague receding shadow. The first step toward putting her out of my life had been taken. As artist she had proved herself. But she must slowly make way for the more human creature who seemed such a stranger at these cross-roads.

Marriage and career had failed to combine harmoniously. Even at the moment, humiliating and difficult months were to pass before the unfortunate tie could be dissolved. There was still another journey to complete, before I took final leave of the professional field—that of the concert world. This would entail the routine I knew well, and carry me the length and breadth of our land, as in previous seasons. The groves of discipline, and the choice of exquisite songs would pleasantly round off my singing career.

In the midst of travel, I was suddenly called home to bury my mother. This shock staggered me, indeed. Somehow, as in my childhood days, I had believed her superior to all mortal incidents. Her rich vitality, fine courage and valiant spirit had never lost power to convince me of her supreme control of our earthly problems. She had been ailing, but no one had foreseen the collapse of so gallant a heart; least of all herself. Quite simply, she had fallen asleep in my father's arms. As I saw her, still and smiling, I could not wish it otherwise. A precept of long ago came to mind—one she had taught me in those early Sunday school classes—"God always knows best;" and I felt He did. The miracle of her sweet face completed my submission to the inevitable; but a precious and inspiring tie to song had been broken. It was never to be the same again.

With my sorrowing father, I kept the schedule of my professional engagements as contracted. My mother would have been the first to wish it so. A demoniac energy drove me on. I resolved that no idle hours should engender self-pity, nor give me fanciful ideas; but I did find myself bewildered—at a loss—to make my proper adjustments to another sphere just then. So we whirled away on the private car, on tours that now seemed endless, so seasonal was their routine and preparation. It was a method of escape I would not advocate to others, but it suited my needs at the time.

Meanwhile, summers found me in the Connecticut countryside where I had brought what was left of my Lares and Penates. This time, in the hope of a happy and permanent domicile. I called it Fairhaven—where I write these lines. And every waking hour, my prayer is that it may continue to justify its name.

To vary the Lieder programs, I condensed *Carmen* into a fantasia with costumes, scenery and orchestra. With 123 consecutive performances in 125 days, in every locale that boasted an auditorium, it was a triumphant record; but I shouldn't care to repeat it. The price exacted was complete nerve exhaustion. At the season's close, I was ordered on a sea trip to Italy for rest and isolation; forbidden even to write a postcard greeting.

That lazy, pleasant voyage in spring sunshine was quite different than the one taken in war-times of 1914! But with Gatti and many of the opera troupe again on board, its company bore a certain similarity to the previous trip. This time Gatti was not my impresario, but we had always remained friends. I like and esteem him. We only fell out during those brief but distressing intervals when money matters or a new contract was the issue. He was entitled to his show of authority; as he often said, he wanted to make the best possible arrangement in his capacity as manager. For this, no one, least of all I, could blame him. But I employed no intermediary; and depended upon plain speaking in person to defend my own interests. It always puzzled him; accustomed to the devious arguments and Italian fine hand, he could not conceive a straightforward proposition—take it or leave it. In fact, I walked off twice and made concert contracts with my best friend, and advisor, C. A. Ellis, who had guided the Boston Symphony Orchestra to its world-wide renown. I knew full well that the sun wouldn't always shine with such splendid favor for me, and so made my hay while the rays were propitious and hot!

There was a great difference between Gatti at the Metropolitan and Cleofonte Campanini at the head of the Chicago Opera. It was there I went on one of these occasions of rebellion. Gatti advocated a small fee and large box-office intake, thereby emphasizing managerial perspicacity. Campanini paid large sums to the singers who were big assets in public appeal. Naturally, the artist felt a little more flattered by this latter treatment and consideration of his prestige. Who wouldn't?

To follow this successful *Carmen*, I had prepared a similar fantasia of *Tosca*, *Bohème*, and *Butterfly*, thinking these pictorial reductions of popular offerings that had earned me acclaim at the Metropolitan would carry me on till the day, already planned, for definite leave-taking from the public platform; but the agent Ricordi, who controlled the Puccini works, would by no means grant any permission for such a project, despite the high royalty fees I was willing to pay. Lacking this attractive material, I embarked on a venture that I hoped would succeed in the manner of the previous *Carmen*, a piece called *Romany Love*, by Franz Lehar.

The chosen Lehar operetta was dainty and melodious, with quite a suggestion of the gypsy girl in its central character. It was, as well, an essay in our vernacular that I thought might please. Unfortunately, it was sadly mangled by Broadway "arrangers." After one unhappy night out of town, I refused flatly to consider further activities in it. Again—and as usual—I was amused to read the highly spiced gossip that emanated from Heaven knows where. I was accused of every petty meanness toward members of the company, the management, and the "backers." As a matter of truth, the troupe was composed of most agreeable and hard-working professionals who knew their business thoroughly. There was no reason to resent them, or vice versa. Nor did they. I shall never know the true story nor the source of resultant confusion and mismanagement that ruined a charming prospect. It is, after all, unimportant now; but no money could pay me for the loan of my name, without my proper artistic contribution to sustain it. And whatever "backers" labored under this mistaken idea were soon persuaded of their error. After much surgery on book and music, I was permitted so little in the entire outline that the electric lettering bearing my name outside the theatre was the most prominent part of my contribution. I withdrew after one night—a disillusioned and very ill woman. However, all in proper order, with a duly attested certificate from my physician. It was a blessing in disguise, no doubt,

196

for I had nearly killed myself to make the venture successful.

A season of rest was highly beneficial to exhausted nerves. Then I returned to the classic Lieder program, satisfied it was the one dignified medium for these last years. With the final Carnegie Hall concert in the fall of 1931, I was definitely off the public platform. I had made no previous announcement, wishing to avoid all possible charge of publicized hysteria. With great care and routine I had worked within the tender compass of my vocal resources. I wanted no charges of theatricalism to deny me serious consideration for my development as a Lieder singer. An affectionate demonstration took place as I spoke a few words of definite farewell when the concert was concluded. My homeward drive had nothing of the hysteria nor fatigue of the opera finale. I had fulfilled my allotted musical years to the best of my perception and ability.

There was no melodramatic retrospection in this leave-taking. The mellow middle years granted precious time, to be used for new pursuits. What they were to be, I had not the faintest idea; but it was glorious to feel release from organized programs and routine living. I almost rejoiced in the first cold of the winter. It could run its course and I could sneeze heartily with no fear of damages to the singing apparatus. No telephone to call me to rehearsals or performances. No hundreds of hands to shake after concerts when one longed for quiet retirement. No autograph seekers, no forced testimonials, no critics to placate, no camera dodging, no parade—no fuss or feathers. In fact, nothing to demand a manufactured *noblesse oblige* attitude toward anyone!

That winter of finality found me ready to indulge in complete relaxation of the mind and body. Thus, I should imagine,

197

would a painter or sculptor lay aside his tools and, contented, look back upon the road he had travelled, knowing he had done his best to bring his measure of beauty into being. The laurel for me had proved a fragrant but heavy crown. To bear this symbol of authority needs the strictest adherence to standards of taste and conduct; to lay it aside graciously is an accomplishment also for which the spirit must prepare itself. My own test had come, and I was happy to believe, because I had given of myself with absolute honesty and abandon, this decision would be easy to effect. And so it was. Gone was the carefree exuberance of singing youth. Gone the precious spontaneity so captivating in its artless charm. No calculated mature artistry can offer that pristine freshness, where the vocal dew is like a gossamer mist of enchantment on a hedge-rose.

Now the riper years offered other interests, no less enjoyable, and motivated by the urge of the new-born moment. I was interested in people and things; in others removed from my own hectic world, which had been bounded on all sides by those dedicated to feverish ambition and unremitting labor. The happenings of every-day living, divorced from the glittering arena of performances, was a more normal pattern of living. Till now, contact in the main had been one of gracious acceptance to public acclaim, behind the flattering screen of the footlights. The artist must always adorn the pedestal where her public places—and keeps—her, till her supremacy is challenged, and a newer sensation causes either a bitter rivalry or eclipse. Adulation had never blinded me to this, usually the closing chapter to all careers. I had fought hard and honorably in my youth for my own place in this law of survival. I was

198

not minded ever to play the party of the second part, in my later years. And so I determined never to plead for indulgence, never to invite apology or reproof, but to make an exit made graceful by discretion and taste.

I had the satisfaction, some years later, of hearing some speculation about this procedure from an eminent musical critic, a Bostonian like myself, who acknowledged that he, too, had shared the same skepticism. He said the press naturally saw in it the spicy flare-up of a spoiled prima donna determined to bring an astute management to heel. In other words, to make them eat crow. Meanwhile, the management would let her cool off from an emotional outburst and reflect upon the advantages of resigning according to their terms. After a period, she would send some suave third party to Mr. Gatti's office to make cautious soundings. There would be a series of polite inquiries about nothing more definite than the plight of opera without Caruso, or Toscanini, and the dearth of great singers! Then a little hint of repertoire difficulty, with assurances of mutual esteem and thinly veiled apologies, would ease the tension—and with love and kisses, both parties would be ready to close a new deal.

But all this did not happen. The astonishment was general, for the traditional tactics were not employed. What complexities and suspicion are invited by simple decisions! And so, according to my critic friend: "There was no further story."

Of course not. You can't make a Forsyte Saga from a statement of a simple fact.

II

REMINISCENCES

I MUST say, with few exceptions, I had enjoyed being "news" to the ladies and gentlemen of the Press; and they had done well by me. However, there was no design on my part for the flaming headlines and exciting speculation that came to be associated always with my professional activities. Naturally, the public's curiosity was not sated, either, by a more than bold peep into my private affairs! But even the most insistent reporter must give up when there is no disposition to converse, and so my life began to run smoothly enough, quite in the character of a private individual, as I desired.

With garden interests, dogs, books and a small circle of intimates, the pleasures of a country life were charmingly simple and without ceremony. Travel also beckoned. Heretofore, my hectic peregrinations had been overshadowed by the singing responsibilities. Outside the opera seasons, I had spent fifteen consecutive years in a private home on rails; in other words, a Pullman fitted up like my own house in miniature. A dining-sitting room with a tiny piano; comfortable chairs; a wall-map on which I might trace my travels; bedrooms for my household; closets for my wardrobe; all in pretty chintz and colorful paint. Dogs and birds also went along. The same crew served me year in, year out; splendid colored men whose attention and efficiency were the best the Pullman service could supply.

From icy Canada to golden California, the dusty Middle-West, the glowing South—along my own Atlantic Coast territory, we whirled merrily into strange auditoriums; week in and week out. The climatic changes were at times cruel, but many were the adventures we enjoyed. Leaking roofs—draughty stages—delayed pianos—and storms that cut off our lighting; nothing stopped me if I was able to sing.

It was not always possible to be in top form under such traveling conditions, but good will and good spirits usually prevailed. There were no complaints from our public; the audiences took small accidents with utmost good humor. In one city, a severe thunder-storm struck down the power lines. We found a little boy who brought us two potatoes with candles stuck in them; with one on each side of the piano, my accompanist blinked over the feeble flame as best he could! I held a taper in my hand to replace the footlights! Rather in the mood of a concert *Tosca!*

Often I begged the indulgence of the public to don a fur wrap—of any icy evening, when backless gowns made the semi-nudity a certain invitation to pneumonia. Once a piano, delayed, was so low in pitch, that the audience of the evening must have thought I was a growling contralto!

In the earlier days when the size of an auditorium was a point of great attraction, with more thought for the intake than the comfort of the patrons, we hired vaudeville houses where trained animals, often confined in the basement, gave lusty obbligato to our efforts. Even so, we were more comfortable under such sturdy eaves than Sarah Bernhardt was when she took to the canvas tents upon her record-breaking road tour at the time theatrical groups were at variance with each other, and theatres therefore taboo.

Crowds of excited people will do almost anything in their

delirious acclaim. I have had my dresses and furs cut to pieces, my hair pulled out, my feather fans loosened, even been swept into strange arms and warmly kissed! Once, I found it was the cold snout of a little dog hidden in its owner's muff. No end of Farrars, members of a family tree that must have had innumerable branches and off-shoots, would spring up all over—to claim a relative's interest, handshake, or personal connection. The autograph seekers never carried pen or pencil, but we somehow managed to make them happy by a hasty scrawl. Those were not the smokeless days of the candid camera, so the post-concert gatherings usually dissolved into sneezes, gasps and chokes in suffocating fumes!

Wherever I went, the stage was laid out in white cloth to protect my long, trailing gowns. The house of Bendel has designed my dresses for street and concert, as well as opera costumes, these many years. There was always a vivid interest in the exquisite, sometimes startling creations I permitted myself for public admiration. Not in the fashion of several good singers, excellent vocalists but indifferent dressers; one of whom wore one frock a year, and sometimes longer. There was a certain black velvet with a soiled ermine trimming that became almost a by-word with us whenever we read Madam So-and-So had appeared! But I revelled in lovely fabrics, with fans, jewels and slippers to match; one dress never served me for more than three concerts. Frequently, I wore a colored wig to complement a gown and add novelty. In consequence, I have often been amused to hear disputes as to whether I was actually a blonde, red-haired, or brunette.

In those days of pompadours, curls, and frisettes, one could permit oneself towers of such silken and abundant tresses, to astonish the beholder! As Bendel has, for over a quarter of a century, dressed me, so John & Company have cared for my wigs, and my own hair, watching it change from dark brown to its present platinum crown, with solicitous care for its well-being. I have always thought it wise to have one's dressmaker and coiffeur know one well and long enough to study and ameliorate one's disadvantages. I always used to say to the former: "Remember that the back of a dress be in perfect order and flowing line. I have no eyes on my shoulders to divert the attention if something is amiss." The New York public is very "costume" conscious and likes its artists to be chic and well turned out.

I recall in the earlier days of my coming to the Metropolitan a truly fine dramatic singer who was so ludicrous in her brown shirt effects as Aida that the ear yielded to the eye most unhappily. When confronted with the lovely Emma Eames and her nobly molded arms under a warm bronze make-up, the Jaeger-clad newcomer was at a decided sartorial disadvantage. We still have some lapses in line and color in the stage costumes of some of our stars which could be corrected, provided, of course, a minimum of discretion in diet could be observed. I do not mean the Hollywood insanity that reduces the human creature to a languorous string-bean anaemia; but some of my preferred artists linger too long and lovingly over the starches and sweets. This is manifest in singing, as well as silhouette. Brunnhilde and Isolde, at a pinch, can sustain the massive effect better than a tubercular Mimi or the lithe, flashing Carmen and tender Butterfly. Kimonos do odd things to prominent hindquarters! Of course, the professional routine is one of constant supervision and denial, even in small things; but, after all, isn't that also the rule of all human existence? Isn't immoderation in any line rather to be curbed for general benefit, if possible?

It is also amusing and astonishing what value the usual professional places upon press reports. Here is an instance to illustrate it, that was by no means isolated in my many experiences. Once, in a pretty but small Mid-western college town, we were greeted by the happy news of a local sell-out for the evening's concert. A young man from the campus called in the afternoon, announcing a pleasant readiness to record anything I wished, or cared to write about the performance to come. With engaging frankness, he explained he only knew how to report on football. Would I be so obliging as to write what it was all about? Then he would attach his name to obviate embarrassment for us both. I scratched off some fulsome compliments while he waited in the private car. To all the assisting artists I gave detailed notice, and contented myself with mention that Miss Farrar lived up to expectations, and was an attractive picture in flashing jewels, etc. Discrimination and welcome on the part of the audience was stressed, even encores were named. (I knew what had been the season's hackneyed offerings.) Praying that all would go according to schedule, I gave the young man the statement. The concert was delightful, and next morning every face wore a smile. One of my colleagues, an excellent artist, but given to the gloomy side of things when the press was not eloquent, was jubilant now. He excoriated Metropolitan reviewers, and opined at last a soul-musician had recognized his true contribution to art. For years this one criticism ran in the Trade papers. I chuckled whenever I read it, but never told!

It is curious to note that the impulse to sing is present at all times; but the urge to work toward that singing leaves much to be desired. I have in mind an agreeable person, with a fine voice, who toured with me; but whom I could never persuade that the joy of singing was not dependent upon the size of the audience. If we had a small house, the obvious boredom and shirking were surprising. In the larger cities, the usual presence of critics left the singer so unprepared to handle emotions that the fine voice never fully showed its worth. There was no love or pride to sustain a daily routine of careful preparation. It takes more than vocal cords to complete a performance!

I recall in our *Carmen* troupe, I would have fared badly had not our excellent conductor, Carlo Peroni, held to a high standard no matter where we performed or what the size of the audience. And again, I am reminded of three young musical goslings who nurtured some stupid false pride that I could not understand. When I was seeking a Micaela for the production, these promising singers were approached. They were deaf to the argument that the experience would be valuable and might lead to definite results elsewhere. No—they explained that in leaving New York their "prestige" would suffer! I knew what their lives in the city were like—the pitiful fare of milk and crackers—on the window-ledge—and the depressing Saturdays when room rents were due . . . and hard to produce! Yet? . . . . . .

Many ingredients must flavor and enrich the vocal soup, but the pot must come to a boil over the flame of plain common sense.

And common sense can mean also a steady head for proper values and organization. Our gallant friend, Scotti never quite lost his wish to play impresario. Since that would never be granted at our Broadway Temple of Art, he took a small company made up of our Metropolitan stars and did excellent business on the road, for several short seasons. Then he approached me for some special performances on the Coast. I found that my concert schedule would permit it—fortunately for me, and greatly to my satisfaction; for while I had sung in concerts in the West, I had not appeared in opera in California, which was a longing I could now gratify.

The business was handled by C. J. Foley, who had then taken over the office of C. A. Ellis. *Tosca, Carmen, Butterfly,* and *Zaza* were to be the offerings. It was a tumultous two weeks that I enjoyed to the full; but our child-like Tony was a poor business man of short vision. We offered him a flat rate per performance. He held up protesting hands, so I suggested a big percentage and small fee, as an alternative I was willing to accept. To which he acceded joyfully. Alas! My confidence in myself turned out beautifully for me, but ill for him! I walked off with nearly all our receipts. When he had finished with the local manager and expenses, he was virtually in tears at the money that was rolling into all pockets save his own. On my departure, I recall a doleful picture as he sat at the St. Francis Hotel, chewing the well-worn stub of a pencil and consulting a little notebook wherein all I could see was the memo for special delivery letters and telegram messages during the season! Thousands of dollars were in the expense account of the auditor, while he agonized over pennies and postal trivialities! In our first *Tosca* of the season, once returned to the Metropolitan, he would dramatically point to me as we took our second act curtain, and hiss, confidentially,

206

"You cost me all my money!" Well—I did. For he erred on the parsimonious side—and missed the gambler's chance.

My father was with me on these tourneés, and that was a signal for all the old-time baseball players to attend opera and concerts. They swarmed backstage—but to greet him! Otherwise, I am certain they would not have endured the stiff shirt, and evening of lesser excitement than that found on their own professional field of sport. Father also had a bouquet for me every night, in memory of my mother; touching little blossoms that stood on my dressing table. Her death tied us so closely, and I know his interest in my musical activity helped him over the difficult adjustment to her loss.

The divorce was shortly pronounced final, and that sad chapter was closed in as dignified a manner as I could manage. The summers were quiet—with rest and work as usual interspersed.

Then came my first return to Germany since the war. There was a delicious feeling of old times returned in arriving once more—though by plane—in Berlin! Word quickly got about and the Press was at my heels. Of course I was happy and excited, and talked a blue-streak to the reporters. To revisit old haunts, see dear friends—and my great Lilli once more—thrilled me immeasurably. Eagerly, I located, and gathered into one glorious afternoon, all the opera comrades of earlier days who had survived the dreadful aftermath of the war. Speeches and toasts came from warm hearts and eloquent lips.

But there were many changes. The Crown Prince's stables were now the archives for all the opera material; a wonderful museum of interest as well, put in apple-pie order and kept so by the curator, my good friend, Dr. Droescher. From where the erstwhile royal steeds came prancing down the Linden, there now streamed forth the youngsters of the ballet, the librarians, musicians, clerks, and visitors also, who were urged to inspect the proudly displayed treasures of the Reich. In a great Golden Book, beautifully tooled, on illuminated parchment pages, are the names of the troupe under the last Kaiser—and there stood my name, in shining letters. A lump swelled in my throat. Across the room our portraits hung; handsome women, splendid men, in the heroic and romantic roles that Imperial Berlin applauded! We were of that last royal company before the deluge. *Sic transit gloria mundi.*

In Berlin I had always made my home at the Adlon—and those gracious hosts, Louis and Hedda, in their hearty greeting maintained a little of the illusion still! And then a familiar voice over the 'phone, Potsdam speaking. It was part of the charm—bittersweet though it was—to find my old friend the Crown Prince warmly welcoming me. That first meeting after so many years—and the incredible happenings in the interim. It will never be forgotten. The world knows something of a throne demolished and heartbreaking exile—but can know so little of the various personal dramas that colored the German scene, before and after the debacle.

The Crown Princess is still a gracious figure. Her stalwart sons I recall as babies, in the long ago, crawling about the Marmor Palast floor at tea-time. Prince Louis Ferdinand—debonair and likeable—has since been a worker, popular with his fellows, in the Dearborn Ford factory. He has been my guest at home, and we agreed, gazing at an early photo which I prize, of his mother in her lovely youth, that a beautiful and distinguished Kaiserin had tragically failed to come into her own. Meanwhile, Lilli Lehmann had gone to Salzburg, where my motor could not take me fast enough to greet her. Regal and handsome, with a flash of the old fire in her great brown eyes, we met at the door of my hotel where she folded me in her arms. For a moment we could not speak for happy tears! Then the torrent burst loose and I chattered interminably. With the first flush of excitement over, I could see the sad changes since our last meeting. Privation and anxiety had taken their heavy toll, from a woman in the sunset of her life.

We spoke of dear departed ones, the sad conditions of the moment, and the lowered artistic standards that seemed so commonplace by the light of her own youth's pattern and companionship with the great names. With grim humor she outlined an evening at the opera in Berlin for a recent revival of *Tannhauser*. Despite all the mechanical marvels that transformed and elaborated the staging, she felt that the entire personnel were a disastrous collection of "untalented nobodies." After the second act, a veteran critic ventured to ask her opinion for publication. With the air of an empress, she rose, drew her cloak about shoulders still statuesque, and announced, in no whispered undertones—as she made her way out—"Say that Lilli Lehmann leaves her loge in disgust at the travesty they call Art in this opera house!" She was as militant as ever in her proud musical integrity.

Meanwhile, we discussed and argued that fine point of the eternal dedication to one's career. It astonished her that I found pursuits outside it, and that the opera no longer exercised its former glamour and claim. We drove to the idyllic Königsee, over the Bavarian frontier from Salzburg, where, on the shores of this emerald Paradise, we lingered in the sun-drenched pines. I had brought her a scarf of silver foxes and begged her to honor them, on the occasion. Tenderly she stroked the soft skins, chiding me for my gesture of extravagance. Luxuries, she said, always alarmed her, and she had had but few! Against that noble head with its snowy crest, the furs lay rich and lustrous, a sumptuous vision—this great Lilli—and my last earthly one. As I said goodbye, who could have dreamed I was never again to behold her? A few years later, on my return, she was gone. There will be no replica of this daughter of Wotan in our time. The Gods received their own. To her and Toscanini, I owe the greatest debt of gratitude for their inspiration in my own musical career. The shadow of their particular greatness looms even larger in the restropect I now enjoy; and, in recollection, I can better estimate and praise them.

My summers in Germany were like the turning leaves of a fairy tale. Each chapter introduced its beauties to stimulate the spirit and refresh the heart anew. I retraced many a way of my early pilgrimages. The Rhineland is ever golden. Cologne's great cathedral still casts its spired beauty in the proud mirror of the mighty Rhine. Terraced vineyards ripple in undulating green at the base of crag and tower; those feudal ruins that ever defy the elements in gallant challenge to the skies.

Knock at the little door in Bonn, and pause in the courtyard before you mount the humble stairway of the house where the infant Beethoven first saw the light. The house will yield a fascinating experience. And if you are bold and reverent, as I was, the caretaker may allow you to lay a worshipful hand upon the mellowed sheets of music, so preciously preserved in their glass case, and to touch the yellowed keys once pressed by a genius' fingers. As you leave, walk not too far away, to the calm green of the village burial ground. A beautiful marble figure of the Muse will beckon you to Robert Schumann's resting place, where the birds sing gayly in the sunshine.

From Coblenz to Mainz, these magic shores invite. Ehrenbreitstein may connote only a war-time fortress to the Army of Occupation who still remember; but from its dismantled turrets, look down upon the confluence of the Rhine and Moselle, those mighty waters that have been in motion since time immemorial. Measureless, they flow on—regardless of man's puny efforts to conquer life and death. Follow the more placid stream of the Moselle to Trier. Forgotten now are the Roman legions that left proof of conquest in their great stone barracks, still standing in the center of the town. Gaul and Teuton have drenched these grounds in bloody fray. But the rivers flow on, unchanging in song and story, to the heartbeat of the centuries—past the treacherous Lorelei rocks, beyond Mainz in the shimmering haze, now on to the Necker, not far away, and its Heidelberg glories!

Among great women of her time, who does not admire that Princess Liselotte of the Pfals? From these ruins, and to save her Province, she went to the marriage bed of dissolute royalty in France. Her brother-in-law, the Sun King, knew how to value her keen wit and surprising energy. Good German thrift and a level head evoked, it is said, a companionship between them that for once was not rooted in amorous dalliance.

Leave the rivers of romance now, and come with me to

mountains and valleys. Munich of superlative delights—the mad Ludwig's glittering castles, so eerie on their shining heights, almost a stone's throw from the city. If you thrill to *Tannhauser*, climb the Wartburg at Eisenach, to its Hall of Song, there bend your head when you enter Martin Luther's tiny study, with the inkspot on the wall, still vivid in its expression of his sturdy impatience and rebellion.

Further down by the market place, open the garden gate to the house of Johann Sebastian Bach—and let your wonder grow. In one room are grouped many instruments of his century. The courteous guide showed me a small pipe-organ, quite like those in the St. Cecilia primitives, with the golden tubes upright against the wall. Imagine my joy at being asked to try it; he was eager to exhibit the mellow if faint tone, still vibrant after decades! Could I do less than essay the Pilgrims' Chorus in such a room? Gradually I noticed a small crowd gather, and as I swung into that grand old Luther's hymn *A Mighty Fortress Is Our God*, their voices took up the inspiring measures with gusto! It was a moment I shall never forget. One elderly woman pressed forward, hand outstretched. "Are you not Die Farrar?" said she. I said I was. She beamed! "I sat for years at the Royal Opera and loved every performance you sang. We Berliners have never forgotten you!" Can you imagine what this simple statement did to me?

Continue your journey of delights to Nuremberg, and sit in Hans Sachs' workshop—look out of his window across the way; perchance young Walther and his charming Evchen may still linger in the doorway. Bayreuth is on your path— and the Wagner dynasty continues the glorious precepts of the Master.

And why have I taken the reader on a few jaunts that might well represent a tourist excursion folder? Because living in, and with, these beauties, the singer's soul will awaken to fuller understanding of those Lieder images, without which he will lose half of the kingdom of song. When, in a narrow view of patriotic outburst—so-called—the student or teacher disclaims the need of European erudition, do not hearken to such foolish talk. We are not concerned alone with vocal fundamentals which are indeed necessary and can be learned anywhere, but are only one part of the artist's pattern to complete himself. Education along all lines but adds to the richness of one's background. The advantages of travel with open eye and enthusiastic spirit are without parallel. Germany happens to be my preference. My youth was spent there; the friends I made, and my early successes, naturally predispose me to this country and its people. I had enjoyed Paris—but my early auditions at the opera had resulted in no stable invitation to return until after I had made a name in Germany. Then, too, the complete loyalty to Lehmann kept me, till the war outbreak, a busy pupil in her hands.

I had never sung professionally in Italy, and only in private houses in London; which absence from the operatic stage in both places grieves me now. Several tentative offers were made for Covent Garden. The extremely low fee I could have accepted—for the charming opera house has no vast dimensions to permit American intake and engagement fees; but the choice of repertoire each time was so unfavorable I could not see the value of underestimating my own worth in roles not suitable. As for Italy, though I loved the land and frequently spent part of my vacations there, I was always apprehensive of the all-too frank expression on the part of the "galleria," as they call the lusty enthusiasts in the top rows under the ceiling. If the great Caruso had been protested, why should I leave my adoring Berliners to invite a possible heartache?

When advantageous proposals were advanced for South America, I was already busy with the movies in California—the summer here being the gay winter season below the equator. Strangely enough, my most ardent movie fans were from South America; they repeatedly called for more and more roles featuring me in a Spanish type. I once asked Lucrezia Bori what might be the reason for my association with so Latinized an impression? This charming artist, who was often a lovely Micaela to my Carmen, and had amiably shared *Bohème* and *Manon* in our joint repertoire, made an interesting reply. She said in Spain there was a gypsy type with dark hair and grey eyes like my own; which, added to my usual vivacity of the screen picturizations, easily conveyed the impression that I, too, might be indigenous to her home country. She thought that I was the last person one might associate with the reserved manner and appearance of my own native Boston, as she knew it.

CHAPTER EIGHT

THE DAUGHTER

1932-1933

ON MANY a wearisome tournèe, while engaged in singing, I had amused myself with verses and translations of
songs. During the time of the war and its aftermath, till the
bitterness had subsided, I used my own English versions of
the German Lieder, thus rendering them unobjectionable to
the public at large.

My interest in translations of the German Lieder led me to
continue the same service for the French and Italian selections
on my concert programs. And above all, the list of Kreisler's
fascinating and popular Viennese violin pieces, spurred me on
to fresh effort in not only contributing verses, but vocal arrangements of them, as well. Thus, *The Old Refrain, Schön
Rosmarin, Liebeslied, Caprice Viennois* to mention a few,
have become available in the singer's repertoire. I found myself easily adapting the musical measures to such expressions
of euphony, as would facilitate pleasant and facile tones; for
many translations are all too literal and indicate a scholar's

215

contact with the dictionary, rather than acquaintance with the restrictions of a tender larynx.

I have many godchildren scattered over a large area, several belonging to the earlier generation of Gerryflappers with whom I keep in affectionate contact. Christmas and Easter have been propitious moments to hold them in especial regard. And for them, I have written original compositions of both music and verse suitable to their years and juvenile efforts.

All these pleasant trifles entitle me to membership in ASCAP,—that valuable organisation for the protection of the composer's interests. With an excellent rating in it and a quarterly check that always comes as an agreeable surprise, I am rather proud of this accidental excursion into an unexpected creative field.

And—as was perhaps to be expected from my early church associations—I incline very much toward sacred music despite my spectacular opera activities. As far as I know, I am the first to put an English verse and vocal arrangement to that divine Air on the G String of Bach, that seems, up to the present, to have invited only instrumental combination. I gave it the title of "Supplication," and one appreciative colleague was so impressed by the noble measures set to reverent verse, that she sings it regularly in her church services.

Perhaps after our snowy, cold winters, the return to spring is so exquisite in beauty and promise that one's senses stir to a lyric expression of the heart. My hills are so lovely in all seasons, many a thoughtful mood has invited the pen. I have renewed my faith and strength often from their serenity. These verses were inspired by a pastor who sought my permission for their inclusion in his parish book, under the title:

216

"What Think Ye of Christ?"

My Christ is the sweep of the lofty elm
That reaches the deep blue sky,
The swaying nest of a fearless bird
In its tiny cradle so high.

My Christ is the shining star above,
The cooling breeze of the night,
The afternoon of a glowing sun,
As it sinks in a misty night.

My Christ is the eye of a little child,
With its earnest glance so clear,
The touch of a dear and friendly hand,
The heart that knows no fear.

My Christ is the sparkling waterfall
That tumbles in merry play,
The fragrant blush of a sweet wild rose,
That brightens a summer day.

My Christ is music and human song,
The marble dreams that delight,
The treasured page of a favorite book,
Or a palette of colors so bright.

My Christ is the beauty of gardens fair,
The lilac of early Spring,
The pungent sap of the evergreen,
A humming-bird's jewelled wing.

My Christ is the softness of falling snow,
That dazzles in shining white,
The moon aloft in silver sheen
As she sheds her radiant light.

My Christ is the growing, happy thing
Be it Earth, Soul, Spirit, or Heart;
For all are His gracious gifts bestowed
And of His Kingdom, our part.

Echoes of my childhood spoke in the urge to write, although for months I would lay aside an idle pen that lacked any incentive. I could not fabricate; it had to flow easily and from a given mood within.

I began to think back upon many an hour at my mother's side, and her discourse upon the esoteric. As long as I can remember, her own daydreams had been colored by sensitive introspection, her actions guided by what she termed her intuition. I realize now how delicately and naturally psychic were her forces, then untrained but nonetheless potent in her; which to my mind's satisfaction clarifies, in these latter reflections, much that was hidden from me as a younger woman. Then, I was not sympathetic to her many peregrinations among astrologers, numerologists, horoscope experts, palmists, and the like. Yet she deduced a working ratio, apparently, from the whole outline, and many of those predictions actuated her daily conduct and beliefs, to our later good. As the subject matter was always myself and the career she ambitiously visualized, there was of course, no clash in the family interests.

Now I have learned, through the years, that much must be

218

taken on faith, and have drawn my own small measure of strength from the miracles of Nature about me. My lack of spiritual eyes to "see" at that time, delayed my real interest in the study and belief of a definite Life pattern which we all must sooner or later recognize. The manner of its performance rests with ourselves.

After mother's death, I was continually advised—from far and nearby strangers—to get in touch with some recognized medium, as she greatly desired to give me a message. I must confess several reasons urged me to disregard these communications, save in courteously acknowledging their reception. A vivid impression of those langourous Swamis, waving eloquent hands before enraptured Boston ladies, rose before me. The hysteria of a friend whose agonized search among charlatans for a long-lost daughter, totally unfitting her for the responsibilities of daily existence, was a sad experience. I saw business men hang upon occult advice to support their Wall Street business ventures. Not much of spiritual value there. Family groups at sad variance in their resentment at any cult save their own, and deaf to reasonable discussion. Perhaps my greatest disinclination came from the fear of exploitation.

In her lifetime, my mother had approached this interesting subject on another plane, clothing her thoughts in terms more nearly approximating a search for guidance and character development. She had always averred that if it were at all possible to communicate from the Beyond, she would do all in her power to be near me, in such a manner as would convince me of her identity. Therefore, when professional assistance was advocated, I was perhaps arrogant, certainly ignorant of Natural laws, when I replied that I needed no intermediary to open an avenue of approach. The later wonders of radio, however, gradually caused me to change my views. If by such delicate impulses this universe we know could be linked in instantaneous contact, I could indeed admit the possibility of other myriad connections affecting me, and heard by ears more attuned in recondite sensitivity of the spirit than were my own. It was I who lacked the knowledge and serenity to provide the proper attitude for those rarified forces that vibrate on high arcana. Nonetheless, I avoided all professional mediums myself, and bided my time for whatever subsequent moment might be propitious for psychic experience.

Meanwhile, things were not going any too well with our poor old world in general. Franklin D. Roosevelt had won a smashing victory in his first campaign for the Presidency. Even the most partisan Republican could admire his party's platform. It won the votes of the majority, but was to come to no fruition in subsequent activity. I did not vote for the genial spell-binder, but I did not wish his program ill. Unhappily this Messiah tampered with his previous concepts, and soon the miasma of politics began to choke and dismay the people. Great unrest ensued. Factions were divided, class hatreds were engendered in a most unpleasant and unnecessary fashion. The unemployed ran into frightening numbers of distressed millions, while the most sympathetic of tax payers and perplexed committees found no solution for permanent rehabilitation. Of course, the money world became chaotic, in consequence of which those organizations and institutions sustained by generous private enterprise encountered serious difficulties.

The opera was one such luxury to suffer. It had always been a center of social brilliance and display, but, at the same time, had afforded the local public ample opportunity to enjoy the finest musical talent available. We were therefore not a little embarrassed to see this erstwhile splendid association about to go on the rocks for want of financial support. Our millionaires were in tight places themselves and could no longer continue their lavish subscriptions. Therefore, the unedifying harangues and pleas for help began to punctuate the entr'actes, while artists and opera groups pledged their efforts to "save the opera" and all that its cultural value had meant in the last half century.

The following urgent message found me at my country place. I had attended a performance and received a hearty recognition from the audience, as I walked down the aisle to my seat.

The great enthusiasm and love again demonstrated other evening at Metropolitan gives me the courage to ask you to come to Metropolitan next matinee to say few words to audience and radio public in behalf of campaign stop I know that a word from our beloved Geraldine will do more than anything else to win the support of opera lovers. Don't refuse. Please call me. Many thanks. Much love.

(Signed)   LUCREZIA.

I responded, of course, for that old house of glorious memories was, and is, inexpressibly dear to me.

It was at a matinee of *Parsifal* that I elected to appear upon that stage I had not trod since my farewell in 1922. Dollar bills began to rain upon me. The glorious-voiced Marion Telva waved a thousand dollar check that an eager usher brought to me. Rosa Ponselle telephoned her pledge. Had the intermissions been as long as the performance, I feel sure we should have attained in cash and pledges, the entire sum, then and there, for the opera's guarantee. The Committee were striving for $300,000. The thunderous welcome nearly unnerved me, and upon retirement to Mr. Gatti's office, I was as exhausted as if I had sung a *Butterfly* performance.

The next exciting event of that season was the announcement of Scotti's farewell. This veteran and beloved figure of opera had carried on to the close of a long and brilliant career—New York and London having known him best. In a superb characterization of the Chinese villain in *L'Oracolo*, he sang a final adieu. The packed house rose as one cheering mass, to clap and yell itself hoarse in affectionate tribute to a favorite artist. Despite long years in American activity, his method of communication was an expressive combination of fluttering hands and corrugated brow, as he stammered through a weird vocabulary of English as he had devised it. It was an entertainment in itself to assist at his fluent but well-nigh incomprehensible linguistic exhibition.

Soon after, he came out to the country to spend the day and in particular to see my father, for whom he had always entertained a real affection. I got together as many of the opera comrades as I could muster, for a gay jamboree that gladdened his heart. Always the gallant, and an immaculately tailored figure, he was easily the "star performer." To many a friendly query as to why he did not open a studio—and impart to our younger generation some of his fine traditions— he would shrug expressive shoulders, and, behind the haze of innumerable cigarettes, remark: "Why I give lessons? Always old singers open studios—no—Scotti not opening studios. Scotti not *learn* to feel—Scotti *born* to feel . . . . nothing to teach."

Perhaps he was right. Privately I added a reservation. Being the most indolent of easy-going Latins, seldom visible before a late luncheon hour, and dreadfully fussed if early morning rehearsals necessitated appearance before noon, he would have hated organized routine with pupils coming and going; then, too, the hours would seriously interfere with bridge, after-noon calls, and evening parties. No, our debonair Scotti was probably more than wise in following his own instinct for a *dolce far niente* existence.

Some years before I had been approached in the following communication for talking pictures:

FIFTH OF FEBRUARY, 1921.

DEAR MISS FARRAR:

The first opportunity to make permanent record of your great art by means of

TALKING MOTION PICTURES

I offered this morning to you, through your secretary, Miss Ketrick.

This is positively the first approach made to any operatic artist on this matter; and before we go any farther with it I do want you to see the pictures for yourself; they will tell you far more than I, or anyone else, could do.

If you will telephone me at the Hotel Seville, Madison Square 5600, and let me know when you could come to the private projection room—it is within a stone's throw of the Metropolitan Opera House—I will have a special run for you; and can arrange

223

for it at any time that will meet your convenience within the next day or two.

The idea is: That you should appear in costume—suitable background and properties supplied—and sing your arias from such operas as you yourself select. The record and the motion picture are in exact accord; and there is thus a permanent record of your voice and appearance for simultaneous reproductions in theatres throughout the world.

This opens to you motion picture opportunities that have never been presented before.

This special opportunity had not been placed on the market—although the market is already prepared for it. That you should make the initial picture—that is, talking picture—be the American woman to flash this great advance to world-wide fame for yourself, is an idea that cannot fail of its appeal to your good sense.

This whole business is so new, so astounding in its effects that we can only say: "Seeing is believing." It will take but a half-hour of your time to come to the projection room; and then you will see and hear for yourself.

Will you kindly let me know promptly if you are interested. There is no obligation whatever incurred in making an appointment to view the pictures; but you will naturally understand that we cannot hold the proposition open indefinitely.

Sincerely yours,

(Signed)   V. B.

As I was very busy then with recordings, opera and concerts, I had not been won over to what then seemed a particularly venturesome innovation in screen activities.

I forget now what may have been my response, but it was not until much later that leisure and a certain curiosity overcame my aversion to the newer interest of radio broadcasts.

I prepared for them in great trepidation. That first Packard

Hour and General Motors program were, I am told, very successful in recording my voice and personality; but I died a hundred deaths, nervous and ill at ease before the microphone and its restrictions. For my part, I was hampered by the newness of it all, and the mechanical delicacy gave me, as artist, a minimum reaction. I missed the warm response of listeners in the flesh. Innumerable ears did not mean quite as much to me as multitudinous eyes would, gazing on me from eager faces, communicating their magnetism to my own.

In the matter of mechanical adjustments I could quite appreciate the amusing story told me by the young man who handled the controls. He had had the honor of conducting Schumann-Heink's first broadcast. Ernestine arrived, in robust humor and exuberance, confidently prepared to deliver an authoritative recital program in her usual superb style and Carnegie Hall manner. Before the awed young man could half venture to explain the little differences in modulation, to be observed in tonal adjustment to the mechanics, she had waved him aside with grandmotherly tolerance. She knew her métier and no stripling needed to advise her in its performance. The evening proceeded. She was jubilant at what she conceded to be her best effort. But upon arrival home, she was greeted by the family with something less than tepid enthusiasm. Frank inquiry on her part disclosed that the major part of the broadcast had been a disappointing series of sputters, crackles, gurgles and blasts. She rushed back to the studio. Yes, such had been the surprising result of practically blowing out all fuses at the release of that great Niagara of sound! Now she understood why the control expert was so eager to indicate those precautions necessary in wooing the microphone. With unexpected humility and fervor, she then and there put herself into such understanding with the mechanics as to safeguard those broadcasts that kept her busy and popular for many years.

When the Victor Company inaugurated its present system of electrical recording, I also had an interesting peep into improved laboratory activities. The earlier manner in its simpler method had allowed each individual a perfect vocal reproduction of the timbre and dynamics. These shadings were effected by the singer, in retreating a few steps backward when volume or emphasis in high tessitura were likely to endanger an homogeneous thread on the smooth surface of the recording plate. This procedure, therefore, in no wise resulted in a change of vocal timbre, but did subdue the quantity somewhat without attendant hollow amplification to increase volume. The danger line for sopranos and tenors usually lay in the upper reaches between G and high C in *forte* passages.

However, John McCormack and Alma Gluck were the outstanding singers who seemed to have no difficulty in accommodating themselves to such high frequency, as I understood it then. I have heard it said that John sat comfortably in a chair before the machine, unloosened a tight cravat, and sang easily and faultlessly into the old-fashioned tin funnel of that early period. His sales were fabulous and rightly so, by reason of beautiful performances of facile song.

The laboratory experts were always patient and helpful, though often not in accord with the singers in the eventual findings, as illustrated by the proof-records. The vocalist, of course, was intent upon the beauty of sound and his particular interpretation of the selection; but when this entailed, by reason of emotional effort, a departure from prescribed mechanical smoothness, the disagreement could become acute between artist and operator.

At any rate, with electrical recording raised to a high degree of fidelity, I was asked to re-make some of my earlier operatic records. I looked at the kindly official who brought me the invitation in surprise. My royalties were still going on from the earlier repertoire, and I was proud of those first Red Seal efforts that had faithfully reported the voice of my very youthful spirits and expression. Therefore, hoping he might understand my point of view, I said frankly, "Why do you ask me to try to duplicate myself of twenty years ago? That is not humanly possible!" Much astonished, he remarked, "But why not? You are singing beautifully—in concerts, to be sure—but what would be the difference?"

I despaired of making him see there *was* a vast difference in the psychological undercurrent that sustained the song and my artistic maturity in another field. I was no longer that exuberant, carefree singer of tempestuous emotions, but a seasoned, cautious vocalist of more delicate line and intention. The opera urge was gone. I was more than willing to record from my repertoire of Lieder to which I had dedicated myself since those years divorced from the Metropolitan. To make a long story short, he shook his head in disagreement, but agreed this decision was better than none, perhaps.

I applied myself with patience and eagerness to the recording. Some of it was sandwiched in between a minstrel group of hot jazz and lively trained canaries! In Studio A of other days this was never the procedure, and I wondered long—but

227

not loud—how the operator would manage the faithful reproductions of three such divergent attractions! I soon found
that a guiding barometer set the vibratory pulse, whether for
jazz or Geraldine! When that indicative red needle wavered
too far to the left or right, into the danger zone, skilled hand
and eye noted the oscillation and returned it to the smaller area
of given chart measure. There seemed no perception demanded
of the ear, but a keen eye reaction for detection of the surface
variations on the recorded plate.

Results of the essay were not unpleasing to me, save a little
too much monotony of color outline. My particular timbre of
voice had always been of irregular fluidity, and these highly
individual qualities were being mechanized into an uninteresting smooth, *sound* wave; which is vastly different, to the
singer's ear, from a *tone* wave. These finer shadings were to
be overcome, to the operator's ear trained for laboratory perfection, by lending amplification rather than intensity. It gave
me the impression of a resilient rubber band stretched too far
for inherent pliancy and quality.

Vainly I tried to explain to the agreeable co-operator this
basis for my own renditions. The value of the tonal phrase as
I felt it guided by an inner emotion, meant careful attention
on his part toward the mechanical interpretation of a smooth
groove. It was not unlike the spectacle of a patient with a
broken leg trying to exercise within a fifty yard distance,
wherein every step must be timed and gaited in equal proportions. The natural impulse must vary according to more sensitive conditions of the individual. I was not bellowing opera
dramatics, but voicing the lyric measures of restrained vocal
effects; tone purity and the translucent coloring of the imagery
228

were the salient results desired. There was no point in repetition of these divergences.

By way of argument, the studio official brought me a Marion Talley record. This charming but tenuous soprano voice was pushed to the amplified limit of large sound—and the tone beauty suffered in consequence, sacrificed to noisy volume.

It is interesting to note that ten years later, my proof records, by default of circulation are being carefully re-recorded for an exclusive Collector's Club, whose subscribers profess, far and near, to find them admirable examples and of great value to their catalogues. I feel, however, they could have been much lovelier, if the operator's ear had been better paired with his eye, for complete survey of the individual endowment and careful re-recording at the moment of delicate nuances.

CHAPTER NINE

I

The Daughter

1934-1938

WHILE the opera was laboring under financial difficulties, the same situation prevailed with the venerable Philharmonic Symphony Society. The magic of Toscanini was seconded by several conductors as guests who shared the responsibility of its musical integrity; in consequence, the performances were not always happily balanced, nor the performers totally obedient to the various leaders. Personally, I had a great admiration for the leadership of Bruno Walter, and would have liked to have seen him not only at this post, but placed as well at the Metropolitan for a share of the operatic duties.

The Manhattan critics and audiences had their own favorites among the several orchestra leaders. I could not agree, however, to some lesser lights, and have recently given up my Carnegie Hall seats. I might add, however, that the poor manners of the listeners are also a handicap to one's complete enjoyment, save when a martinet like Toscanini or Stokowski rises up in justifiable reproof—and thus obtains a silent respect. I find it an interesting commentary to note the hysteria over conductors sometimes based on other grounds than musical appreciation—to judge by the scant attention accorded those concerts where there are no great names. If one has been a constant listener to a Muck, Mahler, Toscanini, or Walter, however, can one respect the crowd's endorsement of mediocre lights, who slip about very uneasily in great men's shoes?

Shortly before Toscanini's retirement from the Philharmonic (which was conceded by the general public to be a definite farewell in America—and, no doubt, hopefully fostered by opposition parties), I was approached to do the same service in solicitation that I had done for the Metropolitan; it was a distressing moment where a general begging campaign for many fine musical organizations was the order of the day. It is a particularly embarrassing thing to do. I think I would rather be a Fuller brush salesman and get kicked out, or invited in, on an impersonal commercial basis, for inspection of my wares. However, I could not well refuse in this case. I suggested a simple statement to the Committee that I urge every interested listener to send only one dollar toward this worthy object—surely a modest plea, likely to appeal. If several million listeners were so inclined to this democratic contribution—or even a fraction reduced to a few hundred thousands, this gesture might well complete the drive toward the amount desired. But I was dissuaded from this naming a particular sum, and half-heartedly read the speech prepared by the conservative Committee in its usual stereotyped fashion.

It was very polite and concise—but lacked totally the cayenne of my own honest enthusiasm.

Now there was to come a very interesting excursion into the radio field, wherein I could employ my own brand of vigor and enthusiasm. The restrictions would be only a time limit. Friends of mine, in a casual dinner conversation, and interested in music as well as industry, proposed my name in connection with the sponsorship of the Saturday matinee of opera broadcasts. Their enthusiasm was based on the unusual feature of my former Metropolitan activities, my present connection with our professional world, and the affection and respect I still enjoyed from a public at large, despite retirement from actual singing duties.

As my personal relations had been pleasantly social with the President of the Lambert Company, Mr. J. L. Johnston, we came directly and verbally to terms agreeable to both of us. Due to such happy approach, there was no commercial intermediary to harass either party to the season's agreement, and I was given full play, in my material, to turn back to some of opera's most colorful pages and bring to the listeners the pictures of past and present glories.

In an especially equipped loge in the upper tier of the opera house, there was arranged for my use a little salon such as would please any woman in her own home. A special engineer was placed beside me, with his intricate and sensitive receiving board; I, in turn, sat at my diminutive Steinway, hauled in from my attic in the country, and dear reminder as well of the many journeys it had companioned me, in the Pullman private car. I wrote all the material used and interjected musical phrases and vocal illustrations whenever the occasion war-

232

Farewell Concert, Carnegie Hall, 1931

Miss Farrar and Milton J. Cross during
Metropolitan Opera Broadcast

ranted. It was interesting also to note that, as our quarters were miniature, I had to reduce all the musical part of the entertainment to the confines of one octave; the scale from lower to medium B flat. Only the vibrations in this range were those easily handled by the engineer without blasts and gurgles; it was quite remarkable that we obtained, even so, anything like a smooth tone and expressive phrasing. But re-recorded examples via remote control, sent me by interested friends, were a delightful souvenir of the occasions and also excellent records to add to my own collection of such a novel activity on my part. Illustrious colleagues frequently joined me for thumb-nail sketches—Bori, Pons, Martinelli, Ponselle, to name a few.

Our first broadcast was on Christmas Day, at a children's matinee of the ever popular *Hansel and Gretel*. Both music and story were a tender recollection of the same composer's lovely *Koenigskinder*—and carried me back to Memory-Land. It was shortly after that I was privileged to announce the exciting welcome offered Kirsten Flagstad, on her debut as Sieglinde in *Die Walküre*. No preliminary press had enlarged upon what was to be the "find" of this, and subsequent seasons. It is an old story now what magnificent aid she lends to Melchior and Schorr, herself an admirable partner in Valhalla's saga, as the Wagner repertoire which enlists their services at present writing is the Metropolitan's most complete and satisfying unit. One must, in justice to the record, add the name of Branzell, the noble contralto, also a favorite, to complete this quartette of pre-eminent singers.

For reasons best known to her capricious self, Ponselle has wearied of her rightful repertoire, to our general regret, and

233

seems determined to devote herself more and more to the concert platform. A supreme Norma, fiery Gioconda, classic Donna Anna—not easily forgotten. When paired with Marion Telva's superlative organ in *Norma* this duet was not eclipsed even by the phenomenal Caruso-Scotti *Forza del Destino* record of unforgettable artistry. Both women gave thrilling exhibition of superb voices in the *bel canto* tradition so seldom to be heard nowadays. Were it not for the consistently fine singing and musicianship of Elizabeth Rethberg, as eminent in the Italian roles as in her native German ones, we should fare poorly in the lyric repertoire. Since Bori has retired— and nobody has assumed the laurel she relinquished—there is pressing need for a stellar attraction in the French and Italian offerings.

It was also my sad duty to announce, at one of the broadcasts, the death of the greatly beloved Marcella Sembrich. She had endeared herself to American opera lovers over a long period of years, as artist and teacher. I noted her passing with reference to the *Marriage of Figaro* of my earlier recollections, when, with Eames and Scotti, we shared the triumph of an almost perfect revival under Mahler. As Cherubino, coquetting between these two adorable women, I had a very special delight in the performance.

I was eager to invite Mary Garden, among other illustrious guests, to our interviews. She had come to town and sent me a loge for her lecture on Debussy—a rare enjoyment graced by a personality still vibrant and unusual. It was not my pleasure, however, to have her, since conflicting dates carried her to distant engagements.

It has been the accepted fact in opera circles that rival sopranos and tenors must necessarily be at each other's throats and reputations. The wild conjectures and spicy gossip would seem to be part of the glamour surrounding the public favorites. I believe Mary Garden shared with me (since neither of us has ever been accused of vacuum above the eyebrows!) the sporting instinct to profit from whatever value the credulous public drew from the headlines. Since such fire must run its course, let it flame toward the box-office, rather than quench it with ineffectual observations or denials toward a back-fire. Like a mighty Niagara, the Press always has the last word.

Both of us have invited more than the usual share of gratuitous speculation and mis-information, with a good measure and reports of a personal nature thrown in, from the grandstand. However, with the Metropolitan and Manhattan companies in animated concurrence, even the artists felt the impetus, while the rivalry was stimulating and beneficial to both houses.

We exchanged written messages infrequently. Once aboard a boat, bound for Paris, she delivered herself of a pithy observation anent *Julien*—then our most recent novelty and most recent production. Her remarks coincided with my own sentiments—not favorable. Once at the Goldwyn Studio, in Fort Lee, we met and posed with the astute Sam Goldwyn, during her filming of *Thais*. Her contract had concluded when my season began in the same locale. We eyed each other politely, but had no occasion to indulge in a lengthy conversation. I think Sam himself was not a little nervous, and relieved when his two tigress-women had not demolished the studio, so tempestuous were we supposed to be! He no doubt felt himself quite a successful animal tamer!

Garden as Thais, Louise, Le Jongleur and Melisande will

have no rivals in our decade, if ever. Two fine artists gave her superb aid in establishing many of her fine operatic portraitures under the Hammerstein regime—Renaud and Muratore.

This latter excellent singer and actor had been engaged by C. A. Ellis, my manager, to support me in a *Carmen* production on tour. He had married the lovely Cavalieri, who labored incessantly, with commendable tenacity but doubtful wisdom, toward a re-establishment as prima donna, after a brief appearance at our Metropolitan. She accompanied him back and front-stage, a pleasant figure, but delivering artistic counsel to her artist-husband that was of little value and often collided with the views of the conductor and other artists. Both of them were indefatigable press agents for themselves, but as their front-page "scoops" were based on his appearance in *Carmen*, that vehicle served him well—and did not disturb my slumbers. For the same grist served my mill at the box office, too.

Colorful as were the stories he told, there was one, however, at this ticklish time of World War difficulties, which was not quite in the picture, nor very gallant. To the effect that once at a rehearsal in my hotel sitting room he had, with calculated gaucherie, sent a photograph of the Kaiser and the Crown Prince hurtling to the floor. This story was demonstrably pure fiction. I never travelled about with the photographs of these distinguished gentlemen. Such honored and inscribed mementos always remain in the privacy of my home.

As a matter of fact, during the period of the World War and its tragic aftermath, most singers were careful to abstain from political or national comment that could draw fire from an overardent compatriot; or inject an unhappy note. While we were a large and heterogeneous musical family, at the Metropolitan, the discussion along these dangerous lines was taboo. There was no fighting on our vocal field.

My own battles—if one wishes so to designate the artist's feverish and unremitting effort toward achievement and supremacy in her elected field—were always conducted before the public in lyric measures, for the final decision. Then let the best man win! And on such terrain, he did.

II

BUT to return to my little radio booth, the event of the season, after Flagstad's acclaim, was the announcement of Mr. Gatti's retirement from the scene of his long tenure and many successes, as Manager of the Metropolitan. Herbert Witherspoon, a favorite American singer and official of the Chicago Opera Company, was elected to succeed him. In the midst of preliminaries, however, his untimely death brought forward the genial Edward Johnson as General Manager. As he was a tenor of renown, being an international as well as a local favorite, this appointment seemed propitious and agreeable to all concerned. At his side was—and still is—the astute Assistant Manager, Edward Ziegler, who had been so long Mr. Gatti's right arm.

I think Mr. Gatti had a pang of regret at leaving the scene, once his decision was made. He had on several occasions visited me in the narrow confines of the opera loge, to observe how I conducted my share of the opera broadcast. The popular announcer, Milton J. Cross, fulfilled all the more technical requirements in the next booth. Gatti was a big man and trod heavily; curious about the coils and wires scattered all over, he stumbled against the microphones, dislocating practically all the fuses, breathing loudly over my shoulder the while. On these occasions, I wondered if the listeners might not fancy that I was wheezing with laryngitis, or struggling in a fog with the hoot of a boatwhistle in the offing, so "muddy" was the reception in the sensitive microphone, under the circumstances. His remarks were priceless anent the mechanics involved, seemingly insurmountable for adequate musical reproduction.

It had been previously quite impossible to persuade him to utter a syllable on the air, but I felt this moment of his departure warranted a personal expression via the radio; and consequently undertook to convert him to the idea. I told him that I realized my arguments would, of course, be more effective if I were younger and he was still under the pleasing emotion of a fine performance of *Carmen, Butterfly*, or *Zaza*, but, in the name of old friendship and musical association, to please grant us all the favor of his consent to a brief interview with me, at the farewell matinee. I promised his part of the interview would be brief, and I would write it according to what he desired to say. I was glad he consented, and he, as well, begged me to compose what I thought would be fitting for the occasion. So I reduced his share of the verbiage to the simplest formula, a week ahead of time, for his inspection. From back-stage officials, I was told he buttonholed everyone to rehearse his careful phonetics, quite like an actor eager to perfect his role!

Fearful he might elude me at the last moment—despite his

promise—I 'phoned before the hour that I would fetch him from his office. He was waiting there, and with a deprecating shrug of massive shoulders, we made our way through the lobby to our loge. Bertha Brainard and William Rainey, those human dynamos of N. B. C., who had so kindly groomed me in my radio tasks and watched over the results with unabated and helpful interest, were on hand to help in case of impromptu jitters. At the given signal, they placed Mr. Gatti before the fearsome little box, and we were off! He covered himself with glory in carefully enunciated phrases of appreciation and farewell good wishes. Suddenly he broke into mellifluous ex tempore Italian, and concluded with a hearty smack on my cheek, after a tremendous clearing of the throat. Then we all adjourned to the lobby for Press photography. He was as excited as a boy.

Gatti could be a most entertaining person when the mood inspired; widely read, he was a mine of historical and biographical information. One time in Milan when I found myself quarantined with measles, and delayed in my plans to proceed for the cure at Salsomaggiore, he waved aside my arguments via 'phone about visiting me while "incommunicado"—and came frequently to lighten the weary waiting in the darkened sitting room, with no end of interesting chat. In New York, he was a "solitaire;" hated fuss and feathers, and, above all, fashionable gatherings which from time to time he had to grace, in view of his position. In such circumstances, he was like Toscanini, a rather glum figure in a corner, with scarcely a phrase to offer to the chatterers about him.

I have previously mentioned a reluctance toward visible

largesse; so the struggle over tips and taxi fare was sometimes rather comical to watch. On one occasion, at lunch in Paris, he was airily indifferent to our lunch check, and the recapture of hat and cane as well. It was my francs that did the trick, and my car that deposited him at his hotel. On another occasion my motor drove up behind a taxi that housed him and Scotti—also of similar indifference to largesse. The most elegant of Scarpias was constrained to separate himself from the fare, while the cumbersome Gatti walked slowly ahead, oblivious of any such trivial gesture; as Director he took precedence over the barytone!

Which brings to mind many a colorful luncheon-hour picture of the old Hotel Knickerbocker days Pavlova would come in, a retiring figure at a corner table. Tettrazini, her plump person followed by a vociferous group of compatriots. Caruso, the generous host to a horde of self-invited guests. Scotti, the solitary gourmet nearby, joining the others for coffee.

And how everyone ate! The blonde Adelina Genee would float in, a veritable "Miss Twinkletoes;" I gave her this as a nickname, so exquisite were her feet and ankles, and so beautiful was her dancing—light as the thistledown it called to mind.

III

ONE midnight I was awakened by the insistent ringing of my private phone.

A call at any unusual hour always quickened an apprehension about my father, whose home was about fifteen minutes away, at the other end of our village. His health had given me concern of late; but it was happily no alarm from that source. A stranger's voice began to inquire if it were really Miss Farrar at the end of the wire? Upon such assurance and the circumlocution of an irritating preliminary, the man said, abruptly, "Well, I'm from the Press and thought you'd probably want to know Lou Tellegen is dead—how do you feel about it, and what have you got to say?" Taken completely by surprise I replied tartly, "I have nothing to say and am not interested," and rang off.

The 'phone continued to ring repeatedly until dawn, adding nothing to soothe my humor of the moment. The following day, the curious-minded and the press hounds kept the wire humming in incessant abuse of inquiry. I left the house to escape the commotion and the attempts at interviews, to pass a few days with a friend. My father was not spared, either, in a morbid attempt to dish up some scandalous observation; of course, no news was forthcoming from him.

Mr. Tellegen had been in Hollywood for some time, and the tragic finale was to be foreseen many years before it actually came to pass. I had, in the latter years, tried to think more kindly of this man who had not only misused his talents and connections, but humiliated me and my family in shameful and ungrateful fashion. It was not alone his complete indifference to the consequences and conduct of a super-ego, and condescending approach to countless women—some of whom deserved better of him than his wretched ingratitude—but his supreme contempt for those great personages who extended a helping hand up the ladder of success all during his early career. Notably Sarah Bernhardt.

Handsome and stupid, as long as physical appeal was seconded by youth, he typified romance and adventure to the casual eye. He could be charming and well-mannered when he wished, but had the perception of a moron, and no morals whatever. It was my own unwisdom to have been misled by a delightful and bland exterior, and I blame only myself for a marriage that turned out so badly for me. For him, it was only another glamorous episode, I suppose. At any rate, I was not desirous of confiding my reflections to the press for widespread relay and conjecture. In the interim since my divorce, there had been plenty of ladies in his life, and a marriage or two as well, I believe, to keep alive his interest and justify his own ego.

I learned only later of the manner of his suicide, which seems so horrible in its sordid and degrading finale, that one would not linger over it. Less than ever was I minded to discuss it, even with friends. Despite the justifiable contempt in which I held him, it was no satisfaction to view such an end to a career that could have been happy and successful. There were many qualifications that pointed that way, but other tendencies and unfortunate surroundings were too powerful for a weak character to resist, much less overcome. How dreadful an illustration on the lesson, and ending, of the flesh-pots! I would not wish any human soul the task of working out such a tortured Karma.

I was harshly judged and criticized—naturally by those who never knew the proper details or sentiments of those concerned—for my apparent indifference and silence to the tawdry services that received their share of display in the tabloids. Some anonymous writers went so far as to send me

photographs of the ceremony, the casket, and the floral tributes, with their pencilled criticisms. It has taken years of effort
on my part to erase the many bitter memories, but I hope I
have come to a fuller realization of the rewards of tolerance
and understanding. May those tormented ashes rest in peace.

The season went on—with many pleasant social engagements interspersed with the radio broadcasts of the opera mati-
nees; but my anxiety regarding my father was to have verifica-
tion in his definite failure in health. Our companionship had
been precious, since our mutual retirement to the country.
Each day, I waited for his cheery hello, as he rolled up in his
motor for lunch. Now I noted a slower step and pulse, foreign
to his usual robust energy. At his suggestion, we consulted
our family physician. Immediate hospitalization was the verdict. Two operations were the outcome; from the latter, he
never recovered, falling asleep quietly in my arms, after many
weeks of suspense.

And now a curious trend of thought began to awaken
within me, with his passing. Upon the loss of my mother, I had
never for a moment worried about her entrance into the realm
of the Great Beyond. She had been so remarkable in vitality,
so filled with initiative, that unconsciously I felt her entirely
capable of self-direction wherever the higher power should
beckon her; but my father had had no such clear perception—
or, shall we say, faith—in the after-life. He had often voiced
his definite belief in the dissolution of all human identity, once
this earthly body had ceased to vibrate along material lines. I
couldn't quite agree to this conclusion, though, as he said,
neither of us could prove our contentions. He had worshipped
my mother, and the thought of her death without faith and

consolation of a later reunion—somewhere, somehow—seemed to me a sad outlook to nourish. Therefore, upon his own death, I own I was very worried about him in particular. He had always been so confiding, so vital a part of my later background and responsibility, I could not bear to think of the possibility of his spiritual bewilderment; that is, if such a thing were possible in a higher sphere.

I am wholly untrained to analyze psychic force, or to penetrate into the delicate and mysterious fancies (or otherwise) of the imagination along these lines. But my mother's early freedom of thought and action, well in advance of her time and circle, had left me with an open mind; and affectionate concern, perhaps, provided a receptive soil for any demonstration or relay of messages that would afford me satisfaction on his behalf.

At any rate, the close friend whose natural forces seem happily attuned to such procedure was, one day shortly after my father's funeral, at lunch with me. Father's usual chair was vacant but we spoke freely of him, and as if he were to join us presently. Suddenly her cheeks paled as her eyes were suffused with happy tears. And when a deeper flush succeeded her pallor, I asked her what the matter was. She said, "Your father spoke to me clearly—and I seem to see him smiling at us from his chair. He says you are not to worry, that he never dreamed his present habitation could be so harmonious and fair; he would not return to be earthbound if he could. You are to have no worry but believe that all comes out right in the end; do your part in your daily life as best you can!"

This was so like my father's vernacular, I could almost hear his voice. And whether or not the reader is inclined toward such indefinite manifestation, I admit my heart was lighter for this assurance, in which I am pleased to believe.

I was to have later evidences of watchful love and care, in messages from both mother and father, though hers were counsels along the lines of endeavor and energy fitted to the incidents of my daily life. I do not expect to be so sensitive that direct communication to me is possible. I realize my driving energy and vitality mitigate against a serenity and relaxation of the will, for entrance into a rarer communion; but I am helped by a faith that if I do my best part, on this confused globe of trials and tribulations, I do not give undue concern about the hazards of the After Life; especially for that one, replete with horrendous penalties for the frailty of poor humans, as prescribed in the narrow ritual of our forefathers.

From this digression, let me resume the retrospection and souvenirs of some of my colleagues.

IV

AMONG popular singers of an earlier decade was the giant Czech tenor, Leo Slezak. A most agreeable comrade and excellent artist, he was bubbling over with high spirits and dearly loved a joke. His two volumes of reminiscences are well worth any reader's attention, and he could laugh as well when the joke was on himself! My favorite among many is his narrative of his first guest engagement in Berlin. Called there to replace a favorite singer, at the last moment he was poured into the *Lohengrin* armor, his long legs sewed into the proper hose, the helmet placed upon a curly wig that gave him the foolish look of a big Kewpie, the while the conductor hurriedly showed him the "cuts" used for the evening's performance. Young, and eager to please, he stepped from the swan boat and began, a little nervously, that difficult address to the stage bird, which does not move till the last note is done. While German audiences are less prone to a spasmodic endorsement of a performer than their more emotional Southern cousins, nevertheless, he says even their growing frigidity could be sensed; it was due to the "home troupe" that he got before the curtain at all to make a salute! What was his chagrin the next morning to read in the most important journal, the following resumé: "Herr Slezak came to sing *Lohengrin;* like the hero, no one knew from where—and, worse still—why! He bleated like an old man and presented himself as a shivering maiden; if he had in the high register what is lacking in the lower voice, one might expect a fairly indifferent medium scale of a none too remarkable voice." And so on. It would take more than this to squelch his determination, however, and he made of himself a first-class singer. At present, no German film is quite so rollicking without his genial personality, massive and mirth-provoking! When I was last in Berlin he was admirable in operetta, still a fine artist in the very abundant flesh. His young son, Walter, is well known in operetta to our American audiences, and is a charming lad.

There are many amusing tales that leak out from the privacy of the prima donna's diary, or backstage gossip. One favorite singer was asked, by a snobbish Fifth Avenue hostess, what her fee was for a musicale. She replied: "Two thousand dollars." The hostess ejaculated a supercilious correction:

246

"But you are not expected to mingle with the guests!" Where-upon the sprightly artist with much more finesse than her questioner, replied: "Oh—in that case, my fee will be half the original amount."

Private parties are not always a social event for the artist; but in Paris, it is—or was—a most charming rapprochement. The host, or hostess, usually would meet the singer upon arrival with an exquisite bouquet—while dangling to its berib-boned beauty would be the envelope with the check and a few written words of pleasant commendation and thanks. In Germany, more ceremony ensued, but the genuine music lovers were quiet and attentive with real appreciation for programs well rendered. The fees, too, could be generous and the hospitality warm. New York was not quite so sure of itself, and the usual entertainment of this kind was either a fabulous splurge, with several costly shining lights, or an intimate circle after a dinner or tea, with women predominating.

I personally disliked the usual run of such parlor musicales, and avoided them when I could. Of course, the perennial Bagby Mornings were an institution at the old Waldrof Astoria. They were the finest of their kind, before or since; but Monday mornings at eleven-fifteen was nonetheless a sad hour to view a popular tenor or glamorous soprano! How much apprehension we might have saved ourselves, had we realized then that a good part of the audience was quite as sleepy as the singers! I think the most wide-awake moment was when a woman artist burst onto the scene in some lux-urious fur or unusual frock to intrigue the feminine element among the listeners.

On one occasion, a singer, more notorious for her jewels

247

than her vocal renditions, was engaged for a private party. All the women were agog at the thought of viewing at close range the superb decorations of the diva—and much speculation ensued as to the donors of what, where and how. Paired with her was a male singer of momentary acclaim; the program offered familiar concert and operatic excerpts in solos and duets. To the irritation of the hostess and chagrin of the curious women, the artist appeared in a simple black frock— without a single glittering jewel to provoke scandalous conjecture. Far lovelier in such classic simplicity, she infuriated these harpies by a genuine impulse to sing, rather than exhibit herself as a living jewel casket. Her ease of manner and charm spoke volumes for inherent good taste.

Expensive fiddlers and pianists usually had a soporific effect despite their famous names. I know that on one occasion there was a great craning of necks when I appeared in a Lanvin *robe de style* of pastel blue, with rows of sable tails cascading from silver lace, supplemented by a huge sable muff, while a turban of Paradise feathers waved above my dark curls . . . an effect of Madame de Pompadour, in her best style. The get-up represented in cost more than the generous fee of the morning; but it was an excellent mode of réclame, and had wide repercussion. Little attention was given to my vocal efforts.

I never begrudged a penny for a handsome wardrobe, on or off stage. I had earlier visions of the beautifully gowned Nordica and Eames. American women are smart and realize this value I think more fully than some European singers who deny themselves a complete visual success. After all, the eye is first in its reaction to a stage picture. Lily Pons, at present, is an outstanding example of exquisite grace and taste. When she steps onto the platform, she is a vision of soigné loveliness.

Some of our larger girthed vocalists do strange things with head veils, floating ribbons, or riotous flower effects, and Mt. Everest moves upon the scene, in consequence. If only they would patronize, and listen to, a first-class dressmaker! Lines and color combinations are so important, particularly when designed for the footlight and distance effects in concert halls or opera arenas. A short skirt of voluminous tulle is delightful on a whirling dancer, but the same is an unhappy inspiration for the concert platform where the motionless vocalist appears to be rising, on two stilts, from a cellophane laundry tub. I know—from sad experience—for I essayed such an effect long ago, with the innovation of the all-too-revealing tunic.

It has often been said—and the men have liked to believe—perhaps—that women dressed for their approbation. But I do not agree to this; I dressed, for my part, primarily for my public and always because I personally love pretty and unusual things; to this day, my extravagances are in the sartorial line, and certainly would not be condoned by a male member of my family, did I now have one. While my father loved investment in cattle, land, and machinery, I conclude my own taste in feminine frippery gives me my modicum of pleasure in return; and, after all, it is one little privilege of self-expression, and so harmless a one to general society in its service of pleasing adornment.

Nowadays there is no excuse for any woman to deny herself the charming and inexpensive wardrobe combinations that can be found for the most modest purse in all stores. A little discretion and taste is all that is needed. With thought and planning, we can all be nearer the dream-woman outline every feminine heart yearns to incorporate. A new frock spruces anyone anew, and a jaunty spring hat acts like a cocktail—ask any woman!

How important for harmonious ensemble are the décor and lighting for opera *mise-en-scène*.

Joseph Urban, the Viennese designer of lush Ziegfeld Follies, was brought to the stodgy podium of our Music Temple, rumor said, by the connoisseur Otto Kahn, who had more than a passing acquaintance with Melpomene, Terpsichore, and Apollo, along with his banking interests. It did our house good to be refurbished under Urban's hand, and discard in several instances the decrepit hangings that had hung for decades so limp and long over the heads of reigning songsters, whose concern had been chiefly for their superb vocalism.

Meanwhile, a new interest was being injected in the opera repertoire, for acting was paired with voice, with the advent of the fascinating Calvé. Mary Garden and I carried out later even more of a determined pattern of the vocal-dramatic combination, so that we were termed "singing actresses." The departure was not always condoned by the musical scribes. There were dire predictions about our frequent betrayal of the *bel canto*. Which *bel canto*, by the way, may need an explanatory "aside", since I have been asked so frequently what was meant by the term:

Bel canto literally means *beautiful singing* and comes from the fundamentals of voice training as practiced and understood by the Italian singers. Their mellifluous tongue, based on the open vowels, seldom interrupted in its liquid flow by the harsher consonants of the Northern speech, already predisposes the throat for freedom of action together with an easy scale of exercises for control, elasticity, and power. Porpora, a great singing teacher of the Seventeenth Century, is quoted as saying: "Give me a voice working for five years on a sheet of exercises devoted to *bel canto* and my pupil will sing anything with unfailing beauty and mastery of tone production." It is to be remembered, however, that the voice alone was involved in such advice for its perfection. And where today will we find any student willing to study even five months in such concentrated fashion?

The mighty Wagner music dramas have always called for a fusion of voice and action, but in such measured indications and *leit motif* observances that most of the statuesque interpreters have needed only to perfect a "count" system of memory for motion and declamation. This was called the Bayreuth tradition, and so detailed upon the scores of the Master that no respectful singer needed to exert an ounce of even a bird brain, provided he owned one, for original nuance or expression.

Nordica told me, when I was a young girl, that resistance, physical and vocal, were the indispensable assets for the big dramatic roles; and I have often had reason to reflect upon her statement, when I see the immobility, long standing or sitting postures, demanded of the Norse heroes and heroines, which is such a tax upon both nerves and voice. Nonetheless, both she and Lilli Lehmann repeatedly cautioned the proper vocal foundation for the general repertoire of any singer, as laid down in the first principles of the *bel canto* method.

This custom of Wagnerian tradition pertains to the costuming department as well. Siegfried must always wear his questionable furs, slung fore and aft, Lohengrin his pewter equipment, Parsifal the none-too-engaging shift, (with its precarious bulge over the likely paunch), and Wotan the moth-eaten eagle-wings perched above a hirsute mass, for the God's effective recognition.

I recall a performance of Bohnen as Wotan, when his lively fancy got the better of the Valhalla tradition. To our general amazement, this excellent singer and athlete, a trifle vain of his fine torso, was stripped to the waist not unlike the Olympian Jove; and looked more like a vigorous Priapus than the aging progenitor of the corpulent Brunnhilde.

The ladies in Wagner's list of heroines are also supposed to obey stringent rules, as set down by the authoritative Richard. The lovely and appealing Lotte Lehmann appeared as Elizabeth with the chin bandage draped so unbecomingly under her crown that I begged her to lay it aside. When she asked me why, I told her frankly she looked from where I sat as if she had the mumps—the effect of unfavorable stage lighting and the distance. Elsa's cloak must employ the azure of her innocent blue eyes, while the Rhine maidens float, in their machine cradles, pinioned in green crêpe and what looks like cellophane sea-weed. Kundry reclines for endless seductive measures under a canopy of cotton roses of dubious vintage, and the frolicsome Flower-maidens, ranging from one hundred to two hundred-odd pounds, startle even the habitual opera lover in their scanty "nighties" and lively gyrations.

More leeway for the imagination is permitted the heroines of the lyric repertoire. Marguerite may choose white, blue or rose for her first act dress, while the darker mood of the church will prompt a more sombre color for tragedy. As Joseph Urban had seen fit to raise a huge purple chestnut tree in the garden scene, down the center of the stage where my spinning wheel would focus all attention, I had to do some quick changes on my previous delicate-hued costume and wig, not to become a negligible phantom in his color scheme. Likewise, for the production of *Reine Fiammette*. The artist was a modernist of violent designs in the squat and shadowy curves, corners, and cupolas that seemed to me decidedly out of place in their Asiatic conception, in Renaissance Italy.

Boris Anisfeld was truly Russian, following that greater Bakst whose gorgeous iconology suited the Russian Ballet, *Boris Goudonoff* or *Ivan the Terrible* of local appeal and tradition. It was hardly applicable to the style demanded for this production, and we were greatly hampered as well by his impractical scenic impedimenta. Windows and doors were placed at angles, where no human figure could accommodate itself, illumination was practically limited to one spotlight, and the orchestra could hardly be seen and, more to the point, very faintly heard. Sanguinary magenta painted canvas drapes so stabbed the vision that in my vaporous dresses I would have been like a phantom clad in veilings had I not hastily ordered them embroidered with the sparkle of diamonds and pearls to catch such light as we could coax from the perplexed master-electrician.

In one scene, I managed to stand out as a human figure, at least, under a canopy of ghastly oversized fruit trees, in a ceremonial cloth-of-gold dress, edged with real ermine. Topped by a vivid red wig, its heavy silver crown set upon jewel-entwined braids, I did manage to create an effect of splendor in a truly horrible mélange of crude colors. I had been canny enough to plead illness at the dress rehearsal to prevent argument about these costumes, so becomingly different from the sketches provided by the artist. For in them I should have waddled about, lost in the voluminous kirtles, sleeves, shawls and ribbons designed evidently for an obsolete Czarina of all the Russias.

Before my first appearance in *Tosca*, I had coached with Sarah Bernhardt, if one could call her enthusiastic interest such. This extraordinary woman was kind, not because I was a singer—a vocation she didn't particularly admire—but because her adored son Maurice had declared I was "une belle fille et une charmante actrice lyrique." I greatly admired the composition of her first act where a huge Gothic chair, placed well down to the center of the stage, allowed a variety of plastic movements and made more of a languishing appeal in the duel of the two lovers, in their ardent embrace, as well as a picturesque frame for my slender form. In adopting this departure for my own assumption of the role, she said sadly, "Pray God you never have to do so for the same reason as I."—And then I realized that her injured knee no longer permitted her to stand erect without some rest, or relief at frequent intervals. This dauntless creature defied Time and the Elements, surviving crucial operations and the final amputation of the limb in question, without relinquishing her activities in the theatre till the end.

Along about 1916, there came to the Chicago Opera Company, where I was a guest performer, a young, modest, and unheralded singer in the person of Amelita Galli-Curci. It needed but a triumphant debut and a few performances in the coloratura domain for this charming little lady to awaken our continent to the fact that we had in her a potential star. It was a voice of rare timbre—like a pansy, in the velvet of its medium scale. A chance remark to this effect to a press reporter, was the means of bringing us together in friendly association.

Before her New York debut shortly after, in *Dinorah*, at the Lexington Avenue Opera House—where the Chicago Opera Company, under Cleofonte Campanini purveyed excellent opera, and resultant disquiet at our Metropolitan—I was questioned about Galli-Curci by one of the outstanding singers. In her early youth she, too, had had a charming coloratura scale, which had in the course of time and in an unavailing battle with the years, become a pure and lovely lyric instrument, while less happy in the realm of altitudinous flight. This defection caused her to look with a sour eye on any coloratura newcomer. With the daily headlines screaming Galli-Curci's name, still she could never remember to call her other than "that new Chicago soprano" in my hearing.

The night of the new diva's New York debut, however, our curious Metropolitan star had joined the throng of other luminaries, well down front for close observation. There they all sat, with their chattering satellites, ready for the facile condemnation of faint praise; but that night made history for the slender and appealing little figure that bowed repeatedly, in happy confusion, at the accolade of thunderous applause that came over the footlights in waves of genuine approval. Only the green-eyed monster could account for the few dissensions.

Such an occasion was repeated more recently when the winsome Lily Pons startled the Metropolitan audiences, totally unprepared for her exquisite bell-like song, that reaches upward in a fabulous high-scale. Canny Mr. Gatti had wisely refrained from advance exploitation of his newest coloratura "find," since the failure of Marion Talley to succeed was still fresh in the public memory. I felt sorry for this young girl whose career promised so well. I could have wished for her the astute and protecting guidance of a mother such as I had been fortunate enough to enjoy in early years. Meanwhile, Lily Pons has become an established favorite in our musical life. In her attractive photographs, we see the largest, softest brown eyes imaginable, and admire, as well, the tiniest feet in the world; so fairy-like indeed, that in our association as friends and neighbors, I dub her affectionately "my little Cinderella."

Could you imagine asking your favorite Brunnhilde if she had ever been a cook? That is what one curious matron did, it seems, in a social gathering given expressly to honor one of our greatest singers. To the surprise of the petrified onlookers, the artist is reputed to have quietly replied: "Oh yes. As a young girl I was employed as cook in your friend's home (mentioning the name). It was the only time her food was properly served, and her kitchen kept clean!"

It reminds me to what lengths the simple-minded and the credulous individual will go in pursuance of light-winged gossip.

Lilli Lehmann showed me the series of letters she received, while I had been absent on my first American engagement. It was the insistent appeal of a childless couple to adopt any one of the several semi-royal children I was credited with having mothered, great stress being laid upon the fact of the couples' loyalty to the Hohenzollern house. Lilli was as angry as my

256

mother was insulted. What would these dear women have said had I told them half the tales that came to my ears?

An amusing incident at the time was the visit of a restaurateur of the Royal Opera, who presented himself in full dress one very hot June morning, to petition my good will for the continuance of his official concession in that august house, serving the noble as well as the more common appetite between acts. I know he did not believe my statement that he had appealed to the wrong source for I had no intention of giving Berlin a Madame Pompadour in my person.

There was at the time a charming and whimsical Parisian tale of the singer whose connection with a personage of high degree was the basis of her successful public career. It came about that she fell in love with a young man with honorable intentions. On the eve of their wedding, she confided that the sensational tales were the invention of envious rivals, which she had had the wit to turn to her advantage, since the tide of gossip could not be stopped by denial. She assured him she would come to him on their bridal night quite the traditional maiden of unsullied virtue. However, it is regretfully noted in conclusion, the prospective husband lost his interest completely, which, he averred, had been stimulated only by the romantic belief she had been at one time "un petit morceau du roi."

I took a leaf from this little book with its peek into the psychology of the human animal. Since truth is stranger than fiction, I lost no good energy bothering with the fantastic legends that even now are circulated as absolute facts. A few years ago, when I was engaged in making records in Camden, at a dinner party I could not attend because of these duties, a

lady very positively asserted that my disappearance from public life was due to my unfortunate incarceration in an asylum,
where I had been for years an incurable mental wreck. It was
useless for a friend present to affirm that, at the moment, I was
tucked in bed at the hotel, resting for the work of the following day. That was too commonplace an explanation.

However, not all the gossip and stories about prominent
singers and musicians are malicious. The gushing opera-lover
means well despite a nit-wit attention to the subject matter.
My good friend Charles Hackett is a popular drawing room
favorite as well as an exquisite lyric artist. His Irish gallantry
is generally equal to any surprise, but he was nonplussed, he
confessed, when a purring lady of fashion remarked, after
lengthy probing as to what role he sang in *Butterfly*, that she
"adored the opera, because Pinkerton was her favorite detec-
tive!"

Then there is the somewhat sleepy box holder who tells me,
after long years of opera attendance, he has never slept so
well as during my performances of the Goosegirl! The effects
were so much more soothing than the noisy Wagnerian offerings, his particular distaste being expressed for the Valkyrs,
who, to his mind, were a group of loud-tongued and scolding
women, very annoying indeed.

Accidents and incidents often make interesting news. A
trapdoor fails to operate and a singer risks a nasty fall. A
lighted candle—such as in *Tosca* once set my hair on fire,
happily with no further results than a scorched hand, hastily
raised to stifle the flame. Scotti warned me of it in a sibilant
whisper before great damage was done. At Baltimore, in the
Conried era, when we were playing *Traviata*, the falling cur-

258

tain crashed on my head as we were taking our calls after the act. He pulled me out beyond it in time to save my neck, if not the diamond tiara I wore. Its resistance probably saved me from decapitation.

It is odd to what extraneous influence the layman will often attribute the success or failure of an artist. Recently, I was warmly rebuked for my lack of enthusiasm as expressed, after insistent inquiry, about a certain charming lady who was not specially endowed as a vocalist. My vis-a-vis took the American public to task for its general endorsement of Flagstad and Melchior while bestowing but a lukewarm reception on the artist she favored. In her opinion, their careers rested largely upon the shoulders of a clever and watchful press agent. This was really too much, and it was a pleasure to remind the lady that no careers endure save by the efforts of God-given larynxes and special intelligence; and since the gifts are so abundantly embodied in both the artists named, this fact in itself should be obvious to the most ignorant listener. If one hears the lamentations and reproaches of those who fail to attain stellar eminence, you may be certain their own incomplete equipment is the more likely reason for their obscurity.

I once told Mr. Gatti, who was making valiant efforts for an argument to deprecate my value to his organization, in our usual financial preliminary, prior to a new contract signature: "Dear Mr. Gatti," I said, "I am not engaged nor valuable to your troupe because I have grey eyes, a pleasant smile, or high protection in this house. I am only valuable to you and myself as long as I render my best service to the public, and continue for this reason to be a box-office attraction." There may be now and again a personal preference that urges the introduction of an artist, but in the long run, to sustain any pretension, the contestant for singing laurels must prove himself worthy to wear them.

All New York knows this story of the witty pianist whose mental agility matches his quick fingers. At the debut of a sensational violinist, he was host to a renowned performer on the same instrument. As the crescendo of approval for the newcomer grew to hysterical acclaim, the guest mopped his brow ostentatiously and enquired if the temperature of the auditorium were not excessively hot. Whereupon the calm host replied, "Oh no, not for pianists!"

Many humorous incidents and otherwise were connected with the question of suitable youngsters to play the baby Trouble in *Butterfly*. Whenever I found a sweet and responsive child in New York, she invariably grew so fast a change was imperative with the next season. This Society that regulates the conduct, age, and choice of juvenile performers was, in the main, agreeable to our wishes, as long as we played in New York. In other states, however, it was a different matter. Sometimes under trying conditions on the road tour, I used a doll (which was hideous) while frequently a girl of the proper age would be so lanky and tall as to make her appearance beside me more like that of a younger sister. In Chicago, a most agreeable little dwarf made the experience as pleasant as he could; though I never did quite master my surprise, in the pathetic scene where he is clutched to the maternal bosom, to feel an unshaven cheek pressed close to mine!

In Pittsburgh, a most exquisite little infant was really a baby of tender years. She became frightened, however, and really ruined our last act with her screams. I tried to still them

260

as Toscanini laid on the brass accompaniment—with little success. The din was awful. The little mother took it all in good spirit, but I was near collapse, in the emotional reaction after the performance. The press spread the story with great gusto that, in a temperamental fury, I had nearly smothered the child. The mother denied it, I denied it; but it was front page news of unwelcome and dubious interest. A recent letter from that same baby, now grown to womanhood, referred to the incident for her identification and recommendation in her inquiry of a personal nature. I was able, in reply, to assure her the lamentable incident involved no aftermath of disagreeable reflections, but contributed its human interest to the data of operatic incidents.

Superstitions, prejudices and apprehensions, all play an important part in the artist's make-up. The Latins usually carry a family portfolio of photographs to which they address a special prayer for their good performance before dashing on the stage. Campanini jingled quantities of gold nails strung on a chain, in his particular gesture to invite good luck. Of course, the dire consequence of the "jettatura"—forefinger and little digit extended over the two others curved inward—cannot be estimated by the Anglo-Saxon mind. Yet it was an American colleague who paled upon seeing me once manipulate a peacock fan, and begged me to lay it aside.

Lilli Lehmann evinced fine scorn for concession to any theatre nonsense, but—bade me beware of putting my slippers on table or chair, before a performance. She, too, never raised her parasol in the house.

When Caruso first went to London, Graham-White was the particular darling of the clouds. An expert flyer, he managed to interest the singer in a short flight at Croyden. Enrico had courage, but as a precaution for the possible need and disposal of his remains on so exciting an adventure, his pockets were filled with little papers on which he had written laboriously all the instructions to that effect, as a codicil to his last will and testament.

He had a good sense of humor, too. In Paris, we had given our services at the Trocadero for an immense benefit matinee. It was a lovely summer evening, and afterwards a small party of us motored to the Bois for supper. The fashionable cars at that moment had prominent high front and rear accommodations, with a door in the middle of the tonneau. After seating the ladies, Caruso disposed his sturdy person upon this central seat, the back of which was not only his rest, but the door as well. As we swung under the portals of Armenonville, the lock became unfastened, and out he was catapulated, in no gentle fashion, to hard earth. We were horrified, fearing he had sustained a nasty injury. Not at all. A roguish twinkle peered out from eyes half shut under tousled hair, as he bellowed, in hearty laughter, *"See how Caruso bites the dust!"* Well, it was the only time he, or anyone, could make such an observation.

And speaking of dust brings to mind an unusual incident that happened to me in my first operatic years. It was during a guest engagement at Magdeburg, near Berlin, where a regiment of smart soldiers were quartered, making a lively audience for any artist. Carl Jorn, a personable young tenor also from the Royal Opera, was my partner in *Mignon, Faust* and *Traviata.* The first two roles naturally involved little adjustment for décor and costumes, but the latter excited interest

262

by reason of its modern dress and my own dramatic conception, heralded from the Berlin success. The local management was agreeable to any innovations and willing in all ways to allow my personal touches. In the first act, when Alfredo and Violetta pledge their growing interest in the *Libiamo* selection, I had arranged a little scene whereby she snatched the wine glass from his hand and dashed it to the floor with feverish abandon, as the cue for a little intimate by-play. Upon this particular occasion, however, what was my consternation and the surprise of the audience, to see a uniformed attendant, with whisk-broom and dust pan, stolidly walk onto the stage and meticulously sweep up the fragments that lay at my feet. This incident was mentioned humorously in the press of the following day, but not the fact that a methodical bookkeeper of the stage accessories billed me for

Glass Breakage —— 25 pfennigs!

A most interesting case of musical amnesia was told me by Mr. Gatti. In his days at La Scala, when countless voices were being tried and refused for the important posts there, a young tenor of handsome presence was brought to him by an agent. Reluctant to hear another aspirant in the course of a tedious series of auditions, he nevertheless granted him a hearing, pleasantly surprised by a fine voice, well trained, and the assurance of a useful repertoire on hand. Though Mr. Gatti had no immediate need of his services, the impression was favorable enough to keep him in reserve on the theatre's call list. As so often does happen, the indisposition of the tenor-lead gave him suddenly his chance one night. But, alas! As he proudly advanced to the martial strains of *Celeste Aida*—

it was to determinedly voice the woes of the unhappy Don José in *The Flower Song* from *Carmen*. This failing was the reason of each blighted attempt at a singing career. I believe he was soon after induced to adopt another profession less spectacular in public appeal.

And now, one more precious story before I bring these chapters to a close. And, of course, it concerns the tenor, who has so often been the scape-goat of opera naratives, ever since Hans von Bulow unkindly referred to their glorious vocal endowments as "eine Krankheit,"—a sickness.

It is too often true that a great voice need not necessarily mean an alliance with musical erudition or unusual intelligence. Its quality and instinctive expression spring from Nature's source, which is the best explanation we can give for its spontaneous outpouring and appeal. It is, however, a wonderful occasion when voice and brain are paired. The ill-fated hero of this last tale had no such credentials. Called hastily to substitute for an ailing Tannhauser, he arrived punctually in his dressing room, to learn the wishes of the conductor and confer with the principal performers. Advised of the substitution, the audience were politely silent, in their German respect, for both scenes of the first act. The curtain was ready for the second scene with Elizabeth waiting for her entrance. It suddenly occurred to the stage manager that he hadn't seen the visiting Tannhauser at his post in the wings. Inquiry along the line, even to the popular beer-hall near by, failed to locate him. The porter, however, seeing the excited gentleman racing to and fro, pointed to a figure in street dress, at the exit, for whom he said he had just called a cab. The agitated manager recognized his fugitive tenor, and leaped upon him. Why was he departing? Had he taken leave of his senses? Was he ill? Did he not realize the second act was about to begin, and shortly he was expected to sing? The abashed singer looked at him in idiotic wonder, with the priceless response: "But—was I expected to sing? I know no second acts—I have never been allowed to sing second acts!"

History leaves him there, still waiting for his cab!

CHAPTER TEN

I

THE DAUGHTER

L'ENVOI

WHEN I concluded my singing career, it was generally understood that I would follow in the footsteps of many retiring prima donnas and embark upon a career of teaching; but never for an instant did I have any such intention. And for good reasons, which were the result of close observation in many studios.

I have high esteem for the intelligent and conscientious instructor. I think many know a great deal about this delicate profession, but no one person is omnipotent in it as they often try to make one believe. The pupil as well, must use some discrimination in her search for the proper fount of knowledge and drink intelligently from its special source. Talent must combat vicissitudes that would discourage the amateur, though ambitious dilettantes may ride forward on the questionable waves of forced publicity, for a time. No permanent

266

results can be achieved without concentration on fundamentals; they are a necessary feature for even a *hope* of singing success.

Great singers would make excellent instructors if they would not too often impose upon young, fresh voices, that same technical trickery that has served them at the end of a career when vocal ebullience wanes and intelligent direction of failing powers becomes necessary. And how often have I heard more than one celebrity remark, "Oh, I shan't bother with the mere A B C's of scale work, but just coach the pupils in interpretation!" Surely this is not a proper attitude to encourage the vocal security on which to build an enduring song edifice. It is too much like putting a roof on walls so shaky that a collapse is imminent.

My early impressions as a student opened wide my eyes to such procedure. A retired singer, herself a victim of vocal abuse, was certainly a dubious guide for pupils led to her studio by reason of a positive and sparkling personality. The walls were decorated with photographs of contemporaries abundant with laudatory data. Naturally the credulous student will not stop to consider that a colleague's endorsement should read otherwise. But how often would truth—and the pupil—be better served if one might read a few dedications couched in the following fashion:

To ——————————

A charming comrade and beautiful woman, unfortunately a poor singer and stupid actress, with the affectionate condemnation of
Hers devotedly,
——————————etc.

No, the careful training of a voice demands the understanding of each individual's problems. The teacher must be specially equipped for a service that has no spectacular appeal in careful examination and exacting routine, note by note, day by day, for the frequently thankless task of vocal development. Students run from one teacher to another, in search of some magic formula for speedy results. They are never permanent. In my day, Mathilde Marchesi was an outstanding teacher, most successful in her handling of the coloratura. But her book of exercises, as well as those of other eminent authorities, such as Lamperti, Concore, Panofka and Garcia, are equally effective for general vocal practice. They should be put in every studio, together with that indispensable mine of musical reference, Grove's Dictionary of Music.

Recently a German dramatic singer asked me how one could obtain the flowing Italian tone-line, so justly admired in the Latin songster. Upon inquiry, she confessed she had never practiced a trill, a scale of short compass, or half-voice exercises to iron out the strain of emotional expansion of a heavy performance. Her complete joy was to unleash warm vibrant tones and let them serve her emotions at will, a purely physical outburst of the moment. When I hear her, I could wish she knew and exercised the rare art of singing as Florence Easton does today. Both were colleagues in Germany, but Time will not continue to be kind to one whose naive alibi embraces the excitements of public appearances, as substitute for the disciplinary measures of careful studio corrections.

Which reminds me of a story of Paderewski, quite as applicable to the singers' throat as to the pianists' fingers.

268

When questioned about his fidelity to practice hours, this great pianist is said to have remarked: "If I miss one day's practice, I notice it. If I miss two days' practice, the critics notice it. If I miss three days' practice, the public notices it."

I once had the pleasure of listening to my favorite Rachmaninoff in some preparatory work. Hour after hour he softly played one phrase, in countless ways, for nuance and dynamics, precisely as a careful singer would try to master a vocal measure.

There is no royal road to supreme accomplishments, but the dedication to them is in itself an inspiration for the truly gifted. There are special voices like Lily Pons', there are dramatic accents allied to opulent tones like Rosa Ponselle's, there are unusual combinations of voice and interpretation like Marian Anderson's. These varied endowments, however, to achieve their ultimate purpose, are molded into serviceable form by the unremitting labor of their possessor to suit their special requirements. To illustrate my point, such specialized artists would hardly shine as teachers. Give me the bona-fide hard-working instructors who are not excited by their own singing memories and visions of past grandeur, but faithfully devote themselves to the pupils' needs in the humdrum routine of the studio.

So I have not, and shall not invade the teaching arena. This decision in no way renders me immune from the contagious enthusiasm I feel for the young singers' problems. For the survey of their musical situation, therefore, I have from time to time read a paper expressing my opinions on the subject, before certain groups sympathetic to the outline.*

*See Appendix.

Gratifying as the reception accorded me has been, I have no mind either, to mount the lecture rostrum in another routine activity that would interfere with my blissful freedom.

II

I AM frequently asked what I do with my leisure, a question which is simple enough to answer, as I never seem to have any.

I live all the year round in my comfortable country house, so near the attractions of New York, however, that I can dash in and out whenever the urge prompts. Opera, concerts and the theatre will always be of colorful interest, and I try to bridge the succeeding decades in their taste, style and interest with an elastic mind, if not always an approving one. Even if we have no group of great stars, such as we knew in an earlier era of opera, still we must enjoy what the times provide. I have enough imagination of my own to lend a little glamour to the scene. I try not to make the error of futile and unjust comparison between Caruso, Melba or Chaliapin and our present standard-bearers.

Melba once told me her early career was hindered too frequently by the observation, "Well—of course it is not Patti" that saddened and maddened her in her reflections upon the public's discrimination. It is ever thus. The younger generation supplants the older as the years roll on, and brings its own idea and patronage to its choice of the moment. If these protagonists are more likely to be drawn from the screen and radio, one must realize the force of the advent of such mechanical and widespread entertainment, and accept the

270

fruits of a new departure for public endorsement. It satisfies the gallery gods.

Meanwhile, the crying need of an intermediate opera stage, between the studio and the Metropolitan, for proper training toward this latter goal, which would be the Ultima Thule, is still as acute as ever. Talent has to eat, pay rent, and most of all, express itself while youth inspires enthusiasm and determination. It must, therefore, and does. Personally, I despise jazz and hold only contempt for the thieving musical distortion of old master works by bandleaders and crooners. But, again, my own generation is not the one to offer criticism on results brought about by a younger one, which is entitled to enjoy all the vulgarities and noise its coarser tastes relish, if that must be its preference.

The craze for speed, the factory systems of mass production, high-pressure salesmanship, unions, and racial confusions, mob fluctuation to the more naive fields of diversion—all influence the moulding of the public taste as we observe it today. Easy and gracious living is a pleasure almost forgotten, and the environment of a home is more likely to be the rabbit warren rental space that entails little domestic responsibility, while the public eating places usurp the erstwhile delights of home cooking. For myself, I revert to the traditional New England housekeeping environment, happy in my lovely retreat, after years of exciting travel and a career that hindered such a dream till professional duties had ceased.

One never knows what surprise may be "around the corner," however, as witness my plunge quite unexpectedly into politics and campaign activities for the most recent Presidential choice.

I was enrolled as a speaker with our Connecticut Women's Branch, which, in its wide scope, was designed to shut out no race or party affiliation but promote a prompt action in vigorous denunciation of the New Deal. I worked often and hard, on public platforms and on the radio. No need to emphasize at this writing how overwhelmingly the victorious opposition again endorsed Franklin D. Roosevelt for another term in his coveted White House chair. The machinery operating to this effect was a transparent one for most observers. A Republican by inheritance and belief, nonetheless I feel a little more constructive scrutiny of our own party might benefit it.

An illustration by that queen of comediennes, May Irwin, is apropos here. I happened in on her recently when a wedding anniversary was in happy progress. Congratulating both beaming parties, I remarked, "May, in this sad day when unions seem so rocky and so temporary, tell me how you managed to steer past the cliffs of disagreement, into the quiet harbor of content and understanding?" With a charming smile, she said, "Well—it is very simple, really. I decided from the outset to correct my own infirmities and concentrate upon their betterment, rather than take my sole text upon my partner's defects." This is an excellent maxim for any group which could profit by self-analysis rather than too minute carping on the mote in the other fellow's eye. It is as effective in politics as in art.

As for the confusion and distressing predictions we are called upon to meet in today's scheme of living, I refuse to harbor gloomy forebodings. My native resilience must meet the outcome of this changing order. I shall pray it does. The tidal waves of radical propositions and actions are no new phenomena in the world's history. The time measure is limitless and the results not to be hastened beyond their normal pendulum swing by the human ants who so feverishly essay to rule the spheres in a given time by their Lilliputian force and ideas. Nature grows strong slowly. So does the soul. And both have their inception in the smallest seed—watered by courage, and sunned by tolerance.

Our old philosopher friend Voltaire holds to this code in his apt remark to Helvetius: "I heartily disagree with what you say, and will fight to the death for your right to say it."

III

MY narrative now draws to a close.

For quite some time I had been approached by several enthusiasts to set down my reminiscences; but I had no inclination to do so, until a quite definite feeling was lately inspired by the gentle insistence of my mother, through a psychic channel. For many years, I wondered if our communication might ever be such as to convince me of its genuineness. The friend whose "sensitivity" provides this assurance, which is one I choose to honor, knows how to relay my mother's messages in such terms as are helpful and comforting to me. Her counsel seems to be along constructive lines that carry an impersonal survey of the great changes in this earthly struggle, and my duties toward adjustment to them. I do not know that my inquiring mind and hesitancy to accept her valuation of these matters without some reflection on my part are entirely pleasing to her. I grant my ignorance in the psychic field, while acknowledging a reluctance to yield my individual opinion without conviction suitable to my understanding; but I prize honesty above all things, and my mother will bear with me in my need and sincere effort for the acquiescence of my own conscience of what she counsels.

Seated one day in my living room looking out over the rise of these beautiful hills that touch the ever-changing glory of the skies, the urge to write suddenly came upon me. The resultant chapters flowed along easily and with little need for after correction, so clear was the message, though in no sense one of automatic writing. Once the material was finished—it was laid aside for some time until other quiet moods called forth succeeding efforts—all finding a resting place in the recess of my desk until now. And so this reminiscence has come about—the duo-recital of two loving, closely knit and ambitious workers in the vineyard of song. It was a beautiful career that my mother guided and shielded, and were I to live my life again, I could not wish one episode other than what I have invited, or perhaps was destined to experience.

Perhaps our generation is too close to evaluate properly the remarkable events that have come about—yet, in restrospect, all of us can thrill to our part in it. I remember a man saying "the horseless carriage will never replace old Dobbin." The new-fangled electric bulb was in itself a startling innovation to one habituated to the kerosene lamp. A telegram in our small town was an event of painful or joyous surprise, according to its announcement of death or birth. The telephone was at the same time no casual friendly transmitter of conversational chat and then certainly no part of one's economical household, but a feature of the important office equipment. In

274

those days, I believe I once saw a blurred jerky affair, in a series of photographs that raced one after another; the central figure was Theodore Roosevelt; pugnacious with pounding fist and, of course, only mutely vociferous. It was my first "movie" recollection.

The radio was yet to quiver on the air, and inventors were still dreaming of and working at the great Leonardo's theory, of some five hundred years ago, that men could fly like birds. My own first airplane ride occurred some ten years ago in Germany. The balloon ascension was the acme of cloud experiences in my childhood. I took my first trip in the Zeppelin marvel of her time, the *Victoria Louise*, in Germany in 1913.

The Spanish-American War was my first experience of a nation marching. I was on the curb when Dewey came home to the hysteria of admiring countrymen. And I recall too well the subsequent cold shoulder turned toward him when the high emotions of an emotional people resumed their normal temperature. Not long ago on a trip to those same lovely waters, I had my first experience of submarine craft. An eerie sensation indeed in these restricted confines, with every inch calculated for use in peace and warfare.

I have been a spectator deluged by the flying mass of ticker-tape and torn directories to honor the contestants for fame, whether they were channel swimmers, South Pole explorers or Lindberghs. If the insouciant magnetic Jimmie Walker ceases to sartorially grace the New York scene at present, his energetic and grand-opera-conscious successor, La Guardia, can lay claim to definite accomplishments in his terms as public official of America's most stupendous city.

Manhattan in my early youth was no such turreted, awe-inspiring metropolis as we now take for granted. I knew the Flatiron Building as unusual architecture, while the Herald Building was voted the most esthetic of commercial edifices. "Time marches on." Peacock Alley in the old Waldorf Astoria saw many a gorgeous beauty on parade, and spectacular millionaires from the local group of plungers, or the cattle and wheat-pits of Chicago. They were men of picturesque piracy—so we were told—and I found some of them most interesting in their simplicity of manner, and pride of achievement. One ruthless steel baron used to like to hear me sing the old English and Scotch ballads at his after-dinner musicales. The effort was never viewed with great favor by his wife, whose shrill cries used to invariably bear the burden of "don't be inveigled into financing any opera company for Miss Farrar." An idiosyncracy that never endeared her to other hostesses was bringing her own wines to their table, avowing her vintage was the best, the most expensive and the only one she cared to sip. In view of many things, I would say something other than "sip," at that.

A blithe young scion of American nobility spent large sums for huge caskets of orchids; whether for me or his chorus-girl affinities was immaterial to him. Mine were sent to the hospitals, but I hope the young ladies were clever enough, as I understand at the time was the practice, to return them to the florist for credit or actual cash.

At Delmonico's and Sherry's, one could see the most beautiful women of the stage, and the less pulchritudinous Fifth Avenue matrons with their "play-boys" in tow. I was to learn with surprise that though these ladies gave glorious parties, whose cost was highly publicized and ran into thousands of

276

dollars, that they were not averse to sharp bargaining with the opera star for the singer's services for their entertainments. As my contracts were for opera appearances, and a private musicale could not be construed as a performance, I was pretty top-lofty myself, and the plea of the hostess for a discount met with a discouraging refusal. Nor did these ladies think anything of buttonholing one with the demand to loan one's costumes, wigs and jewels for some masquerade of the moment—all for sweet charity's sake. On one occasion I was gracious, and sent half a dozen of my prettiest things to oblige a committee of pleading millionairesses. They were returned to me in such shocking disorder that I vowed never to be so agreeable again, and kept my word. One buxom Juno was possessed to don my second act *Tosca* costume and harassed me, at a luncheon, with constant recrimination for my reluctance to oblige her. Whereupon, I turned on her, exasperated, and said clearly for the benefit of those curious about us, "Dear lady, until you can lift your façade and restrain your posterior, you would need not one but several of my *Tosca* dresses. You would do better to choose something from Madame X————'s wardrobe." I mentioned a singer of the moment whose dreadnaught construction was the cartoonist's delight.

I was also wary of the hostess who asked you in for a cup of tea and would expect you to entertain a roomfull of guests, impromptu. At such a gathering, a lady once said—oh so coaxingly—"Dear little songbird, do please sing that heavenly *Butterfly* entrance, I so seldom hear it." Whereupon I gathered up my furs, and, ready to exit, replied, very graciously, "I am so sorry, but if you would arrive in your box

277

before the middle of the second act, and stop chattering, you *would* hear it, in the opera house, where it belongs!"

For these, and many other similar replies, I was judged frequently to have a very saucy tongue and independent manner. It may be true. I grant that if a polite hint is unavailing I lose no time in administering the *coup de grace* of finality. There are, perhaps, social ladders that are agreeable, but hardly profitable, for the artist who relies on her profession for advancement. I never believed in mixing business and pleasure, nor did I. If I was engaged to sing at a private party, I arrived prepared to do so, an artist. If I was asked as a guest, that, too, was another matter, entailing no musical duties. People respect you to the same degree to which you respect yourself, and I was never a gratuitous entertainer. Now that I am retired from public performances, it is a particular delight to make myself agreeable at the piano for others, who lift their voice in song.

IV

THESE pages of retrospection have been in the main a pleasant labor. Though the memory of some incidents carries the echo of a heartache and a tinge of melancholy, it in nowise disturbs the general content of my present pattern of living. Light and shade must combine and merge eventually into harmony for every design. Lessons are learned through joy and sorrow, to enrich our lives and open the way to an understanding of the world and ourselves.

I conclude these reflections on a day of indescribable summer beauty, as the distant chime of a church bell floats over the still air, to consecrate the Sabbath morning. The village church nearby is typically New England, the kind familiar since my childhood. Set on the brow of a hill, it invites one and all. White and refreshingly cool, its slender spire points upward to a flawless blue, and watches over the sleepers below, so peacefully at rest on generous Mother Nature's bosom. In this pleasant village churchyard, each tablet carries a bouquet or plant in sweet remembrance, while crickets sing in the green folds of the grassy mounds. The little train of worshippers slowly treads the narrow pathway up to the open door where a simple service is in progress.

Here at home, June roses and honeysuckle are rampant over my stone boundary walls, the laurel frames the garden borders where tall spikes of delphinium and lilies, foxgloves and hollyhocks raise their fragrant banners to the vagrant breeze. My favorite robins trill lustily from the sweeping arches of the elms. This is my New England; not so very different, I imagine, from the picture my forbears viewed and enjoyed on that seventh restful day, which they observed so cautiously but obstinately, with the Bible in one hand while the other clasped a musket. I feel they bequeathed to me a precious heritage, drawn from their own stubborn purpose and sturdy strength to reason, combat, and conquer their frequently self-invited obstacles. I belong to this hardy strain of God-fearing, earth-loving people.

The pilgrimage of my earlier rapturous youth with its singing goal is ended; but I travel on my road, nonetheless, toward that summit where existence still challenges the spirit and warms the heart. The valley spreads below—one sees the detours—while upward, beckons the peak. Press onward, for our ascension shall be as high and successful as God in his infinite wisdom will allow.

279

As the following lines have so often been of comforting philosophy, I can do no better than to quote them in my leave-taking:

> *Then say not Man's imperfect, Heaven in fault;*
> *Say rather, Man's as perfect as he ought;*
> *His knowledge measured to his state and place,*
> *His time a moment, and a point his space,*
>
> *If to be perfect in a certain sphere,*
> *What matter, soon or late, or here or there?*
> *The blest today is as completely so,*
> *As who began a thousand years ago.*
>
> *All nature is but Art, unknown to thee;*
> *All chance, Direction, which thou canst not see;*
> *All discord, Harmony not understood;*
> *All partial Evil, universal Good;*
> *And spite of Pride, in erring Reason's spite,*
> *One truth is clear, whatever is, is right.*

Pope's Essay on Man.

Concluded on a Sabbath Day, July, 1938.

Fairhaven,

RIDGEFIELD, CONNECTICUT.

Miss Farrar at Fairhaven, in her Garden

APPENDIX

APPENDIX*

I AM often called upon to give my views of the future of opera in America. Music lovers of all ages seem to feel that the opera in America is on the wane, that its glories are all in the past, though why this should be, particularly in America, I am at a loss to comprehend. Civilized European centers, for example, have long and successfully included in their business of government, subsidized opera and drama organizations. The honorable post of Minister of Fine Arts was created to further their activities, and it is safe to say that the post has invited no more political suspicion or criticism than we are accustomed to levy upon any official appointed to handle and distribute public funds. Perhaps the unhappy spectacle of artists as objects of charity may be eliminated from the scheme of present-day emergencies, and these artists, so deserving, may come to enjoy not an emergency movement of insecurity but rather a well planned organization and a permanent contribution toward a national expression of pride and interest founded upon graded qualification and not based merely upon pressing economic need or political expediency.

*A brief digest of a short talk given by Miss Farrar at the Museum of the City of New York, January 1937.

When I sang my farewell in 1922, wealthy and generous patrons still made the opera possible, and its presentations were social functions as well as great music. The star system was still in its heyday and the finest artists then available were proudly presented on the Metropolitan stage. It was, however, the close of a splendid era. Perhaps it was inevitable that with the departure of Toscanini and the shrewd Gatti, and the passing of the management into younger hands, the golden era had to pass.

And with the increasing scope of the radio, with its mechanical marvels, new problems have arisen, a new medium has been brought forward to compete with its own expression. This medium has the distinct advantage of reaching several millions of listeners simultaneously. This is commendable, but I am not wholly convinced that the hidden millions of attentive ears can give me, as a performer, quite the magnetic thrill I experience when facing a visible audience. The glory of symphonic music surging over the air under the baton of Toscanini is unquestionably an offering of overwhelming generosity. But while all this "front window" magnificence is going on, what about the aspiring opera singer?

I come in contact with many lovely young voices, gifted students who always ask the same question:

"Where and how shall I make a career?"

Twenty or thirty years ago the answer would not have been difficult, for in my early student years we were sent to Europe because one could be certain of finding opera institutions, great and small, where the necessary debut and routine were eagerly offered to the singer of talent, once released from the studio.

284

In Germany, for example, our engagement was made for the entire year, at a small fee to be sure, but so arranged as to guarantee a monthly salary plus an extra compensation for each performance. One sang not five performances a season, but perhaps three a week: Siebel in *Faust*, a gypsy girl in *Carmen*, Musetta in *Bohème*, Nedda in *Pagliacci* or Maddelena in *Rigoletto*. Stage experience was thus acquired at no great vocal fatigue by the ambitious beginner. It would not be long before the fledgling would show her mettle and effect her entrance into the important stellar repertoire. In the meantime her training before the public had been well grounded. The privilege of going as a "guest" from one opera house to another broadened and educated the aspirant as no other experience could. A real career would be in the making—not to mention the sheer joy of being able to sing while one was young, while the impulse was fresh and eager.

Why cannot we in America turn our interests and energies to some such practical undertaking and evolve a system under which our own talented singers could enjoy similar development on home soil? It is almost unbelievable that after all these years we own but one famous opera house and one that is hard put to it to survive for a few short weeks out of the year, and forced almost to beg, at that, in order to exist. It is a sad commentary on our national pride that such is the fact. And yet I can find no one who can advance any sound reason, other than the usual uncertainty of a commercial return, why we have no chain of subsidized opera houses in this country. Are the movies offering too keen competition? I think not. Or rather, I think that there are just as many millions in the country who would gladly choose to pay a small sum to hear operas in their local opera house, if one were provided. And there is always the pride that comes from seeing a local singer perform. Radio could be enlisted, too, to bring the performances to a wider field. But the performances would require performers, and the advent of television could be looked upon as a means of bringing the visible as well as the audible performance to those who could not travel the distance to the opera house.

At present we have one weekly performance broadcast from the Metropolitan stage, and now and again a sporadic excerpt from some association of the moment. We shall never believe that these meager concessions to operatic interest will satisfy the listener completely. Therefore why not form some sort of liaison between municipal pride and interest in local opera houses and radio?

With an appropriation—not necessarily gigantic—we could sustain an operatic project in several centers of this immense country of ours. Municipal and State opera houses scattered throughout the country giving performances of high standard, attended with pride by the members of the community and broadcast to all the land at the same time. Why not? Is it too fantastic a dream? For *America?*

In this way musicians, singers, orchestra leaders, chorus masters, ballet dancers, carpenters, electricians, costumers, scene designers, stage-hands, yes, and even scrub women and ushers would enjoy a compensation for a legitimate group activity. Not to underestimate the joy of actual performance with hundreds in attendance and millions listening to the radio broadcast. Let us imagine a sample week under this system:

286

Monday—*Carmen*	Broadcast from	Boston
Tuesday—*Faust*	"	St. Louis
Wednesday—*Butterfly*	"	Chicago
Thursday—*Aida*	"	San Francisco
Friday—*Meistersinger*	"	New York
Saturday—*Manon*	"	New Orleans

And so on.

These local companies need not be large in number nor extravagantly paid, and admission fees could be graded so as to meet all purses. When I see the crowds that storm the motion picture houses, I wonder why opera cannot be put within similar reach, and made available to the modest purse. A permanent group based entirely upon qualification and talent, and not upon the humiliation and uncertainty of emergency relief measures.

Recently I heard four voices. Excellent material, attractive young women. All aspire to, and have trained for, opera and the serious concert stage. I think they can achieve a commendable position if they are given a chance. But where shall I find the smaller opera organization in which they can be given the routine and essential experience?

The Hippodrome in New York, under the direction of Maestro Salmaggi has a brief season of week-end operas— the operas sandwiched in between prize fights and political meetings.

The San Carlo operates as an uncertain road company.

The Chicago Civic Opera opens for a few weeks and stellar names must be utilized to make a sufficient financial return to justify expenses.

San Francisco has a gala excitement lasting a few short weeks with Metropolitan stars as a dependable nucleus for winning public support.

These uncertain ventures, however, offer no real proving-ground for the development of the young singer. Consequently one of my girls must try her luck in a night club and eat her heart out in this tawdry kind of entertainment. A second, whose splendid stage-presence and fine dramatic voice stamp her as an ideal exponent of Wagnerian roles sighs for the days when Germany was less conscious of non-Aryan pretensions. The third has settled to teaching: she must live respectably. And the fourth haunts the Broadway agencies looking for any kind of a walk-on part.

"Where and how shall I make a career?"

After thirty-odd years of professional activity, I am ashamed and abashed not to have a constructive and encouraging reply for these girls who represent thousands who are eager and young and talented, who are waiting for the chance to try their wings in their native country. Must they remain mute because we lack a national pride in our artists?

A Complete List of Miss Farrar's Operatic Rôles

by Edward Wagenknecht

(Reprinted, by permission, from *Geraldine Farrar, An Authorized Record of her Career*, published, 1929, by the University of Washington Book Store, Seattle, in a Limited Edition of 350 copies, signed by Miss Farrar. Copyright, 1929, by Edward Wagenknecht.)

Miss Farrar's operatic appearances have not, of course, been confined to the cities here named. Under "Berlin," "Monte Carlo," "Warsaw," and "Paris," are given the rôles which Miss Farrar sang for the first time anywhere in the cities named. Under "New York," all rôles sung in that city are given, regardless of whether they had previously been sung in Europe or not. Other cities, European and American, in which Miss Farrar sang but created no new rôles are not mentioned in this list. The date given is, of course, in each case, that of Miss Farrar's first appearance in the rôle in question.

A. BERLIN
Royal Opera

1. "Marguerite"   FAUST   *Gounod*
   October 15, 1901. Miss Farrar's début in grand opera. Grüning (Faust); Mödlinger (Mephistopheles); Hoffmann (Valentine); Gradl (Siebel). Conductor: Muck.

2. "Violetta"   LA TRAVIATA   *Verdi*
   November 29, 1901. Jörn (Alfredo); Hoffmann (Germont). Conductor: Edmund von Strauss.

3. "Nedda"   I PAGLIACCI   *Leoncavallo*
   March 7, 1902. Sylva (Canio); Berger (Tonio); Hoffmann (Silvio). Conductor: Edmund von Strauss.

4. "Zerlina"   DON GIOVANNI   *Mozart*
   November 23, 1902. Bertram (Don Giovanni); Destinn (Donna Anna); Rothauser (Donna Elvira); Soriser (Ottavio); Nebe (Leporello); Krasa (Masetto). Conductor: Richard Strauss.

5. "Juliette"   ROMEO ET JULIETTE   *Gounod*
   December 2, 1902. Philipp (Romeo); Hoffmann (Mercutio); Dietrich (Stephano). Conductor: Muck.

6. "Leonora"   IL TROVATORE   *Verdi*
   February 2, 1903. Sommer (Manrico); Berger (Luna); Schröter (Azucena). Conductor: Edmund von Strauss.

7. "Manon"   MANON   *Massenet*
   December 1, 1903. Berlin prémiére of *Manon*. Naval (Chevalier des Grieux); Knüpfer (Comte des Grieux); Hoffmann (Lescaut). Conductor: Muck.

8. "Mignon'   MIGNON   *Thomas*
   November 17, 1904. Naval (Wilhelm Meister); Hartmann (Lothario); Dietrich (Filina). Conductor: Edmund von Strauss.

9. "Angela"   LE DOMINO NOIR   *Auber*
   October 28, 1905. Naval (Massarena); Berger (Juliano); Rothauser (Brigitte). Conductor: Richard Strauss.

10. "Elisabeth"   TANNHAEUSER   *Wagner*
    December 20, 1905. Grüning (Tannhäuser); Destinn (Venus); Berger (Wolfram); Knüpfer (Hermann). Conductor: Edmund von Strauss.

11. "Gilda"   RIGOLETTO   *Verdi*
    October 4, 1906. Naval (The Duke); Hoffmann (Rigoletto); Rothauser (Maddalena). Conductor: Edmund von Strauss.

B. MONTE CARLO

Casino

1. "Mimi" LA BOHÊME *Puccini*
   March 10, 1904. Caruso (Rudolph); Renaud (Marcel). Conductor: Vigna.

2. "Marguerite" LA DAMNATION DE FAUST *Berlioz*
   February 28, 1905. Rousséliére (Faust); Renaud (Mephistopheles). Conductor: Jehin.

3. "Amica" AMICA *Mascagni*
   March 18, 1905. World prémiére. Rousséliére (Giorgio); Renaud (Rinaldo). Conductor: Poiné.

4. "Sita" LE ROI DE LAHORE *Massenet*
   February 13, 1906. Rousséliére (Alim); Renaud (Scindia). Conductor: Jehin.

5. "Margarita" L'ANCÊTRE *Saint-Saëns*
   February 25, 1906. World prémiére. Rousséliére (Tebaldo); Litvinne (Nunciata). Conductor: Jehin.

6. "Queen Elizabeth" DON CARLOS *Verdi*
   March 15, 1906. Chaliapin (Philip II); De Marchi (Don Carlos); Renaud (Rodrigo). Conductor: Poiné.

C. WARSAW

Imperial Theatre

"Maddalena" ANDREA CHENIER *Giordano*
In October, 1904, Miss Farrar filled a special engagement in Warsaw. The only new rôle sung here was Maddalena in *Andrea Chenier*, which Miss Farrar never sang elsewhere. I regret I have not been able to trace the exact date of this performance. Except for Battistini, the cast was made up of locally known Russian artists. Vigna conducted.

D. PARIS

"Zephyrine" LE CLOWN *Camondo*
a. April 26, 1906. World prémiére. Nouveau Théâtre. Rousséliére, Renaud, Delmas, Margyl, Mérentié. Conductor: Cathérine.

b. May 16, 1908. Opéra Comique. Thévenet, Bailae, Salignac, Périer, Fugère. Conductor: Ruhlmann.

E. NEW YORK

Metropolitan Opera House

1. "Juliette"   ROMEO ET JULIETTE   *Gounod*
November 26, 1906. Miss Farrar's American début. Rousséliére (Romeo);
Plan͵on (Frère Laurent); Journet (Capulet); Jacoby (Stephano).
Conductor: Bovy.

2. "Marguerite"   LA DAMNATION DE FAUST   *Berlioz*
December 7, 1906. Rousséliére (Faust); Plançon (Mephistopheles);
Chalmin (Brander). Conductor: Vigna.

3. "Marguerite"   FAUST   *Gounod*
December 31, 1906. Rousséliére (Faust); Plançon (Mephistopheles);
Stracciari (Valentine); Simeoli (Marthe); Jacoby (Stephano). Con-
ductor: Bovy.

4. "Elisabeth"   TANNHAEUSER   *Wagner*
February 6, 1907. Fremstad (Venus); Burrian (Tannhäuser); Van Rooy
(Wolfram); Alten (Ein Hirt); Blass; Reiss; Bayer. Conductor: Hertz.

5. "Cio-Cio-San"   MADAMA BUTTERFLY   *Puccini*
February 11, 1907. Caruso (Pinkerton); Scotti (Sharpless); Homer
(Suzuki); Reiss (Goro). Conductor: Vigna.

6. "Violetta"   LA TRAVIATA   *Verdi*
February 28, 1907. Caruso (Alfredo); Stracciari (Germont); Dufriche;
Bégué; Tecchi. Conductor: Ferrari.

7. "Mimi"   LA BOHÊME   *Puccini*
March 15, 1907. Caruso (Rudolph); Scotti (Marcel); Journet (Colline);
Alten (Musetta). Conductor: Vigna.

8. "Nedda"   I PAGLIACCI   *Leoncavallo*
March 22, 1907. Caruso (Canio); Stracciari (Tonio); Reiss (Peppe);
Simard (Silvio). Conductor: Vigna.

9. "Margherita"   MEFISTOFELE   *Boïto*
November 20, 1907. Chaliapin (Mefistofele); Martin (Faust); Rappold
(Elena); Girerd (Marta); Jacoby (Pantalis). Conductor: Ferrari.

10. "Zerlina"   DON GIOVANNI   *Mozart*
February 12, 1908. Scotti (Don Giovanni); Eames (Donna Anna);
Gadski (Donna Elvira); Chaliapin (Leporello); Bonci (Ottavio);
Barrochi; Blass. Conductor: Mahler.

Appendix

11. "Mignon" MIGNON *Thomas*
March 6, 1908. Abott (Filìna); Jacoby (Frederick); Bonci (Wilhelm Meister); Plançon (Lothario); Lucas; Mühlmann. Conductor: Bovy.

12. "Micaela" CARMEN *Bizet*
December 3, 1908. Gay (Carmen); Caruso (Don José); Noté (Escamillo); Fornia; Niessen-Stone. Conductor: Toscanini.

13. "Cherubino" LE NOZZE DI FIGARO *Mozart*
January 13, 1909. Eames (La Contessa); Sembrich (Susanna); Mattfeld (Marcellina); L'Huillier (Barberina); Scotti (Il Conte); Didur (Figaro); Paterna (Doltore Bartolo); Ananian (Antonio); Reiss (Basilio); Tecchi (Don Curzio). Conductor: Mahler.

14. "Manon" MANON *Massenet*
February 3, 1909. Caruso (Chevalier des Grieux); Scotti (Lescaut); Noté (Comte des Grieux); Sparkes; Van Dyck; Mattfeld; L'Huillier; Bégué; Reiss; Bozzano; Sibelli; Paterna. Conductor: Spetrino.

15. "Charlotte" WERTHER *Massenet*
November 16, 1909, at the New Theatre. Clément (Werther), début; Gluck (Sophie), début; Gilly (Albert), début; Pini-Corsi (Le Bailli); Devaux (Schmitt), début; Bourgeois (Johann), début. Conductor: Tango.

16. "Floria Tosca" LA TOSCA *Puccini*
November 22, 1909. Martin (Mario); Scotti (Scarpia); Gianoli-Galletti (Sacristan); Ananian (Angelotti). Conductor: Tango.

17. "Die Gänsemagd" DIE KOENIGSKINDER *Humperdinck*
December 28, 1910. World prémiére. Jadlowker (Der Königssohn); Goritz (Der Spielmann); Homer (Die Hexe); Didur (Der Holzhacker); Reiss (Der Besenbinder). Conductor: Hertz.

18. "Ariane" ARIANE ET BARBE-BLEUE *Dukas*
March 29, 1911. Rothier (Barbe-Bleue); Wickham (The Nurse); Maubourg (Selysette); Sparkes (Ygraine); Van Dyck (Mélisande); Wakefield (Bellangère); Fornaroli (Alladine). Conductor: Toscanini.

19. "Rosaura" LE DONNE CURIOSE *Wolf-Ferrari*
January 3, 1912. Jadlowker (Florindo); Alten (Colombine); Maubourg (Beatrice); Fornia (Eleanora); Murphy (Almoro). Conductor: Toscanini.

20. "Susanna" IL SEGRETO DI SUSANNA *Wolf-Ferrari*
December 13, 1912. Scotti (Count Gil). Conductor: Polacco.

21. "Louise"
    "La Beauté"
    "La Jeune Fille" } JULIEN   *Charpentier*
    "L'Aieule"
    "La Fille"
    February 26, 1914. Caruso (Julien); Gilly (L'Hiérophante, Le Paysan, Le Mage); Duchène (La Paycanne); Ananian (Un Casseur de Pierres, Une Voix de l'Abîme, Un Camarade); Reiss (L'Acolyte); Murphy (L'Officiant, Une Voix de l'Abîme); Bada (Un Ovrier); Audisio (Un Bucheron). Conductor: Polacco.

22. "Carmen"   CARMEN   *Bizet*
    November 19, 1914. Caruso (Don José); Amato (Escamillo); Alda (Micaela); Rothier (Zuniga); Reiss (Dancairo); Braslau (Mercedes). Conductor: Toscanini.

23. "Caterina"   MADAME SANS-GÊNE   *Giordano*
    January 25, 1915. Martinelli (Lefebvre); Amato (Napoleon); Althouse (Conte di Neipperg); De Segurola (Fouché); Leonhardt (Leroy). Conductor: Toscanini.

24. "Thaïs"   THAÏS   *Massenet*
    February 16, 1917. Amato (Athanael); Rothier (Palemon); Garrison (Crobyle); Delaunois (Myrtale); Howard (Albine); Botta (Nicias). Conductor: Polacco.

25. "Lodoletta"   LODOLETTA   *Mascagni*
    January 12, 1918. Caruso (Flammen); Amato (Gianotto); De Segurola (Franz); Didur (Antonio). Conductor: Moranzoni.

26. "Suor Angelica"   SUOR ANGELICA   *Puccini*
    December 14, 1918. Perini (La Principessa); Sundelius (La Zelatrice); Fornia (La Badessa); Arden (La Maestra della Novizie); Belleri (Suor Osmina); Ellis (Suor Genovieffa); Sparkes (Sorella Infermiera); Mattfeld (Suor Dolcina). Conductor: Moranzoni.

27. "Or!anda"   LA REINE FIAMMETTE   *Leroux*
    January 24, 1919. Lazaro (Danielo); Rothier (Cardinal Sforza); Didur (Giorgio d'Ast). Conductor: Monteux.

28. "Zaza"   ZAZA   *Leoncavallo*
    January 16, 1920. Crimi (Dufresne); Amato (Cascart); Howard (Amaide); Bada (Malardot). Conductor: Moranzoni.

29. "Louise"   LOUISE   *Charpentier*
    January 15, 1921. Harrold (Julien); Whitehill (Le Père); Berat (La Mère). Conductor: Wolff.

30. "Anita"   LA NAVARRAISE   *Massenet*
    November 30, 1921. Crimi (Araquil); Rothier (Garrido); D'Angelo (Remigio); Paltrinieri (Remon); Ananian (Bustamente). Conductor: Wolff.

294

INDEX

INDEX

A

Abbott, Bessie, in *Martha*, 109; 111
Accidents and Incidents, 258
Africaine, 124
Aida, 109
Alvary, Max, 125
Amato, Pasquale, 109, 137, 140, 148
American Women's Club, Berlin, 33; Defends Name of Geraldine Farrar, 50 et seq.
Amphion Club, 11
Anderson, Marian, 85, 269
Anisfeld, Boris, 253
Appeals for Funds to Save Opera, 221 et seq.
Ariane, 131
Arrival in Berlin, 33
Audition at Berlin Royal Opera, 40
Autobiographical Narrative, Withdrawn from Bookstores, 143

B

Background, 4, 57 et seq.
Bara, Theda, 165
Barker, Reginald, 180
Bates, Blanche, 104
Behind the Screen, 179
Belasco, David, 104, 151
Bel canto, 25, 35, 234, 250, 251
Beldert, Charles, 173
Benjamin, Dorothy, 154

Berger, Rudolf, 110
Berlin Opera Audiences, 112, 113
Bernhardt, Sarah, 113, 146, 176, 241, 254
Bittersweet, 187
Black Domino, 64
Blech, Leo, 35
Bohème, 102, 108, 109, 112, 154, 195, 214
Bonci, Alessandro, 109, 111
Bond, Belle, 14
Bond, Charles H., 14 et seq.
Bori, Lucrezia, 130, 156, 214, 221, 233, 234
Boston Concert, First, 22
Boston Symphony Orchestra, 141, 195
Bosworth, Hobart, 173, 176
Brainard, Bertha, 239
Branzell, Karin, 233
Bushman, Francis X., 165
Butterfly, Madame, 64; Preparations for Singing Role in New York, 102 et seq.; with Florence Easton at Garden Theatre, 107; with Geraldine Farrar and Andreas Dippel in Boston, 109; Recordings, 110; Box-Office Acclaim, 112; 113, 141, 191, 195, 206, 258, 260

C

Calvè, Emma, 24, 97, 109, 125, Accident in Carmen, 138; 250

Campanini, Cleofonte, 195, 255

Carmen, 23, 63, 123 et seq., **Press Reports on Acting**, 126, 132; 137 et seq., in Moving Pictures, 144, 166, 169, 170, 186, 188; 191, 195, 206

Caruso, Enrico, 69, 71, 90, 104, 107, 108, 109, 112, 125, 133, 137, 148, 149, 152 et seq., 171, 214, 234, 240, 261, 262

Caruso, Gloria, 154

Cavalieri, Lina, 73, 128, 236

Cécile, Grand Duchess, The, 53

Certowicz, Tola, 80

Chaliapin, Feodor, 71 et seq.; 111

Chaney, Lon, 165

Chaplin, Charles Spencer, 165

Charpentier, Gustave, 132

Chicago Opera Company, 195, 254, 255

Child, Calvin, 109

Childhood Characteristics, 6, 19, 20, 21

Church Social, 9

Clark, Marguerite, 165

Classroom, Conduct in, 10

Clément, Edmond, 129

Concert, First Boston, 22

Concert given for a pet charity of the Crown Princess, 95

Conried, Heinrich, 90 et seq.; 98; requests Geraldine Farrar to sing *Salome*, 102; 108, 109, 113, 153, 258

Coquelin, 76, 112

Cordoba, Pedro de, 167

Covent Garden, invitation to appear there, 66

Craig, Gordon, 77

Cross, Milton J., 237

Crown Prince, The, 35; visits to Geraldine Farrar, 47; newspaper reports of romance and intrigue, 48 et seq.; 135, 208, 236

Crown Princess, 53, 54, et seq.; 95, 208

Curtis, Dr. Holbrook, 26, 27, 148 et seq.

D

Dalton, Dorothy, 165

Damnation of Faust, 106, 107

Damrosch, Walter, 124

Dancing Class, 7

Debut at Metropolitan, proposed and deferred, 28; Choice of role for debut, 97; preparations, 97 et seq., description of debut and reaction of the press and critics, 98 et seq.

Debut in Berlin, 43 et seq.

Decision to leave opera, 189, 190

De Mille, Cecil B., 144, 166 et seq.

Departure for Europe, 30

dePougy, Liane, 73, 74

Desti, Mary, 83

Destinn, Emmy, 65, 87, 104, 107; in a moving picture 143

Devil Stone, The, 177

Devotion of "boys" backstage, 97

Dinorah, 255

Dippel, Andreas, 109, 114 et seq. 124

Disagreement with Toscanini, 121 et seq.

Divorce, 207

Don Giovanni, 84, 111

Donne Curiose, 131

Duncan, Isadora, 77 et seq.

Duse, Eleanora, 113

E

Eames, Emma, 58, 96, 97, 108, 109, 111, 113, 128, 234

Easton, Florence, 107, 148

Elliott, Maxine, 179

Ellis, Charles A., 26, 138, 195, 206, 236

Ellis, Melville, 169

Eltinge, Julian, 185

Eugene, Archduke, 83

298

F

Fairbanks, Douglas, 176
Farewell Concert at Carnegie Hall, 197
Farewell party in Sweden, 79
Farewell performance at Metropolitan, 191, 192
Farnum, William, 165
Faust, 40, 61, 63, 64, 83, 102, 107; sings role of Marguerite in Boston, 108, 262
Fay, Maude, 88
Fiammette, La Reine, 150
Figaro, 127, 234
Fitch, Clyde, 105
Flagstad, Kirsten, 233, 237, 259
Flame of the Desert, The, 184
Foley, C. J., 206
Forza del Destino, 234
Four Horsemen of the Apocalypse, The, 185
Frederick, Pauline, 179, 183, 185
Fremstad, Olive, 102, 109, 125, 128
Fu-ji-Ko, Madame, Japanese actress, coaches Geraldine Farrar in role of Butterfly, 102 et seq.

G

Gadski, Johanna, 84; as Isolde, 109; Red Seal recordings, 109; 111
Galli-Curci, Amelita, 254, 255
Galli-Marie, 123
Garden, Mary, 76, 102, 140, 149, 179, 180, 234, 235, 236, 250
Garden Theatre, 107
Gatti-Casazza, Giulio, 113 et seq., 135 et seq., 139, 148, 149, 156, 170, 171, 190, 194, 195; 237 et seq., 256, 259, 263
Gay, Maria, 125
Genee, Adelina, 240
Gentle, Alice, 139
Gerryflappers, 133, 116
Gest, Morris, 144, 165

G (continued at top of right column)

Gish sisters, 165
Glaum, Louise, 165
Gluck, Alma, 129, 226
Gogorza, Emilio de, 110, 137
Goldwyn, Sam, 149, 166, 179, 180, 181 et seq.
Grau Opera Co., The Maurice, 15
Grau, Madame Maurice, 27, 28, 90
Graziani's Studio, 34, 37
La Guardia, F. H., 275
Guitry, Lucien, 76

H

Hackett, Charles, 258
Hammerstein, Oscar, 102
Hansel and Gretel, 233
Hatton, Ray, 174
Hauk, Minnie, 123, 124
Hell Cat, The, 181 et seq.
Hempel, Frieda, 112, 156
Hochberg, Graf von, 38, 39, 40
Holmes, Burton, 104, 105
Homer, Louise, anxiety at rehearsals over her babies, 104; 107

I

Ideas on acting, 40; on stage settings, 98; on presentation of *Carmen*, 137 et seq.
Independence of Character, 24; at rehearsals, 103, 114 et seq., 121 et seq.
Ingram, Rex, 185
Interview with the press upon arrival in New York, 95, 96

J

Jeritza, Maria, The Viennese "Thunderbolt," 139, 140, 155 et seq.
Joachim, 35
Joan the Woman, 168, made movie history, 172; 173 et seq.
Johnson, Edward, 237

Johnston, J. L., 232
Jorn, Carl, 262

K

Kahn, Otto, 115, 120; Geraldine Farrar begs him to cancel her contract, 122; 250
Kaiser, The, 34, 57, 66; gives permission to Geraldine Farrar for leave of absence to go to America for Metropolitan debut, 94; 112, 135, 208, 236
Kaiserin, The, 34, 57
Kalisch, Paul, 67
Kaulbach, von, 89
Kennedy, Madge, 180
Knote, Heinrich, 88
Koenigskinder, 131
Kosloff, Theodore, 177
Kreisler, Fritz, propaganda directed against him, 142; 186

L

Ladies Home Journal, The, 143
Lasky, Jesse, 144, 165, 178, 179
Leave of absence from Berlin Royal Opera granted by the Kaiser, 94
Lehmann, Lilli, 12, 26, 33, 34, 38, 61 et seq., 66, 67, 83, 107, 125, 145, 151, 189, 207, 209 et seq., 251, 256, 261
Lehmann, Lotte, 251
Leisure time, uses of, 270 et seq.
Lenbach, von, 89
Leopold of the Belgians, King, 79
Letter of protest to Metropolitan Board of Directors, 118 et seq.
Life in retirement, 197
Lloyd, Frank, 183
Loan, First, 15
Lodoletta, 148
Long, Mrs. J. H., 25
Louise, 154
Loyalty to German friends and the

royal family, 145; to Lou Tellegen, 183
Lind, Jenny, impersonation of, 9
Louise, 76, 132
Lussau, Zelie de, 124

M

Mahler, Gustav, 35, 84, 111, 231
Mack, Willard, 179, 181 et seq.
Macpherson, Jeannie, 170, 177
Manon, 55, 62, 63, Aroused Berliners to frenzy, 64, 65, 124, 127, 214
Manon Lescaut, 129
Maria Rosa, 144, 166, 167
Marriage of Figaro, 127, 234
Marriage to Lou Tellegen, 147, 155 et seq.
Marshall, Tully, 174
Martha, with Bessie Abbott, 109
Martinelli, Giovanni, 68, 140, 148, 152, 233
Massenet, Jules, 62, startled by Mata Hari's dancing, 70
Mata Hari, 69 et seq.
Matzenauer, Margaret, 88, 138
Mefistofele, 111
Meistersinger, 39
Melba, Nellie, sings for, 26; 28, 29, 32, 77, 97, 109, 113, 124
Melchior, Lauritz, 233, 259
Mérode, Cleo de, 79
Mignon, 28, 64, 109, 111, 262
Monte Carlo, first season there— meeting with Caruso, 69
Moore, Grace, 77
Morena, Berta, 88
Mottl, Felix, 88
Mounet-Sully, 76
Mozart, 84
Mozarteum, cornerstone laid by Lilli Lehmann, 84, name of Geraldine Farrar engraved on bronze plaque, 85
Muck, Dr. Karl, 35, 40, 42, 64, 84, 111, 141, 142, 231

Munich, engagement to sing there, 86
Musical amnesia, 263
Muzio, Claudia, 156
McCormack, John, 109, 226

N

Naval, Franz, 64
Navarraise, La, 160
Newspaper reports on interest shown in Geraldine Farrar by German Royal family, 48 et seq.
Negri, Pola, 185
New Deal, The, 272
New York, winter in, 25
Nikisch, 35
Nilsson, Christine, 76
Nordica, Lillian, 12, sings for 26; 33, 34, 58, 97, 113, 251
Normand, Mabel, 165, 180
Notzing, Baron Schrenk von, 89

O

Observation anent *Mayflower*, 57
Opera, first attendance at, 23
Opera in English, 64
Oscar, King of Sweden, honors Geraldine Farrar with Order of Merit, 77
Otello, 67 et seq.
Otero, 73, 74

P

Pagliacci, I., 108, 109
Paris, first visit to, 31; efforts to locate singing teacher, 32, 33
Patti, Adelina, 92
Pavlova, Anna, 240
Pelléas and Mélisande, 76
Philharmonic Symphony Society, 230 et seq.
Phonograph recordings, 109; 226 et seq.
Piano Lesson drudgery, 7
Pickford, Mary, 165, 176

Plançon, Pol, 98, 107, 109
Pons, Lily, 233, 255, 256, 269
Ponselle, Rosa, 140, 222, 233, 269
Puccini, Giacomo, 103, 107, 108, 195

R

Radio broadcast activities, 224 et seq.
Rainey, William, 239
Rawlinson, Herbert, 180
Reasons for not teaching, 266 et seq.
Red Seal Record series, 109, 110, opinions on modern recordings, 226 et seq.
Reid, Wallace, 144, 167, 174, 176
Rejane, 76
Renaud, Maurice, 72, 86
Repayment of loan to Mrs. Webb, 127
Reszke, Jean de, 15, 97
Rethberg, Elizabeth, 156, 234
Retirement from opera, 160 et seq.
Ricordi, Tito, 103, 107, 108, 195
Rigoletto, 112
Roberts, Theodore, 144, 174
Rogers, Will, 185
Roi de Lahore, Le, 69
Romance and glamor synonymous with her name, 95
Romany Love, 196
Romeo and Juliette, 38, 61, 64, 98
Roosevelt, Franklin D., 220, 272
Roosevelt, Teddy, 35
Rousséliére, Charles, 97
Royal Opera (Berlin), 39, 40; debut, 43 et seq., gossip about Geraldine Farrar and royal partiality, 47 et seq.; 64 et seq., 94, 107, 112, 115, 145, 212, 257, 262
Ruffo, Titta, 109

S

Salome, Attendance at première at Dresden, 86; invitation by Strauss to sing title role, 86, 87; refusal to

sing role in New York for Mr.
Conried, 102
Salzburg, 83 et seq.
Sanderson, Sybil, 63
Sans Gêne, Madame, 134, 140
Santschi, Tom, 181, 182
"Sarah-Ann Wireback," 8
Savage, Henry, 107
Savage, Marie, 153
Schuch, von, 35, 64
Schumann-Heink, Ernestine, 109,
experience on radio, 225, 226
Scotti, Antonio, 84, 92, 104, 107, 108,
111, 112, 113; the peerless Scarpia,
128; matrimonial intentions to-
ward Geraldine Farrar, 132; non-
plussed by Jeritza, 139, 205, 206;
farewell performance, 222; opin-
ions on teaching, 223; 234, 240, 258
Segreto di Susanna, 131
Segurd-Weber, 76
Seidl, Anton, 125
Sembrich, Marcella, 109, 112, 118
et seq.; 234
Shadows, 180
Sills, Milton, 181, 182
Slezak, Leo, 68, 245 et seq.
Spencer, Janet, 13
Spiritualism, 89, 243 et seq., 273 et
seq.
Strauss, Dr. Richard, 35, 86, 111
Stronger Vow, The, 182
Stuck, Franz, 89
Sunday School Class, 5, 7
Superstitions of artists, 261
Supervia, Conchita, 139
Suor Angelica, 150
Sylva, Marguerite, 139

T

Talley, Marion, 229, 256
Tannhäuser, Elizabeth in, 65, 86;
appearance at Metropolitan in role
a momentous occasion, 107; sings
in Boston with Fremstad, 109

Tellegen, Lou, 144, 146, 155 et seq.
166, 178, 179, 241, 242
Telva, Marion, 221, 234
Temptation, 144, 171
Tetrazzini, Luisa, 109, 240
Thais, 140, 147, as a moving picture,
180
Thursby, Emma, 26
Tibbett, Lawrence, 77, debut in
Falstaff, 92
Tosca, 102, 108, 128, 129, 139, 140,
155, 156, 191, 195, 206, 254, 258
Toscanini, Arturo, 64, 68, 84, 113 et
seq., 121 et seq., 138; 210, 230,
231, 239
Trabadello, 33
Traviata, 38, 46, 61, 102, 108, 112,
258, 262
Trovatore, Il, sole performance as
Leonora in, 64; 109
Turn of the Wheel, 180

U

Ugliest man in Paris, 112
Urban, Joseph, 250, 253

V

Valentino, Rudolf, 185
Verses Composed by Kate Douglas
Wiggin in honor of Geraldine
Farrar, 105, 106
Villa Serbelloni, 128
Vocal Teacher, First, 13
Vom Rath, Frau and Herr, 33, 36,
38; arrange concert, 39; 40, 43, 90

W

Wagner, Cosima, 36, 38, 39
Wagner, Richard, 7
Wagner, Siegfried, 36, 39
Walker, Jimmie, 275
Walter, Bruno, 230, 231
Ward, Fannie, 177, 178
War-fever directed against Geral-
dine Farrar, 141

Warsaw, engagement at, 79, 80, 81
Webb, Mrs. Annie, sings for, 29; loan arranged with, 29; conditions of loan, 29, 30; repayment in full, 127
Werther, 128
Wesendonck, Matilde, 36
Whispers over Berlin, 55
Wiggin, Kate Douglas, composes verses for Geraldine Farrar, 105, 106
Witherspoon, Herbert, 237
Wives of Impresarios, 27
Wodak, Madeline, 80

Wolff, Albert, 132
Woman and the Puppet, The, 185
Woman God Forgot, The, 176
World and Its Women, The, 183

Y

Young, Clara Kimball, 165

Z

Zaza, 150, 151, 191, 206
Zerlina, in *Don Giovanni*, 84, 111
Ziegler, Edward, 237